Frederick Whishaw

The Romance of the Woods

Frederick Whishaw

The Romance of the Woods

ISBN/EAN: 9783744693592

Printed in Europe, USA, Canada, Australia, Japan

Cover: Foto ©Thomas Meinert / pixelio.de

More available books at **www.hansebooks.com**

U_, _ _+

THE ROMANCE of the WOODS,

by

F. J. WHISHAW.

Author of "Out of Doors in Tsarland".

'a bear, a bear'

London,
Longmans Green & Co.
and New York.
1895

CONTENTS

THE

ROMANCE OF THE WOODS

.

CHAPTER I

ON A RUSSIAN MOOR

I ONCE had a strange dream. I dreamed that I
was dead, and that dying I suddenly discovered
all my preconceived ideas as to the future state to
have been entirely erroneous, at any rate in so far
as concerned such persons as myself—the respectable middle class, so to call it, of mundane sinners.
Had I belonged to the aristocracy of piety and
goodness, which, alas! I did not, or had I occupied a position at the lower end of the list, other
things might have befallen me, better or worse, as
the case deserved ; but being, as I say, one of
the decently respectable middle-class sinners, I was
shown, in this foolish dream of mine, into a committee - room marked No. 2, and there informed

A

that since I was neither very good nor very bad, my present destiny was to continue to inhabit this planet for a number of years—I forget how many —not, indeed, in my present corporeal form, but as a spiritual essence; and that I might select any place this side of the dark river, the Styx, as my temporary abode, there to live in Nature's bosom and to assimilate and be assimilated until the simplicity and beauty of Nature, uncontaminated by man, should have purified me of all the harmful taints which I had acquired during my terrestrial existence among fellow-mortals.

And I remember that, in my dream-foolishness, I clasped my hands and fell on my knees, and with streaming eyes assured the committee of Mahatmas (for such, in the dream, they appeared to be) that I wished for no more beautiful heaven than this that they had offered me; and that I implored them to allow me to stay on for ever in the paradise they had prepared for me, and never to pass me onward and upward to attain further joys, however blessed !

And then, in my dream, those Mahatmas flashed their shining eyes at me (there was very little *but* eye and flowing cloak about them, I remember), and said "Silence!" and frightened me thereby out of my dream-dead wits.

That, they added, was not my affair nor theirs. All I had to do at present was to make my choice of a place from among those I had best loved during life, and to do so as quickly as I conveniently could, because their hands were somewhat full of business this morning, and they could not spare me more than, at most, five minutes.

I remember that I looked over my shoulder at this and perceived an innumerable host of persons, all, presumably, in a similar position to my own, and all ready to take their turns, in strict rotation, before the committee of Mahatmas in room No. 2 ; and I could not help reflecting that the middle-class sinner must indeed be a very large class, and that I should do wisely to select some rather unfrequented spot for my future home, lest my domain should be trespassed upon by other spiritual essences, and my peace marred by—to use a mundane expression—unseemly rows.

And then I became conscious of a great difficulty in the matter of this choosing of a place to live in. Picture after picture came up before my mind's eye, each more fascinatingly beautiful than the other. There was a lovely little bit of Devonshire coast, and another shore in Pembrokeshire; there were delicious spots in half the counties of England —woods, and hedgerows, and rivers, and waving fields wherein my spiritual being might disport itself in the contemplation of the teeming secret life of Nature; there were Kensington Gardens, a certain central glade of which I had loved well enough, and which my spiritual essence might find a handy spot in case the longing for human fellowship were to assail me—when I could so easily perch myself unseen amid the branches of a tree overlooking Bayswater Road, and drink in, to my heart's content, the familiar sights and sounds of London, or even take a ride on the top of an Acton 'bus; but at this point of my reflections one of the Mahatmas wagged his head at me and said:

"Oh no! You can't do that, you know. No 'bus-driving. Twenty miles from any town, if *you* please!"

It did not strike me as curious that this Mahatma should have read my thoughts, neither did it occur to me to wonder how he knew that I was animadverting upon the delights of the twopenny 'bus. However, his remark narrowed my field of selection,

and I thought on as intensely as I could. I crossed
the seas and flew, in spirit, to Finland, to a lovely
island in the midst of a beautiful river—the Voksa
—teeming with trout, great and small, and with
silver grayling; and then I thought of Ostramanch,
the home of the capercailzie, of the blackcock; the
scene of a hundred and one superb days with the
gun, and of as many nights spent in the perfect
happiness of solitude and observation beneath the
tall pines and the bright stars of the northern sky,
in the hush and the solemn majesty of the darkness
and silence. And I had almost cried, "Give me
Ostramanch!" when I remembered that this dearly
loved spot would not, after all, do. It had passed
from English into Russian hands, and my spiritual
self could never be really happy there under such
circumstances. What if my essence were suddenly
to happen upon a Russian sportsman taking a family
shot at a young covey of blackgame or willow-grouse,
huddled together upon a sand-dune, or hiding behind
a tuft of purple-fruited bilberry? Could my spiritual
voice cry out upon such a deed, or my spiritual fingers
close upon the throat of the delinquent, or my phan-
tasmal toe perform a corporeal function? Could I even
spread bony arms before his eyes and play the common

vulgar ghost upon him, to punish him withal? Alas! I thought, no. Ostramanch will not do. And then, at last, the picture of Erinofka rose before my eyes, and I knew that I had found my Fate. I pictured myself strolling year-long over the purple moors, through the dark belts of forest, by bog and morass and snipe-haunted waste. I remembered many trudges—days of delight—in those same woods, gun-laden, full of ardour, unwearied by day-long tramping, oblivious of hunger, impatient of oncoming darkness; and I imagined myself repeating such delightful experiences *ad infinitum*, and laughed aloud in the joy of my foolish dream-heart. The Mahatmas immediately interfered; they flashed their great eyes and fluttered their long black mantles at me, and cried:

"No guns, no guns!"

"And no fishing-rods!" added one of them.

"What! no guns and no rod?" I said, growing grave very suddenly. To be at Erinofka and never to hear the popping of another cartridge seemed a dreadful prospect.

"Oh, you can carry a gun if you please," said the presiding Mahatma, who was growing strangely like a London police magistrate, "but you must use smokeless and noiseless powder, and no shot."

" And a rod without a reel," said another Mahatma.

" And a line without a hook," added a third.

" And see that you have a license," put in a fourth.

" But, sirs," I began, " what am I to do with myself, if I may not——"

" Take life ? " interrupted the Chairman. " Silence, prisoner at the bar, and learn to be happy without killing ! To Erinofka with him, gaoler ! "

" How long, your worship ? " said that functionary.

Four thousand five hundred years was, I think, the figure, but it may have been four hundred thousand. I was still puzzling over the matter when I awoke. Afterwards, when I thought upon this dream of mine, it struck me that my sentence was, after all, a most enviable one. Thousands of years at Erinofka, with no terrestrial cares to weigh me down ; face to face and heart to heart with Nature, learning her secrets day long ; a life-atom among myriads of others ; a little part of an infinite whole ; harmless, free, careless, contented, in fellowship with bird and beast and insect, and with every form of life that has a vested interest in wood and moor and wet morass. For such an existence I had chosen, I

thought, the right place. At any rate my spiritual
essence, if weary of wandering about armed with a
gun that would not work, could amuse itself by
recalling those dear, unregenerate days when guns,
unprohibited by stern Mahatmas, popped freely, and
reels craked, and when the glad voice of the sportsman was heard upon these moors, and among them
my own, together with the popping of many terrestrial cartridges. One day, especially, and that the
day of my first acquaintance with the place, lingers
more fondly than others in the memory, and would
afford material for much spiritual contemplation,
perhaps even unto forty-five thousand years, if there
were nothing better to do! And it is of that particular day that I propose to tell, now that this somewhat extended preface has been got through.

It was Jemmie, of course, who introduced me to
Erinofka. Any one in St. Petersburg will tell you
who Jemmie is, for he is a popular character there,
and is known and loved by all. Well, it was Jemmie
who proposed a day at Erinofka, a day among the
juveniles; the younglings of the blackcock and of
the willow-grouse, and perhaps a peep at the princelings of his majesty king capercailzie. It was early
in the summer, perhaps too early; but shooting in

the Tsar's domains begins considerably earlier in the year than we, in this country, are accustomed to take gun in hand, and the sportsman may there sally forth on July 27, if it please him, and shoot young game without breaking any laws. It was not quite so early as this when Jemmie carried me—a willing captive—to Erinofka, but August was still very young, and so were some of the coveys; though, thanks to a fine warm season, many or most of these were marvellously well-grown; but of this anon. Erinofka is blessed, or cursed, with a most marvellous little railway of its very own, a kind of toy track from town, laid down for the convenience of a peat-cutting establishment not very far from the shooting-box which was our objective point. The railway is very narrow, and the omnibus-like carriages, which the public are allowed to occupy for a consideration and at their own risk, are very top-heavy; and the driver of the little engine is generally very drunk, all of which circumstances combine to make this Erinofka heaven quite as difficult of attainment as the very highest of Mahomet's, and the journey a matter not to be undertaken without deep thought, much repentance, and a visit from the family lawyer. The line looks something like the toy track at Chatham—that upon

which youthful officers of the Royal Engineers are or
were wont to disport themselves; a pastime devised,
I believe, by the War Office, for the twin purposes
of teaching the British officer how to drive a loco-
motive, and how best to fall off it with dignity when
the engine runs off the rails.

Jemmie tells me that before the peat-people built
this line it had been necessary to bump along to Erinofka as best one could, over the most awful roads that
human bones ever creaked upon, a distance of forty
or fifty miles; but that now, if only you can secure
the sober, the *comparatively* sober driver, the journey
is a sweet boon. It appears that there are three drivers
on this line—Matvey, who is always very drunk
indeed; Ivan, who is always rather drunk and sometimes highly intoxicated; and Yegor, who has been
known to be sober. I have not seen the man who saw
Yegor sober; but it is confidently asserted that he has
been observed in this unusual condition, and that he
is rarely more than half drunk.

Well, I seldom have much luck, and when I went
with Jemmie to Erinofka upon that little narrow railway, in a wide long carriage that might have served as
a portion of the G. W. R. rolling stock in its unregenerate broad-gauge days, we had Matvey to drive our

engine. Matvey had, to put it mildly, been drinking, and he desired to drink again. Now, Matvey knew very well that he could get no more vodka until he reached Erinofka, and this is why we travelled at a pace which was bound to end, and did shortly end, in disaster. In a word, we ran off the line three miles or so from the start, and that we did not also run down a steep embankment into a river was certainly not Matvey's fault; we could not have gone much nearer the edge than we did.

However, Erinofka was reached in safety at last, and—since our accident had delayed us at least two hours—right ravenously did we fall upon the good cheer set out for us by the head-keeper, Hermann, and his wife. One item of this repast, at least, I remember vividly : an enormous dish piled to the height of nearly a foot with luscious wild strawberries. It would be unfair to give my friend away in the matter of those strawberries ; but I will say that Jemmie partook with freedom of the fruit, and that I myself tasted, well, a few berries. The armchairs in the Erinofka sitting-room were remarkably comfortable, I remember, after that repast, and the conversation languished. But we were to be up and away at half-past three A.M. ; for we must drive a matter of seven miles to the moor we intended to work on the morrow, and the courteous Hermann—who had cleared away the large empty dish which had contained so many strawberries with but one. convulsive movement of the facial muscles and a quick glance of polite consternation in the direction of the reposing James—this courteous Hermann very gently reminded us that it was now eleven, and that between that hour and three was embraced the entire period devotable by us to sleeping off the effects of railway accidents and arctic strawberries, all of which was so very true that we sighed, and rose from those blest armchairs and went to bed.

The baying and barking of four excited dogs (who knew as well as we did that the first shoot of the season was to come off on this day) rendered unnecessary Hermann's polite knockings at the bedroom doors, and his gentlemanly intimation that the day was all that could be expected of it, and the hour—three. When Shammie, and Carlow, and Kaplya, and Bruce are performing a quartette at 3 A.M., even Jemmie cannot sleep, and we were both wide-awake and discussing matters when Hermann came to hound us to breakfast. Breakfast was somewhat of a failure, I remember. Did I mention that we had taken a few strawberries at 10.30 P.M. ? Well, we had ; and it was

found that the circumstance militated against a hearty
British appetite at 3 A.M. However, this being so, the
less time was wasted before starting for the moor.
There is something, to me, peculiarly fascinating and
exhilarating about this starting out on the first day of
shooting ; but oh ! that seven mile drive to the moor.
The roads were so absolutely and utterly vile, and the
cart so unspeakably uncomfortable, that no reader
would believe me were I to attempt to describe the
misery of driving under such conditions. But Jemmie,
bless him ! smiled on and smiled ever ; and I—not to
be outdone in exuberance of spirits this superb morning—pretended that I enjoyed being bumped about
like a hailstone on a hard lawn. All four dogs were with
us. They lay, at the start, quiescent enough at the
bottom of the vehicle ; but alas ! not for long. In the
first fifty yards Shammie was on my lap, and Bruce
with his arms round Jemmie's neck ; in the second I
found, to my surprise, that a cartridge-box had usurped
Shammie's place on my knee, and that Shammie's
head and my shin were exchanging civilities at the
bottom of the cart. Occasionally the driver was
sprawling on the back of the shaft horse, and now and
again he was shot violently upon the top of Jemmie or
me, or suddenly appeared, wrong way up, between us.

Occasionally also we found that the dogs and we had changed places, and that we lay struggling on the floor of the cart while they stood on their heads, or sat with surprised and pained expressions upon the seat. Nothing mattered. Jemmie smiled, and I tried to. What though our shins were black and blue with the misplaced attentions of cartridge cases and gun stocks ? What though the dogs whined and grew absurdly angry with one another, showing signs of an imminent general engagement? What though Jemmie bounded into air—bird-like—and nested upon the top of my head, or I on his ? Nothing matters on the first day of shooting ; disasters are a joke, and battered heads and limbs are contributions to the hilarity of the pro-ceedings. Ah, well ! the dogs limped ostentatiously when we arrived, and Jemmie and I were very, very stiff, but oh ! so happy, and I, at all events, grateful and amazed to find myself all in one piece, and we paced slowly through the first belt of thick, gameless pine-wood, thinking unutterable things, and with a decided tendency to quote poetry when the tongue would wag.

Half a mile of barren trudging and then the forest begins to lighten ; the young day sends golden smiles to greet us through the trees ; wherever there

is room for a ray or two of his glory to pass, he
stretches a hand to us. "Come," he seems to
say, "come out upon the moor and bathe yourselves
in my full favour; my good, gigantic smile is over
all this morning!" And here is the moor itself,
a sight to set the heart a-beating on this first day
of the season; stretching wide and rich before us;
miles across; limitless, apparently, from end to end;
and, as we believe and hope, teeming with game if
only we can hit upon the coveys.

What a lot of trouble it would save, I suggest
foolishly, if one had a divining-rod that showed
the whereabouts of the birds! *"Proh pudor!"* says
James, and rightly, "the dogs are our divining-rods."
As to these dogs, Shammie and Carlow are setters—
Shammie a red Irish, Carlow a blue Belton, and
wild at that. The other two are Russian-bred
pointers of English parentage—good animals both,
and well trained, according to his lights, by Hermann.
The setters both hail from a Scottish moor, and
are to-day on their trial in this unfamiliar country.
Their journey has lost them none of their keen-
ness—look at them now! Shammie, cool and collected, businesslike, making no false move, but ardent
and determined; Carlow, half a mile off, but back

again in no time and hundreds of yards away on the opposite tack, the quickest and wildest dog, surely, that ever ranged. Kaplya and Bruce hunt close to their trainer—we are giving all four of them a breather just to settle their nerves; but presently two will be taken in while two do the work.

Suddenly Shammie stops dead; so do, for an instant, my heart and pulses. Kaplya and Bruce back instantly, stiff as marble. Carlow is coming in at racing speed, but sees the others when fifty yards away, and lies down automatically. Shammie's tail wags slightly, and we feel that there may be a disappointment before us; but he turns and looks at us; and observing that we are taking him seriously, stiffens into a dead point. It must be business.

"You take first shot," says generous Jemmie; "if it's a covey, your birds are on the right and mine on the left."

The first shot of the season! how absurdly my heart is beating. I wonder the birds do not hear it and get up wild.

Suddenly, twenty yards from us, there is a rustle and a flutter of strong wings, and a grey hen rises without clucking, and lifting herself gracefully over the young birch saplings, floats away over the moor.

" *Matka !* " (Hen !) shouts Hermann, and to the surprise and disgust of the dogs, no cartridge explodes. Shammie smiles and pants, and looks round at us in a pained though kindly manner; he hopes it is all right, but reflects that they generally get their guns off in Scotland when he shows them the game. Jemmie declares that, if it were lawful, he would spare none of these old barren hens ; he is convinced, he says, that they do great damage by bullying the younger hens and chasing them from the moor, in order themselves to monopolise the attentions of the gentlemen of the family.

Oh ! the jealousy of the female sex. Jemmie may be perfectly right ; and I fancy that he is ; but what do the old blackcock, or (for the matter of that) the young blackcock, think of such proceedings ? What would the marrying men of our branch of life think or do, if the old maids should succeed in banishing all that was young and beautiful in order to promote their own chances of mating ?

But it is very hot, and Jemmie suggests that the birds will be lying at the edge of the moor beneath the shade of the pines, and thither we trudge through the heavy moss and heather. The going is always terribly heavy until the first bird is grassed : after

B

which event, I have observed, the tramping loses
much of its weariness and the shooting-boots their
weight, and when a dozen brace or so have been
secured, the feet that bear the delighted trudger are
winged feet.

Nevertheless, we walk for a full hour and are
still—as to our game-bags—as empty as when we
started. We see no beauty in the lovely moor, at
this period. The dogs, we feel, are failures, all four
of them. Hermann, too, is a fraud, for did he
not declare that there were eight fine coveys within
a radius of a mile upon this very moor. Where
are those coveys, Hermann? Did we submit to
be shuttlecocked over your ghastly parody of a road
in order to be humbugged by you at the end of it?
Where are these coveys? I say. Such, or to this
effect, were the remarks of Jemmie. I think during
those first two hours of unremunerative trudging,
he vowed to shoot all four of his dogs, sell his guns
and his cartridges, give up shooting, and devote
his entire energies to gardening and lawn tennis,
with a little fishing and a trifle of archery; I rather
think Hermann and the other keepers were to share
the fate of the dogs; I forget whether I was to die,
I think I was; but at the end of two hours the

luck changed and Jemmie smiled, and dogs and keepers and I all breathed again.

It was Kaplya that stumbled upon the first covey. Carlow was being led just then and so was Bruce, and good Shammie had by this time formed unflattering opinions as to the Russian moors in comparison with those of Scotland; consequently he was cantering about scientifically enough, but half-heartedly, ranging in an unconvinced and unconvincing manner, ready to oblige by doing his share of this foolish work, but feeling that in his case it was time and talent wasted. Probably he was wondering when the next train started for Scotland, and deciding to take it and go hence to places where the moors were not dummy moors, but the bonâ fide habitations of grouse and blackgame, when he suddenly caught sight of old Kaplya at a dead point in front of his very nose, while perhaps that organ was at the same instant assailed by the unexpected evidence of the proximity of something better than heather and bilberry plants. At any rate, down went Shammie as if shot, in as correct a pose as a "backing" setter can assume.

Instantly, also, Carlow and Bruce sat down, the former so suddenly that Ivan, the under-keeper, who held him, tripped over him and measured his length, letting Carlow go, chain and all, to join the party of stiffened doghood at our knees.

This time there was no disappointment. After a moment or two of that intense waiting which every sportsman knows and loves—while the birds, hidden somewhere in the heather or greenery, are eyeing their human and canine disturbers, and wondering what is best to be done, whether to run or fly, or remain crouching—there came the usual pulse-fluttering rustle, and up and away went three superb young blackcock, nearly full grown, two to Jemmie's side, one to my own.

For all I know to the contrary, my blackcock may still be alive and entertaining his friends with the narrative of how a foolish and excitable English-man once drew a bead upon him in his youth, and drew it awry. In a word, my too agitated pulses blinded my eye and unnerved my hand, and I missed that lordly youngling handsomely and en-tirely. Not so James and his brace of beauties. Jemmie is a deadly shot, and I would as soon sit on a fizzing bomb as play the blackcock to his unerring barrel; he grassed both his birds; and I knew that the dogs and keepers were now safe, and that the guns of my friend would not, yet awhile, be put up for sale.

But trusty Kaplya and Shammie still stood on; there were more of this interesting family to come. Recaptured Carlow pulled and strained at his leash; Bruce softly whined and trembled spasmodically, sitting on Stepan's foot.

Up started a fourth blackcock, accompanied by his mother; with bewildering suddenness they rose and hurtled away, the old lady dropping a last word of advice to the youngsters still remaining vacillating behind. I imagined her clucks to mean, "Oh, you foolish little creatures! why do you not fly when your mamma gives the lead? Fly always after a shot, when the guns are empty."

This time black death darted from my right barrel, calling to his last account a very beautiful young blackcock, nearly as large as his mother, who of course escaped scot free, triumphing – as she supposed —by reason of her wisdom. But the dogs still stood on.

This is the best, as it is the pitiful foolishness of the blackcock younglings. Their fathers are birds of great wisdom and cunning; their mothers are sagacious and experienced; but the little ones are

headstrong and foolish, and love to act indepen-
dently of their elders. Instead of flying altogether
as grouse and partridges do, and thus enjoying
each a chance of escape as well as participating in
the common danger, they rise by ones and twos,
and each bird becomes the sole objective for the
charge of the sportsman, thereby immensely lessen-
ing his chance of flying between the pellets.

The first covey of the season was a grand one
indeed, thirteen birds, including the mother, and
of these we slew, without leaving the original spot,
no less than nine. Jemmie beamed. He said
sweet things to Hermann, the lately abused and
condemned; he patted the dogs and "praised them
to their face;" he declared that I had slain a full
half of the dead birds, whereas I knew well that
three only had fallen to my fire and six to his; he
discovered that the walking was easy enough when
one grew used to it; he liked the sunshine; in a
word, my friend James had donned those spectacles
whose glasses are of the colour of the rose.

It was now seven o'clock; the heather and bilberry plants were still "dew - pearled," and there
were diamonds on every gossamer thread that ran
from leaf to leaf and from plant to plant; but the

sun was hot enough, by this, to dry up an ocean, and I knew these morn-gems would not last much longer. I was glad when Jemmie proposed a short rest (nominally for the dogs' sake), for there was all the beauty of the morning to take in, and thàt is best done in a sitting or lying posture. The panting of the dogs is almost the only sound—that and the indescribable evidence of teeming life which you may hear in the dead of the silence. Who makes that sound? What is it? Where is it? I think it is Nature in travail; it is growth and development, the never-resting activity of the spirit of life that moves upon the face of the land.

Our nine little victims lie upon the heather before us, and Jemmie weighs each in his hand and tries, very unnecessarily, their beaks in order to be assured of their youth, and admires their growth, and beams upon men and dogs in high good humour. I, too, criticise the birds and am conscious of a stifling feeling of regret. Here are nine beautiful little lives taken in as many minutes, taken so easily —alas! but who could ever give back to these feathered ruins the thing we have bereft them of? I know it is foolish to sentimentalise thus over the dead creatures I came to destroy, and will destroy

again the very next time that I have an opportunity; but the triumph of the sportsman is always a
little marred, I think, by this feeling of guilt—the
guilt of having robbed mother Nature of some of
her beautiful children. She does very well without
them, I dare say, and if we had not secured them
doubtless the kites and hawks and foxes would
have taken their share—probably as large a share as
this of ours; nevertheless, here they were an hour
ago upon this moor, alive and busy and beautiful;
and now they are not, and *we* did it.

Nevertheless, again, we are up and about and
ready to "do it" once more after a quarter of an
hour's repose; and the next thing we chance upon
is a covey of chirping and twittering little willow-
grouse, scarcely free of the egg-shells, a tiny, confiding flock that flit chattering and scolding after
their brown and white mother, annoyed to be disturbed and made to use their lovely little mottled
wings in flight, and anxious to settle again before
twenty yards have been covered. We send a laugh
after the little family, instead of a hailstorm of No.
7, and leave them to grow and fatten; they shall
enjoy the delights of life on this moor for three
good weeks, if not four, ere the leaden death shall

make Erinofka the poorer by their perfectly marked
little persons. Then an old blackcock, unaware
that Jemmie and his choked left barrel are about,
foolishly lets us approach within fifty yards of his
sanctuary, and rising with a crow of defiance, sub-
sides instantly at the bidding of the unerring James,
with a groan and a gasp—dead.

Presently a superb covey of willow-grouse (who
are the parents of our own red variety of the family)
rise with a whirr and a loud laugh from the old
cock, leave their tribute of four upon the heather—
and vanish. We see them flit like a white cloud
over the open moorland, rise like one being to top
the bushes, flash their wings in the sun as they
wheel round in the traditional manner of their tribe
before settling, and then we suddenly lose sight of
them and see them no more.

" They are down among the aspens," said Jemmie.
Hermann dissented.

" They wheeled right round the spinney," he
says, "and settled well beyond it."

Ivan takes the side of Jemmie, and Stepan sides
with his chief. I am neutral. I saw them up to a
point but not beyond it ; I saw the sun tip their
white feathers with fire as they wheeled and then

lost them ; but I know how many there were—there were nineteen, no less, that journeyed over the heather and into the spinney—a gigantic covey indeed!

"Two coveys," says Jemmie; "the willow-grouse have a passion for massing even in the chicken stage," which is perfectly true, while in the autumn you may find a community of a hundred of them living together.

Now were these birds little white ghosts, or real flesh and blood and feathers? If not spectres, then where are they? This was the question we asked of one another as, for a full hour, we paced and repaced, as we believed, every inch of a square half mile of ground within which the little wizards must inevitably be somewhere hidden. Hermann explained the matter by declaring that they had settled altogether in a huddled mass, and had not moved a muscle since ; knowing, perhaps instinctively, that by preserving absolute immobility they would give no scent. We may, and so may the dogs, have passed within a yard of the hole or tuft in which the beady-eyed little creatures lay crouched, watching us, scarcely breathing for terror, their poor hearts and pulses going very fast as we come near and pass by and see no sign of them.

But Carlow has the luck to stumble upon them. I am watching the dog, and I see him stop suddenly in his mad career (Carlow's career is always mad!), and bend over in an extraordinary position. There is the covey, under his very nose. Alarmed, indeed, they are now, and their necks are held straight and high; they attempt no further concealment; their only anxiety is how to take wing without falling into the jaws of this ogre—fox or whatever he may be. Carlow would sooner perish than touch one of them; but they do not know this, poor things, and peer helplessly and timidly this way and that in the extremity of terror and uncertainty. I can examine them now at leisure for a moment or two, and oh! what beautiful creatures they are. Where was ever so soft a brown as this of theirs, or so pure a white? What bird ever matched the graceful poise of their heads? What—there! they are off, and I have missed them with both barrels; this comes of moralising. Jemmie did not moralise, and he has dropped two of the beauties; but there is a chance for me yet, for the covey has settled in the open, no doubt about the exact spot this time, and not more than one hundred and fifty yards away.

So we take in all the dogs excepting old Kaplya,

who is as safe and steady as the Rock of Gibraltar,
and head straight for the place in which we believe
the birds to be lying. Old Kaplya raises her nose,
half turns towards us, smiles and winks (she positively
does both), as though she would say, "All right,
keep your eye upon Kaplya; I'm *on* these birds
already—follow me!" and away she goes straight
as a line, first cantering easily, then trotting a few
yards, then cautiously walking as many more, then
slowly stopping, stiffening, turning her nose now
slightly to this side, now to that, then finally fixing
herself into the very perfect picture of a sure point.

Up they go, and off go my two barrels, rather too
rapidly and excitedly; off go Jemmie's also, but with
more deliberation. To my first shot a bird falls in
tatters; to my second two succumb. I have shot
three of them, and Jemmie his usual brace. But,
alas! my first bird is but a mangled mass of feathers
and broken bones, and there must be a burial. Hide
him deep beneath the moss and heather, Hermann,
and for pity's sake say no more about the circumstance; for in truth my heart is like wax within me by
reason of this wasted life. It is pardonable and right,
though perhaps regrettable, to take these lives when
we intend to use the shot-riddled carcases for our

food, but to blow a beautiful creature to pieces and
to be obliged to bury its remains is unpardonable.

We decide to leave the rest of this covey; we
have levied sufficient tribute upon it. And now the
day is growing into middle age, and Jemmie says
that we will find one more family of willow-grouse
or blackgame and then take our mid-day meal and
our siesta. We will diverge into the thick belt of
forest on the right, he says, and see if we can find
a covey of capercailzies.

I long to see another capercailzie before I die.
For many a year I have been absent from those
moors whereon the great king of game-birds holds
his high court. Oh! if I could but come face to
face—but once—with the royal family, I could return
to far-off England content.

But, alas! the king was not to be found. Deep
in the sanctuary of mid-forest, somewhere beyond
those tall, dark pines—perhaps miles away—he had
listened in proud disdain to the popping of our
cartridges upon the moor, and had laughed at our
impotent endeavours to outwit himself and his family
of princelings. To-morrow, likely enough, he would
stalk about the moor from end to end, he and the
long-legged princes and princesses, his sons and

daughters, and the haughty lady his queen; but to-day, no, thank you! Not while James and his deadly Holland were about!

We stumbled, however, upon a covey of black-game, and levied full tribute upon them in default of their big cousins; but now the splendid August sun had

"Clomb up to heaven and kissed the golden feet of noon,"

and Jemmie declared that if we did not instantly settle down to our legitimate lunch, he would not answer for it if he suddenly fell upon me, or Hermann, or Shammie, or even perspiring Stepan and devoured him. Accordingly, therefore, we selected our camp in a shady spot by a moss-pool—for this bog-water was all that we should get to-day, and we must use it or none for tea-making—and Hermann was instructed to unpack the luncheon basket. Out came the good things, a profuse and welcome procession of luxury —spring chickens, tongue, well-iced butter, two bottles of claret, *Alexander Kuchen* (oh! blessed Alexander, whoever you may have been, to have invented so delicious a dainty; may the sweet maidens of Valhalla feed you for ever with your own Kuchen, oh Alexander! and may you eat heartily of it without suffering or surfeiting), and arctic strawberries. For half an hour we toyed, did James and I, with the viands, after which for two hours we slept or rested; for during this time of high noon the birds mysteriously disappear, and nor man nor dog may find them; and I lay and dreamed dreams, a few sleeping and many waking ones; and the peace and silence and restfulness of that mid-day in the forest entered into my soul and abode there in a sense of infinite and lasting content, which may be recalled—as through a phonograph—and reproduced at will to this hour.

And then again, after a cup of tea concocted of bog-water, but delicious notwithstanding, and after counting and recounting our twelve or thirteen brace of victims, we pulled ourselves together and trudged for four more hours, during which time we doubled our tale of slaughter, or nearly so, and when the moment came that we must head for the carts and return home to dine and catch the night train for town, it was with sadness that we wended our way homewards. We had spent twelve hours upon this pleasant moor indeed; but who would be content with twelve? Twelve thousand were all too little of such delight. On mature reflection I am quite determined that if my friends the Mahatmas give me another dream-chance I shall jump at the offer of Erinofka as a place of abode, however long the sentence be. What if the spirit-gun will not go off? So long as I may tramp the heather and see the game and carry over my shoulder the semblance of a gun to point at it, even a dummy gun; so long as I may see the dew-pearled gossamer, and feel the broad smile of the August sun, and hear the hum and buzz and crackle and cluck of teeming life around me, I really do not think I care so very much about the killing. And this is why I declare that if the Mahatmas again offer me the Erinofka heaven I shall accept it, ay, even unto forty-five thousand years! Nevertheless, if they allow me a breechloader and cartridges instead of that foolish spirit-gun of theirs, I shall certainly shoot.

CHAPTER II

IN AMBUSH AT THE LAKE-SIDE

IT is spring—such spring as is vouchsafed to the high latitudes, and I am in my night ambush, prepared to welcome any living thing that is good enough to come forth from its sanctuary within reeds or forest, and to parade itself in the open for my inspection. My ambush is a pine-branch tent, or *shalashka*, the little edifice which has been my refuge and centre of observation for many a cold northern night—spring-time nights, indeed, but nights of more degrees of frost than the sportsman or naturalist of temperate Britain has dreamed of in his coldest excursions into the realms of imagination. My tent on this occasion is not pitched upon one of those open spaces in mid-forest, whereon the blackcock love to hold their nocturnal or early-matutinal tournaments, where the laughing willow-grouse—that faithful lover—sports with his pretty white mate, and the dark forest trees form a romantic background to the proceedings of both. To-night I am placed in the midst of the marshy approach to a wide sheet of water—an annexe, in fact, to the great Lake Ladoga. Fifty yards or more in front of me the waters, but lately released from their entire subjection to the yoke of winter, may be heard softly lapping the shore in a series of gentle kisses, stolen in the darkness; for it is but three in the morning—if that, and I can see nothing but the broad wing of Night still stretched over land and lake. On either side of the *shalashka* there extends, I believe, a spur of moorland; behind is the forest : never far away in a Russian landscape.

I am still in the dreamy, semi-conscious condition superinduced by the long ride through gloom and silence which has intervened between supper last evening, twenty miles away, and my arrival here. The little ponies to whom we are indebted for our conveyance in perfect safety, through darkness which even the marvellous eyes of a Finn pony could hardly have penetrated, are some little way off behind us, hidden among the pine trees, waiting with the philosophic content of their tribe until it shall have pleased us to accomplish the object of our nightly pilgrimage and return to them.

The Finn pony, good, faithful soul, accepts everything at his master's hands with unquestioning
docility and good temper; he is never surprised or
annoyed; never taken aback by an obstacle in his
way, but rather sets himself to seek out the best
means to circumvent such obstacle. If his master
happens to be drunk or asleep, this is a matter of
supreme indifference to the little animal between the
shafts of the inebriate's cart or beneath his saddle,
for he is perfectly able and ready to manage the
whole business of getting himself and his master
safely home, without the slightest interference from
the latter. One of the canniest and best of animals,
one of the handiest of the servants of mankind
and the most faithful and reliable of his friends, is
the Finn pony; and I am glad indeed to be able to
put this fact forward, and thus do a good turn for a
little-known hero among those who are not personally acquainted with his claims to that title.

Asleep at my side is Ivan, and Ivan is—I am
delighted to say—too tired or too considerate to
snore; I do not care which it is so long as he does not
play his usual nocturnal tunes and spoil this dreamy
unreality in which I am steeped. I am here to take
notes; but what notes can a man take when, not

only is there nothing to be seen, and nothing to be heard—save the gentle plash of the lake, but when he is not even convinced of the fact that he is himself, or at all events that he is awake and not dreaming? Such is my condition at present. Everything seems far, far away. My old self, my own history, even the point of time, three hours ago by the things we used to call watches, when I left the lodge and started upon my long, dark, silent ride—seems to be separated from me by an eternity of space and tranquil, incidentless existence. What shall I do to pass away the next hour or two? Sleep? Heaven forbid—the stillness is too good for that! Review my past? Heaven forbid again—nothing half so unpleasant! Whatever I do must be done in consciousness and must be connected with the immediate present or the future; no ghostly past shall be admitted into the sanctity of these hours. I shall recline and watch the dark plumage of night, and listen to her soft sounds of peace, and satisfaction, and maternity, as she broods over her nest and her little ones, until the hunter Day shall come and chase her from it, and drive her far away over the sea to her sanctuary beyond the eastern gates of the world.

And, first, what a marvellous thing is this darkness!

Far away at home, in bed in one's own room, the
darkness is nothing; because the bearings of each
object in the chamber are known to you whether in
light. or darkness. You can, if you please, sit up
in bed and point with the hand and say: "There
is the window, and there the door, and there the
wardrobe," and so on. But here, where I lie and
stare out into the blackness, I can determine nothing
of the million animate or inanimate objects around
me; I may people the darkness with what beings I
please until the light arrives; it is an area in which
imagination may disport itself freely and there is none
can contradict its tales, for who knows what bantlings may not be concealed here beneath the shelter
of Mother Night's extended wings? How do I know
that a company of elves are not disporting themselves within a yard or two of my tent—as ignorant
of my proximity as I am of theirs? How can I tell
that some dreadful wild beast is not, at this instant,
feeling his way down to the waters of the lake, in
order to allay his thirst after having feasted upon
our poor ponies, behind there in the wood? I can
imagine an interview between a ferocious bear or
two gaunt wolves and our faithful little quadrupeds,
whose one idea in life is to do their duty and eat

the breakfast, each day, that the gods provide. I can see the wolves arrive and find the ponies, and say :

"Good evening, my friends ; we regret to say you are required for our supper."

"That's impossible," the ponies reply ; "we are needed to carry our masters home to Dubrofka."

"Oh, *that's* all right," say those wolves, to whom a lie is an unconsidered trifle ; "your masters sent us on to tell you it was all arranged !" Whereupon the ponies believe the tale and are ready to be eaten, because it is part of the day's work as ordained by their master, which is another way of spelling God in their language.

I think I know pretty well, however, what I should see, or some of the things I should see, if an electric light were suddenly switched on and illuminated the ground around my tent. Close at hand, here, on the shingly sand at the edge of the lake, there are seven or eight or more little grey and white sandpipers, fast asleep—perhaps standing on one leg apiece— among the stones, which are so like them in tint that it is difficult to distinguish the one from the other, even by daylight. Then, somewhere within eye-shot, though maybe half a mile off, there is a

flock of cranes standing, like a body of sentinels
met to compare notes, or relieve guard, also probably employing but one leg each to balance themselves upon during the hours of repose. I wonder
whether they use a different leg on alternate nights,
or whether the same one is told off for night duty
each time? If so, it is very hard indeed for the one
limb thus employed to receive no share of the repose
enjoyed by the rest of the body, but to be obliged
to toil on night after night, and day after day, while
its lazy fellow-limb gets all the rest and only half
the work. But such is life. I am sure there are
cranes near, for I heard their outposts give the alarm
when we splashed through the marshy approach to
this spot on our arrival here. Luckily Ivan knew
the password, which was the grunt of an elk, as which
animals—in search of a drink—we were permitted
to come within the precincts of craneland without
alarming the big grey birds to the departure point.
In a very short time we shall hear them going through
the business of waking up, and complaining of the
hardship involved in keeping early hours. Then
again, there are ducks, numbers of them, I feel sure
of it, though not one of them has yet uttered a
sound, because this place is a paradise for ducks,

and Mother Night covers many a fond couple of them—paired by this time, and tasting the sweets of love and the lovely anticipations of nest-time and prospective flappers. Perhaps there is a pretty pair of tiny painted teal within a biscuit toss, little lovers nestling in a ridge of the coarse moorland, or amid the yellow grass which waves all around me, though I cannot see a blade. Perhaps they woke up when we came tramping by, and peered with long glossy neck outstretched, and beady eyes straining to pierce the gloom, on the very point of rising and disappearing together into the sanctuary of the darkness, but quieted down when we entered our *shalashka*, and ceased to approach their nestling place. Or a pair of snipe, or a ruff and a reeve, the former, at this season, a thing of exquisite beauty by reason of the Elizabethan ruff which gives him his name. Each male member of his family is furnished with one of these, and not one is like another in hue, though all are beautiful. They are of every conceivable tint and variety, and certainly metamorphose the bird completely, giving him the handsomest possible appearance so long as they last; but alas! when the courting days are over, and the fair one has capitulated to the beautiful besieging party,—presto!—his principal beauty exists no more, and he becomes without his noble collar, the dullest and least interesting of birds. Hard on the hen bird, I call it, and savouring of unfairness. How would Angelina like it were Edwin—the luxuriance or rakishness of whose moustaches or beard had been instrumental in captivating her affections—were Edwin, I say, to shave off those appendages so soon as her fond heart was fairly his own? If Angelina threw him over, under the circumstances, I am sure no one could blame her. But if the darkness is mysterious and wonderful, and full of subtle, hidden potentialities, what shall we say of the marvellous silence? The repose of it is almost *too* great. I feel at every instant as though something or somebody *must* suddenly break out into sound. Either the heavens themselves must— this moment or the next—burst forth into a great, grand chorus of divine music, or a bird must sing, or a beast roar. There is something in the air which *must* out ; any sound would do, but a loud hymn would be the most satisfying at this instant. What a silence it is! The tension is oppressive when you come to listen to it, yet, if you were in the humour, how you could lean your very soul against it, and rest—and rest ! But to-night I must have sound

soon—my nerves demand it—I cannot bear this
hush much longer; if no wolf howls within the next
few minutes or no crane gives tongue, if no sandpiper
whistles or duck quacks, I must wake Ivan and bid
him talk.   I am outside the beat of the willow-grouse,
else he would have broken the oppressive spell an
hour ago.   Oh, for a chord of music !   Oh, to hear
on organ swell out, but for a moment, and then die
away again ; or to listen, close at hand, to the soul-
deep song of the nightingale !   Something is going
to sound forth in a moment; I feel it—now—now !
there ! . . . I knew it must come just then, I had
a presentiment of it.   It is a snipe high up in the
air, tracing his embroidery upon the sky-line overhead, and swooping at intervals with a sound as of
a sheep's "baa ;" this is the male snipe's curious way
of wooing his mate ; the "baa" comes dropping
upon the ear at intervals of a few seconds.   If that
snipe had not come to save my reason I believe I
should have shouted like a lunatic the next minute,
which would assuredly have given Ivan a fit.

    There goes a night-hawk, flitting by in the darkness
like a ghost.   Oh, what a voice !   When he gives
tongue I wish the silence back again.   Go hence,
noisy spirit of night, and hunt your moths elsewhere.

No wonder you can scream loudly with a mouth like that, for when you open it your head seems to split in two pieces. There will be no more silence now ; the night-jar has murdered sleep. Listen to the sentinel crane—or is it the boots or the chamber-maid of the community awakening the family? He screams loudly to them, but they answer drowsily. "Have you not made a mistake in the time?" they are saying. "It cannot, surely, be time to get up yet?" It is though, Madame Crane, and you must quickly let down that other leg and see about the breakfast. In a minute or two there will be such a clamour of conversation among the crane community that any person within a radius of five miles will be aware of their presence. I should say that the cry of the crane is a better traveller than any other sound I have heard. These birds require a good voice for communicating with one another during flight, for a large flock will often separate into many little bands of two or three while on the "march," and the strag-gling units must be picked up by nightfall. They must have strayed far away indeed if they cannot hear when their friends hail them at the full pitch of the crane-voice!

Now comes another sound. Far away at first, but

nearing at each repetition. A sad, melancholy note, falling at intervals of a second or two. I have heard it often before, and wondered what it could be. I have heard it as they who produced it—whoever they might be—passed at night far above the sleeping city, and have felt a great pity for the sad wandering spirits flying and wailing through the darkness—whither? Perhaps they were the souls of the unbaptized, I have thought, which must wander, according to a Slavonic tradition, over land and sea for seven years, seeking and entreating to be baptized.

But Ivan does not allow my thoughts to wander into folk-lore this night. The cranes have awakened him, and he has heard this last mysterious sound also. It has excited him. His finger is at his lip, and he is listening. "What is it, Ivan? Speak!"

"Hush!" says Ivan. "This is what we came for!" (There *was* a *raison d'être* for our presence here; I forgot to mention this circumstance before.) "It is the geese!"

So this is the wild geese arriving! Then beat, heart, and strain, eyes, through the darkness, for this is an exciting moment. Not that there is the remotest chance of a shot at them at present; but it is enough if they alight close at hand and tarry, breakfasting, until daylight doth appear. How close the sound seems in the still air, and yet the birds may be a mile away! I can hear the slow, measured beat of their great wings as they approach, a solid phalanx, conversing quietly at short intervals. Surely they are very close indeed? They are all talking at once now. Perhaps they have seen the water and are excited, knowing that their journey is at an end. The beating of their wings seems almost to brush now the topmost boughs of the *shalashka*. I fancy I can feel a movement in the air, fanned by their big pinions. Thud! There goes the leader; he has alighted. Thud again—and yet again! It is true—they are here; they have come!

To judge from the noises which they are making, there must be a considerable number arrived—thirty or forty. They are chattering to one another happily and sociably, and uttering very different tones from those weird, melancholy cries of theirs while on the wing. They are no longer the lost spirits, the poor wandering unbaptized souls, but a party of merry travellers just arrived, so to speak, at the tavern where a comfortable breakfast is spread all ready for them. They are sure to do justice to it, for this is their favourite feeding-ground—all over this marsh,

so Ivan says. It is growing lighter. The conglomera-
tion of sounds of life seems to have startled the
Night, and reminded her that she must hurry away
and attend to her duties in another hemisphere. She
is gradually withdrawing her soft wings—those dark
and motherly wings which have guarded so well her
little ones for many a long silent hour. Go in peace,
Mother Night, for the broad Sun will take good care
of your bantlings during your absence. He will
open upon them his "good gigantic smile," and they
shall laugh and sing and be merry. Already I can
catch a pale, sickly gleam of light, where the Waters
look up to the grey sky and cry, "How long, Sun,
how long the gloom and the cold?"

Be silent, lake, for soon the bridegroom will arrive,
and you shall bedeck your waters with gems, and
sparkle and glitter in leagues of dancing delight.

The sandpipers are merry and active, and dart from
place to place in pairs and companies, whistling and
rejoicing; they pass, now and again, so close to me
that I can see them, and their whistling seems to
come from the very air within the *shalashka*. And
the snipe overhead, he never tires of his lightning-
flight and his wheeling; and his "baa" is one of the
sounds which continues without ceasing. There is

yet another voice—a croak and then a whistle, and the same repeated farther away, and yet again in the distance: a woodcock, I believe, but I cannot see him. He is taking his spring-flight, followed or preceded by his spouse. They will flit across a given space, then alight and dally awhile in pretty courtship, then return the way they came; and so again, *da capo*.

What are those tall posts yonder, outlining themselves against the paling sky? They are motionless, apparently—no, they move, as I stare through the uncertain light; they shorten, and lengthen, and bend, and dip, and glide slowly forward and bend again: it is the cranes, I am sure of it, for the clamour seems to come from that very spot. But where are the geese? I can hear them but they are still invisible, for they are feeding head down, and show no outline against the sky. Listen! another band of melancholy air-wanderers is approaching— how weird, how pathetic is the sound of their coming! Do they then so hate the trouble of travelling? or is it merely that they have discovered which tone and note of the gamut carries furthest through the ether, and that this happens to be the most doleful of all notes? They are very close now—stay! What is this? are they not going to alight and join the happy breakfast-party below there? Apparently not: they are overhead, they have passed, they have gone on— I can see them; they are travelling in wedge-like formation, a big triangle of beating wings that flog the air with measured sound and slow. How deliberate and yet how swift and powerful is their flight! Why did they not stop here? Their cry was answered from below, and yet they did not pause but continued on their course. Why was the invitation to breakfast not accepted? Who can say what is the etiquette of the wild goose? Perhaps it was not an invitation, but rather an intimation that this place—this tavern —was already occupied by a rival community.

One or two of my former friends take wing and join the other party; no doubt they have some reason for this step, but what that reason is no man may conjecture. Perhaps they are scouts sent forward to find out who these new arrivals are; perhaps they have been badly treated here and have gone over to the enemy in order to "better themselves." Luckily the bulk of the party remain behind, however; and now, in the strengthening light, I can plainly see a body of stout grey fellows waddling about among the yellow grasses and the soaked moss, and feeding in the well-known manner of geese in any field in far-off England. Forty yards, I reckon, separates my *shalashka* from the nearest goose : one of them may wander nearer—it is worth while to be patient and to allow the light to intensify before hazarding a shot which will disperse every living creature within hearing, and end the delight with which this spring morning is stored.

Slowly the sky, due east, yellows and then reddens ; it seems to be shooting up pink cloudlets, and letting them fly over heaven in order to herald the uprising of the King of Morning ; for the Sun is coming—there can be no doubt of it ! Redder and redder are the clouds that precede him ; now the mists that veil his bed are growing golden and radiant, and fly right and left as he pushes his head through them and looks out upon the earth, and smiles in a broad pathway across the lake. As though by magic a thousand song birds instantly fill the air with hymns of praise ; even the tall cranes cease their gabbling and gobbling, and look for a moment at the apparition ere they resume the business of the hour. They are splashing about in shallow water, and each step they make throws a shower of bright gems around them. The geese—hungry no doubt after a long journey, and

D

being naturally rather of a practical than of a romantic turn of mind, take but little notice of the Sun-god; he's all right, they think, and is sure to turn up at daybreak every morning, surely one need not interrupt one's breakfast to look up at him? The pace is too good! Look at the ducks—here a pair and there a pair—swimming out into the shining water, dipping their heads as they go and sending diamond-baths over the sheen of their necks and shoulders. They pursue one another, and quack and court, and bathe, and are perfectly and entirely happy and content, as who would not be in their place? A curlew sails by, calling to its mate, who is circling over the lake further to the left. And all the while the busy little company of sandpipers flit and whistle, and alight and run, and are off again on the wing—life is all movement and 'go' for them; they cannot be still.

There is an osprey! He is floating motionless in air, high over the lake. He, too, is thinking of breakfast. Soon he will drop like a bolt from heaven, disappear entirely or partially in the wave, and in a moment reappear with his meal safely held in those business-like talons of his. There he goes—splash! he has missed his mark. A cry of rage, and a circle or two over the water, and he is aloft again—hanging

like an impending doom over the bright lake. He
will not miss again! But Ivan is touching my arm :
I know what he means : he means that I must blot
out this picture of peace and life by sending a
message of grim death and noisy ruin into the very
midst of it. Let me wait awhile, Ivan, and watch.
It is so little for you who live amid all this and can
see it at any time; but it is so much to me—a
dweller in towns, where there is no free, happy
nature-life to watch and feast upon, and no daybreak
save that of the London cat and the strident, brazen
cock. Give me another hour of it, Ivan? No?
Well, half an hour? But Ivan says " No; " the
geese may depart at any moment, he whispers;
shoot while you can! I have no doubt Ivan made
a mental addition, "and don't be a sentimental
English idiot ;" but the former words were all I
was permitted to hear. So there is nothing for it :
I must shoot; I must, with my own hand, blot
out all this beauty, and smudge the picture which
Morning has painted for my delight—and all to
see a grey goose flutter and die who is now so busy
and happy! The game is not worth the candle;
but it must be done! One shot as they stand, says
pitiless Ivan, and another as they rise—unless I

prefer to hazard a cartridge after one of yonder cranes. Crane me no cranes : it is goose or nothing; give me the gun, Ivan !

There ! the deed is done, for good or for evil. The goose who stood to receive my shot lived on, and I trust still lives ; his feathers are thick and tough, and I hope in mercy that if he is hit at all his plumage has turned aside or suffocated the shot, and that he is not much hurt. He is gone, anyhow, flying strongly. The goose which rose to receive fire will rise no more. He is dead; he will utter never more his sad pilgrim-notes; he will feed no more in these pleasant pastures. Go and pick him up, Ivan, and he shall be cooked and tentatively eaten, and perhaps pronounced very nice, and perhaps condemned as very nasty.

Now turn and see what we have done. The last crane has taken wing—running a few yards and jumping clumsily into the air, rather like a cyclist mounting his machine. He will fly a hundred yards before those long legs of his are comfortably stowed away ! What a slow flight it seems, yet it carries him wonderfully far away from us in a short time !

And the ducks? Gone also; circling high in air, taking stock of us. When they have made up their

minds that we are bad characters and not to be
trusted, they will head for a distant point and disappear. The curlew is far away, so is the osprey;
the sandpipers are still in the neighbourhood, they
are too inquisitive to go far from us; they must
needs watch us and find out all about us first. And
away there in the bright distance floats, receding, the
triangle of geese—one less than it came, and one,
perhaps, in pain and suffering, though Heaven forbid
that this should be so.

All this we have done, friend Ivan, with our banging and bloodshed! See what a transformation scene
the act of man works, in an instant, upon a lovely
landscape? Of life he makes death; of busy, happy
places, full of colours and of sounds, and of song
and of joy, he makes a barren waste, with himself
the sole living creature remaining to look upon the
face of it! Let us go home, Ivan, we shall see no
more of bird-life this morning; take up your poor
grey victim and come along—the place will be the
better and the happier for our departure, and perhaps,
after a while, all its evicted tenants, save one, may
return again to their own.

But Ivan only remarks that I ought to have shot
that first goose in the head, and then we should have

had two instead of one. Then he scratches his own head, gazes long and intently over the sparkling waters of the lake in the direction where the departed geese are now but a dark smudge in the distant sky, spits on the ground in contempt of muff-shots and lost opportunities, and strides away towards the ponies. As we disappear in the forest I look back and see some ducks returning, and hear the sand-pipers whistle us a taunting farewell! Amen! No one wants us here : they are all happier without us.

CHAPTER III .

A DAY AFTER CRAWFISH

THERE are certain days of one's boyhood which have made so deep an impression that they seem to stand out like mountain peaks in the misty plains of the memory, clear and distinct against the sky-line, when all else is dim and hazy and distorted by distance. One of these landmarks in the early life of the writer is a certain day, long years ago—though the recollection of every detail of it is as green as though it all happened but yesterday—when, in company with two or three kindred spirits, he made his first grand expedition after crawfish. It was summer—the summer holidays : holidays long looked forward to as to be among the most delightful that ever boy spent ; for they were to be passed in Mourino, the paradise of our youthful imaginations, where the long Russian days were not half long enough for the multitude of delights to be crammed into each, there being " more to do " at Mourino, as we always thought, than any-

where in England, seaside or otherwise. As a matter
of fact, the northern haven of our schoolboy desires
was the very place for boys home from an English
public school, and fond of healthy outdoor pursuits
and recreations. There was a river at the bottom of
the garden in which fish of many kinds might be lured
to their doom; there was shooting, in a mild way;
there was riding *ad lib.*, if galloping about the country
on the spiky backs of the little Finn ponies of the
place can be dignified by that name; there was boating, of course, and canoeing, at our very doors, as
well as the usual English games which the true Briton
takes with him however far afield he may roam. No
wonder then that Mourino was the place in which we
preferred, *par excellence*, to pass our summer holidays;
for, as I say, the days were not long enough to contain
all the joys to be crammed into them.

There were crawfish to be had at the bottom of the
garden, but these were neither sufficiently large nor
sufficiently numerous to tempt us to engage very
frequently in their capture. When we wanted crawfish of a size to do their captors credit, we knew well
enough where to go for them, just as well as the
giant crawfish themselves knew which part of the
river suited them best as their headquarters. It was,

however, some little distance to the favourite haunt
of the monsters, a matter of ten miles or so ; a journey
not to be undertaken lightly over the unspeakable
roads of the neighbourhood, so that we did not very
often disturb the scaly warriors in the cool depths of
their chosen pleasure-grounds ; when we did organise
an excursion, therefore, in their honour we fully intended to "do the thing in style," and to create some
considerable gaps among the ranks of their best and
mightiest. When a day was to be devoted to the
capture of big crawfish at Sairki, preparations were
made over-night in order that no time should be
wasted on the morrow ; the usual miscalculation was
made as to the number of sandwiches required—
food sufficient for an entire regiment was invariably
provided for us, yet I cannot recall that we ever
brought any back. The stock-in-trade of the complete
crawfisher, a strong hand-net and a pound or two of
slightly high meat, was in readiness for each of us ;
our pike rods and tackle were seen to ; the most particular instructions were issued as to our awakening
as soon as daylight should appear ; the vehicles, or
rather their peasant owners, were hunted up for the
hundredth and last time and warned, with all solem-
nity, as to the awful consequences that unpunctuality

would bring down upon their heads, and then we all
four went to bed and wished for day.

When morning came—the particular morning I
am now recalling — things were propitious. Two
telyegi stood awaiting our pleasure at the door, each
with its pair of small Finn ponies ready harnessed and
impatiently whisking away the horseflies with their
long tails. The *telyegi*, I may explain, are springless
carts upon four wheels. They are provided with so-
called "cushions," which consist of a square bag of '
sacking with a certain amount of hay inside it. The
sensations of the traveller who has once been bumped
about in a *telyega* over Russian roads are memorable
—indeed, I have spent the rest of my days since my
boyhood in wondering how in the world I managed to
remain "all in one piece" throughout the awful joltings
to which my body was submitted during those *telyega*
days. Has the reader ever seen a Russian country
road? It is not a road at all, as we are accustomed
to understand the term, but a mere succession of deep
and wide holes worn in the natural sandy soil. The
Finn ponies think nothing of such trifling drawbacks,
however, and pursue their headlong course without
regard to the feelings of the evil-entreated passengers
behind them. Perhaps the good-natured creatures

experience a mischievous delight in thus "taking it
out" of those who weary their flesh by causing them
to drag a heavy load at breakneck speed through all
the heat and dust and breathlessness of a Russian
summer day. The pair are harnessed in an original
manner ; one, the better trotter of the two, is between
shafts, while his companion canters alongside, attached, in a happy-go-lucky way, to the vehicle by
means of a couple of loose ropes, but otherwise free
to do pretty much as he pleases, consequently he
is sometimes close enough to his comrade to make
that animal, if irritably inclined, put back his ears
and snap at him as a gentle reminder that he is
taking liberties, and sometimes a yard or two away,
frisking over puddles or shying all over the road on
his own account. When a pit of more than the average
depth is encountered, both horses will jump it in
preference to running down to the bottom and up
again, and at such a moment the fate of the passenger
in the cart behind is melancholy. He is tossed up
into the air for all the world like a spun coin, sharing
also the uncertain destiny of that coin as to the
manner of his descent — whether "heads or tails."
It must not be for one moment supposed that we, in
the exuberance of our happiness, and in the all-

accepting, unquestioning, all-enjoying spirit of the
British schoolboy, cared a farthing for the depth or
width of the very vilest hole that time and horseshoes
ever wore in a Russian road; on the contrary, we
loved the sensation of being sent flying up into the
air every other minute, and if we came down upon
the top of one another or of the luckless driver on
his hard box-seat, or even into the six-inch dust of
the road in the rear of the *telyega*, why, I believe we
liked it all the better.   As every one knows, a special
Providence watches over drunken men and schoolboys, and I have often reflected that we must have
caused our particular bodyguard a terrible amount
of anxiety, and kept it very hard at work during
these wild *telyega* drives of ours at Mourino, for we
were racing, most of the time, with the wheels of
the two carts interlaced, the horses—all four of them
—galloping *ventre à terre*, and the demented Russian
drivers—quite as far gone in lunacy as our British
selves—shouting at the top of their voices and bumping about half in air and half in cart, like a couple
of demon Jehus let loose for the occasion, and for
our especial and particularly complete destruction;
and yet I cannot remember that any one was ever
hurt !   Truly that special Providence of ours was

well up to its arduous duties, and performed them admirably.

Sairki was reached at last, and the horses put up at the village. As for us, we unpacked the carts before a group of admiring Finnish children ; for Sairki, like many a score of other villages within twenty miles of the Tsar's capital, is inhabited exclusively by Finns, who cannot speak a word of Russian. Hand-nets and rods were got out ; the crawfish meat was produced (extremely unsavoury by this time, owing to the intense heat of the day, but all the better for that from the point of view of the crawfish, who likes his dinner to be attractive to his olfactory senses) ; huge fishing-baskets were strapped upon our shoulders, containing our food at present, but to be used for another purpose soon, and away we headed for the riverside. The Ochta is a tributary of the Neva, into which it flows close to St. Petersburg —a pretty little river as one would wish to see, if he cares for the sort of scenery that Ruysdael loved to depict. Down by the river there grew countless clusters of leafy young birches and aspens, and to these our attention was first directed, for from them we must draw one of the essential items of our stock-in-trade. Provided with large knives as we were, we soon possessed ourselves of the necessary number of long sticks, about a dozen each, and stripped the leaves off to the end. In order to explain the exact object of these sticks, I will now, with the reader's permission, make him acquainted with the *modus operandi* of the scientific crawfisher. I have said already that a lump of meat is required. This is cut into small sections of about an inch and a half square, one of which is firmly tied to the end of each stick with a piece of string or " machalka," the birch-bark ribbon known to gardeners. This is the nastiest part of the proceedings, and it is better to get a friend to do it for you if you can. The preliminaries being thus completed, the next thing is to take the twelve baited sticks one by one and place them in the water, the meat downwards and resting on the bottom, while the top end of the stick is allowed to project a foot or so above the surface and to rest against the bank. The sticks must not be placed too close to one another. The proper distance is about ten yards between each. It will be remarked by the intelligent reader that the crawfisher thus requires a considerable portion of the stream to himself, for no two sports-men can find scope for their energies within a hundred and fifty yards or so ; while a party of four or five will occupy the best part of half-a-mile of bank. When the sticks are all placed scientifically, according to the fisher's knowledge of the spots likely to be favoured of crawfish, the sportsman must possess his soul in patience for a quarter of an hour at least, in order to give time to the gentlemen of the claws to realise the good fortune that has come their way in the shape of a lump of meat dropped apparently from the skies. After the interval indicated, the hand-net is taken and the sticks are visited one by one. Now comes the moment when the skill and science of the performer is put to the test. The water is not very clear. It is not muddy, but the colour is dark—a brownish tint—caused, as we always believed, by the quantities of iron in it, so that we cannot see to the bottom or near it. Hence, the first part of the proceedings must be done in faith and hope, and with an extremity of caution and lightness of hand not attainable without considerable practice in the art of crawfishing. The stick is taken firmly in the left hand, while the right grasps the handle of the net. Then the stick is raised from the bottom, but so gradually and imperceptibly that the movement is, presumably, unnoticeable down below. The baited stick is thus slowly and carefully lifted inch by inch, until the lump of meat at the end of it is visible. If a crawfish is clinging on to the meat the stick is raised no higher, for the hand-net now comes into play. This latter instrument is brought cautiously up against the current, placed deftly underneath the clinging feaster, the stick and the net are raised together, and as the crawfish reaches the surface of the water, and at length realises that he had better quit this perambulating breakfast, he lets go, only to discover that he is too late and has been outwitted, and that his place henceforth is in the fishing-basket, or a watering-pot half full of water, until such time as he is taken out and boiled for the use of man. It is very simple, and were the crawfish not the most criminally greedy and careless creature in the world, he would never allow himself to be captured in so ridiculously elementary a way. But it is his nature to, and no amount of experience will teach him the foolishness of his conduct, for you may, if you please, catch and return to his element the self-same crawfish a dozen times in an afternoon. In a good place, the fisher may find two or three, or even more, of these hungry fellows clinging to the same piece of meat, and, if clever enough, may easily capture the lot at one swoop.

Such, in brief, is the *modus operandi* of the craw-fisher. We all knew the way to do it, we of the Sairki party; and the tying on of the bait and the placing of the sticks were finished as quickly as these operations could be performed with a due regard to efficiency, lots having decided the portion of bank to be worked by each of us. Then came the quarter of an hour during which it is the etiquette of the crawfisher to allow his prey to discover and to enjoy undisturbed the refreshments provided for him. I do not know whether schoolboys possess souls—presumably they are provided with a special schoolboy quality—but in any case we, at least, were entirely unable to possess those souls in patience, and that little quarter of an hour was spent by each of us upon his own portion of bank under a carking sense of grievance. We felt that we were conceding too much to the crawfish. Personally I passed my fifteen minutes at full length in the long grass, within a yard or two of the water, and any one but a schoolboy would have been glad enough of the opportunity to lie thus beneath the brilliant northern August sky upon a bed of wild flowers, which, if one chose to

E

sit still and pick one specimen of each, would have filled his hands with a hundred delicate stems without the necessity to stretch beyond an easy arm-reach. I have never seen any place that equalled the country about Mourino for the wealth and variety of its wild flowers, or the luxuriance of the ground-berries in the woods—Arctic strawberry, bilberry, cranberry, raspberry, and a berry which I remember as making the most delicious bitter-sweet jam, called brousnika. As for the flowers, the anemone is the only representative of our familiar spring visitors, but the summer months are gorgeous with every blossom that our own English fields can boast, with few exceptions, besides lilies of the valley, linnæa borealis, a lovely creeping plant with a tiny starry flower ; " star of Bethlehem," and other varieties not often seen in this country.

But the longest and most vexatious wait must come to an end in its season, and at last the crawling minutes had sped by and we were at liberty to commence the business of the day. Oh, the delightful excitement of the first visit to each stick ! How my heart beat, I remember, as I grasped the first of them, and with somewhat trembling fingers raised it cautiously a few inches towards the surface, peering

the while into the dark brown depths to catch the
earliest possible glimpse of the desired visitor. The
water seemed extra dark in colour to-day, to spite one,
and the stick had to be slowly lifted to within a foot
or so of the keen eyes watching above it before the
meat could be distinguished at the end of it. There
it is at last—now then! Is that the claw of a crawfish
sticking on to it, or not? It may be, but if so it
is a tiny one. Carefully the hand-net is drawn
towards the bait, up the stream, for otherwise the
current bulges the network inside out, and deftly
the string-prison is placed underneath the end of
the stick—there! If it is a crawfish I have got
him safe. Up comes stick, and up comes net with
it to the surface—alas, no! It was but the split
end of a piece of "machalka," and not the claw
of a crawfish. Down goes the stick again to its
place at the bottom of the stream, and away go I
to the next one. Here a strong waggling at the end
of it when it is raised from the bottom tells me
that undoubtedly a guest is availing himself of my
hospitality; caution must be observed—yea, caution
must be doubly cautious. It is a big fellow by the
feel, and he is still tugging away as I raise the stick
with breathless care towards the surface. Now I

can see the bait, or rather I can see the place where the meat may be supposed to be ; for there is nothing visible but a dark mass which hides the bait from view. Now comes the tug of war. The current is rather strong, and the exertion of bringing the broom-handled net against it is considerable ; but this is not a moment to think of difficulties. Down comes fate upon the thoughtless reveller ; a turn of the wrist with the right, and a swift upward motion of the left arm, and anything there may chance to be busy-ing itself at the baited end of the stick is my own. What do I see ? A big crawfish ? It is indeed a big crawfish, and with it a second and yet a third, true Sairki monsters, all three of them, seething and glistening in their dark brown armour at the bottom of the net, and laying hold angrily of each other wherever they can fasten a claw, as though each were chastising his companions for having brought him into this mess. They must be taken up carefully, one by one, and held by the back, else those cruel-look-ing claws will lay hold of one's fingers and inflict a pinch which will be a memorable circumstance for some little while. These three fellows, exactly like lobsters made in a smaller mould, so far as the unscientific eye can judge, are about six to seven

inches in length from head to end of tail; one of
them has one large claw and the other quite a
miniature member, as though it had never emerged
from its baby stage; the truth being that the warrior
has lost one of his natural weapons, probably in a
fight with a rival, and that a beneficent nature is
providing him with a substitute as quickly as can be
managed. If I place one of these creatures upon
the ground, instead of in the watering-pot prepared
for his reception, he will instantly set off backwards
in the direction of the river. I have tried this at all
distances from the water, placing a crawfish as far
as several hundred yards from his native element, and
pointing him in the wrong direction; yet in defiance
of all obstacles, the poor fellow invariably and without
hesitation made straight for that point of the compass
in which instinct told him lay the stream which was his
home. And so was made the round of the sticks;
one producing nothing, another a single tiny victim, a
third four at once, and so on to the twelfth and last;
the net results of the first round being seventeen
crawfish of a fair average size. Then the proceedings
began again, *da capo*. The sport generally improved
up to about the fifth round, while the inhabitants
of the stream were gradually becoming aware of

the feast spread for them at easy distances all down the river. After the sixth round the numbers fell off again, until, eventually, a second portion of the bank had to be worked, the original lie having been exhausted. The largest haul that I ever made from one stick at one swoop was six crawfish, all good ones, and one of them a giant. We had agreed to put back the babies, the very tiniest, that is ; though we invariably took a great number home with us which we did not intend to eat, in order to let them go at the bottom of the garden as stock for our own portion of the river, and to afford us sport when they should have grown to more respectable dimensions. They always accommodated themselves to circumstances, and remained contentedly where they had been put in.

When we grew tired of capturing our crawfish in the orthodox manner we adopted another plan ; this involved, first, the finding of a shallow place in which, when found, we waded about with a short stick in one hand and a net in the other. When we caught sight of a crawfish wandering along or trying to hide the too expansive volume of his tail beneath a stone designed to conceal a junior member of the family only, all we had to do was to suddenly place the stick in front of his nose, at the same instant holding the net immediately behind him, when the simple creature would promptly commit suicide by running backwards into prison.

Then there was trolling for pike in the quiet pools when we were weary of the crawfish. There were good pike to be had at Sairki, and their favourite food was spoons—so, at least, one would suppose from the voracity with which they endeavoured to devour those we offered for their destruction. Many an exciting half-hour was afforded us by the good-natured Sairki pike; they generally got away in the end, but always thoroughly entered into the fun of the thing and obliged us, while the game lasted, by pretending to be doing their best to escape our un-scientific attempts to bring them to book. Probably they could have rid themselves of the bait and us at any moment if they had been so disposed, but they were too good-natured. Now and then we caught one, but very rarely.

And so the summer day would pass with its sport and its bathing and its incalculable sandwiches, until the brilliant sunshine began to wane and the time came to shoulder our nets and hoist our heavily loaded watering-pots and mount the hill to the village. As for our sticks, we hospitably left these in the water in order that the crawfish remaining in the neighbourhood might enjoy themselves to the full and learn to laugh at those of their fellows who were disposed to look with suspicion at bits of meat attached to the ends of sticks. They might now finish the food with absolute impunity, and would come to the feast at our next visit without a thought of danger.

A memorable ceremony was the counting of the victims up at the village. This was performed in the midst of a gaping and ejaculating crowd of Finnish children, a score or so of scantily dressed, fair-haired little maidens and their brothers, who expressed their delight with the outcome of our prowess in a ceaseless chatter of their own language, monosyllabic, but full of extremely expressive inflections. We put ourselves upon the best of terms with these little foreigners by letting loose a number of our scaly captives among their naked toes, a move which caused them to jump about and scream in the wildest delight. The dis-tribution of a few copecks among them completed our popularity thus easily acquired. The Finns are a good-natured, inoffensive race, when properly treated; but proud and stolid and somewhat lazy, and withal

dignified and extremely jealous of their personal
independence. The commonest Finn peasant con-
siders himself the equal of any other man. Destiny
may have put the Tsar in a warmer corner than himself, perhaps, but that does not make the Tsar the
better man of the two. "The Tsar has a pair of
legs exactly like my own," a Finn peasant once remarked to the writer, and the saying sums up very
concisely the attitude of this quiet but dignified
member of the human family towards his fellow-men.

Six hundred and thirty-seven was the sum total of
our day's netting, besides many others caught and put
back: not a bad tally! It was sufficient to supply
the whole of the British colony in Mourino, which is
a good large one, with crawfish enough to last them
for some time. These are most delicious eating, as
highly flavoured as the lobster, but much more
tender and less stringy. A certain soup made of
crawfish is declared by gourmets to be simply un-
equalled by any other decoction known under the
name of *potage*.

And so, sped upon our way by the shouts of our
admiring friends the little Finnish maids and urchins,
we set forth once more to brave the perils and dis-
comforts of the return journey. I know not what the

unfortunate creatures in the watering-pots and the fishing-baskets may have thought of the bumpings and jars that marked our progress along that terrible road, but I do know that the day's wading and netting had not damped our own spirits in any appreciable degree. The ponies, knowing that they were directed homewards, flew along like mad things; breakneck races were once again the order of the day, and once again did our special Providence preserve us from the destruction we courted. Swiftly, too swiftly for us, the miles were left behind, and the last rays of the setting sun had scarcely lighted up the green cupola of Mourino church when, with whips cracking, drivers shouting, dust flying in clouds, and six human beings (counting schoolboys as coming under that category) and 637 crawfish bumping about like peas on a drumhead, we raced up to the lodge gates—and the day was over.

CHAPTER IV

A FINLAND PARADISE

FINLAND, or Fen-land : the land of fens, "the country of a thousand lakes"; in Finnish Suomen-maa : "the swampy region." The root *suom*, if not related to our own *swamp*—which is a matter upon which the present writer can give no opinion worth having—at all events appears to have the same meaning, and is quite similar enough in sound to please the ear of plain people with a neat, amateur appreciation for roots. It is indeed the country of a thousand lakes—ten thousand. Glance at the map; it almost makes a man's eyes water to look at it! As represented there, the entire country appears to be more water than dry land; the inhabitants must surely be obliged to get about the place in boats—or goloshes, you will think—and, oh! what a place for the fishermen! Not the people in smacks and trawlers, I mean; but for men with rods, and lines, and reels, and flies, and phantoms, and landing nets, and so on : think of it—all these fresh-water lakes—a network of ideal corners for the *Salmonidæ*, communicating one with another and with Ladoga and the Gulfs of Finland and Bothnia by means of glorious fishing rivers ! A place for fishermen indeed.

Look at the map, my dear reader, and consider the province from the point of view of the fish and their habits; it is the fishes' heaven, and being so it is certainly the paradise of anglers. A glance at the map will show that between Uleaborg in the north and Wiborg in the south there must be many spots which, to the keen fishing man, would in all probability present such piscatorial attractions as would entitle them to be called, as I have called one particular spot about to be described, "A Finland Paradise." I believe that the salmon fishing on the Ulea at Uleaborg, for instance, is so excellent that those who have deserted Norway or Scotland in favour of this remote Finnish spot are inclined to go no more a-roving, but to cry "Eureka," and spend the rest of their days by Bothnia's placid waters. But of this I can only speak from hearsay and from the printed reports of others, and will only add that I have been informed that fishing rights are easily obtainable at Uleaborg ; that such rights are absurdly inexpensive; and that there is some one in that distant city who can speak English, and who can put the traveller in the way of getting an introduction into the best salmon society.

But my Finland Paradise is not in far Uleaborg, nor yet in any of the thousand or ten thousand other places which on the testimony of the map of Finland must be equally worthy of the title. I must warn my readers that there is no admission to my paradise, excepting by favour of those happy ones who possess the right to inhabit it. In other words it is not, like Uleaborg and hundreds of other places, accessible to the ordinary travelling man and the itinerant sportsman. Its doors are closed to the public; the fishing is preserved, rightly and jealously preserved.

There is a railway, the Finnish Railway, as it is called, which runs from St. Petersburg to Hango, at the mouth of the Gulf of Finland. On this railway, at a distance of four hours from St. Petersburg, is Wiborg, the very ancient capital and castle of the Karelian Finns, who were conquered by Torkel C'nutson in 1293. From Wiborg there is a branch line to Imatra, built for the accommodation of tourists anxious to visit the wonderful rapids or falls at the last-named place. Imatra is on a river known variously as the Vuoksen, or the Voksa, which connects the great Saima Lake with the still greater Ladoga ; which, again, is connected with the open sea, as all the world knows, by the Neva. The Voksa is, I should think, one of the most beautiful rivers in the world. Wide, and clear as crystal, we have nothing like it in England ; it has no tide to yellow it, no navigation to stir and distress its calm depths ; the fish—grayling and trout—love it, and so does every human creature who has ever set eyes upon it, and who knows how to appreciate a big, free, clean, noble river when he sees it.

Lake Saima is a long sheet of water measuring from end to end one hundred and fifty miles or more, being quite as long as Ladoga itself, though much narrower and studded all over with islands. Saima is full of fish—great lake trout and others of the *Salmonidæ*, together with numberless other finny creatures of less exalted birth and parentage. Now all these fish occasionally pine, if not for actual sea travel, at least for such change of air and diet as a little wandering in running water can afford them. This they can only obtain by visiting the sole existing outlet (excepting the Saima Canal, leading to the Gulf of Finland, which cannot count as a river) to the entire hundred and fifty miles of lake, the Voksa.

Now, just where the Voksa takes its departure from the Saima upon its journey of fifty-or-so miles to the Ladoga, the Saima Lake narrows into a round basin of about one-third of a mile in diameter, which basin forms a kind of ante-room to the river, which starts out bravely from the western end thereof in a glorious rapid, the descent being considerable, and the consequent draw of current throughout the basin very strong, though not very perceptible at the surface. Through this basin, or ante-room, known as Harraka, every single fish which desires to visit the river from the lake, or *vice versâ*, must pass as through a turnpike gate; and many are the fish that have had to pay blood-toll for the privilege. The basin is at all times crammed with fish; it is their recognised rendezvous; it is Harraka, the paradise *par excellence* of the Voksa; the place to which all good fishermen should go when they die, unless they know of a better. I don't.

This paradise was, until a few years ago, in the hands of a few Englishmen, residents in St. Petersburg, who discovered it and acquired the rights of enjoying it as a fishing club. They built unto them-

selves a comfortable and most convenient lodge, just
at the very spot where Voksa, in froth and delicious
chatter of bounding rapids, bids farewell of Saima
and starts exuberantly on his race to Ladoga, little
dreaming of the fearful gauntlet to be run, a few
miles away, at Imatra. These thrice happy Britishers,
I repeat, acquired Paradise : they planted their feet in
the Garden of Eden ; they tasted of the delights of
Harraka for several seasons, and then by misfortune
they lost it. By some most deplorable accident or
misunderstanding the letting of the place went past
them, and Harraka, the paradise of anglers, became
a beautiful memory and nothing more. The flaming
sword of jealous proprietorship stood for ever between
them and the lost Eden of their happiness.

Then those men did the next best thing open to
them. They secured a small island a few miles
lower down the river, together with the fishing rights
around it for a space of a mile or so, and upon
that island, known as Varpa-Saari, they pitched their
tent, building a charming house, engaging fishermen
well acquainted with every inch of the newly acquired water, and, in a word, making the best of
what was distinctly a "bad job."

Varpa-Saari is not Harraka. But since, according

to some learned commentators, there are seven heavens, and since Harraka is certainly the seventh or highest of these, Varpa may surely lay claim to be called one of the remaining six. It is, in truth, a very delightful place. The river is here some three hundred yards in width, and is divided by the island into two channels, both of which show their teeth as they angrily pass the obstruction in a tumult of noisily chattering and scolding rapids on either side. Around the island platforms have been built jutting out into the turbulent water for the convenience of those who wish to try for the favours of grayling or trout with fly, in preference to spinning for them with a minnow from a boat.

It was the delightful privilege of the writer to spend a portion of the summer of 1894 in the land of the Tsar; and to me, ready and anxious for every kind of exploit, whether with rod or gun, came my friend C. G., whilom a member of the Paradise Lost of Harraka, now one of the proprietors of Varpa-Saari, with hospitable proposals, which ended in the speedy getting together of our respective gladstones, and the collection, on my part, of a great number of borrowed rods and reels and flies and minnows and other piscatorial paraphernalia, and

F

our prompt departure upon a three days' sojourn in
the delicious retreats of Varpa Island. It cannot, I
should think, be much more than sixty miles from St.
Petersburg to Wiborg, but the trains of the Finnish
line are imbued with all the dignity and deliberation
which are inherent in the Finnish character, and they
do not hurry themselves. A good English express
would do the journey in an hour; the Wiborg express
occupies the best part of four. But the carriages are
certainly comfortable and run very smoothly.

There is a custom-house somewhere between the
two great cities named—I think it is at Tereyoki—
but we are not asked to disclose the secrets of our
gladstones or to reveal the riches of our superbly
appointed commissariat, for C. G. is the most hospitable of hosts as well as the most talented of caterers,
and his arrangements for our three days' exile in the
wilds of Finland are such as to strangle in the birth
any vague ideas of prospective "roughing it."

So we glide slowly and smoothly through the
south-eastern portion of the Land of Fens, which, so
far, greatly resembles the Russia we have just left;
and if we look out for one of the thousand lakes we
do not see it, and shall not until Wiborg itself is
reached; though, as it happens, I know of several

further inland—old familiar places where in former
days I have angled for many large perch and pike,
killed many a duck, missed many a snipe, enjoyed
many a happy hour. It is hot with all the closeness
of the Russian July; but, fortunately, this is the
Finnish and not a Russian railway, and though we
manufacture a delightful draught by opening the
windows on both sides of the carriage, we are not
threatened for this reason with the terrors and tor-
tures to which those are subjected who infringe the
bye-laws of the company. It was but a few days
before that, travelling upon a Russian line, and
feeling asphyxiated by the heat of the carriage, I
had, in my innocence, let down the windows on
both sides. Instantly a guard rushed up and closed
one, that on the side from which the infinitesimal
air that existed happened to be blowing. I protested.
The guard expressed horror: there would be a
draught, he explained. I hastened to assure him
that that was exactly what I most wished to bring
about, and made as though to reopen the window
which he had closed. But this the guard would
not permit. I should catch cold, he said, and the
company could not dream of allowing their passengers
to catch cold. I argued, I entreated, but in vain,

and eventually I went to stand upon the balcony
outside. But, alas! this also, it appeared, was not
permissible just at present, and that for a peculiar
reason : a train conveying some member of the
Imperial family was to meet us presently, and no
man might stand outside until it had safely passed.
In the end I was compelled to return to the stifling
carriage, wherein I was cooked to a turn by the
time I reached my destination.

But if the train from St. Petersburg to Wiborg is
slow, what shall be said of that from the latter place
to Imatra? Yet why, after all, should anything be
said? There was no hardship in travelling now,
for it was evening and cooler, and the country
had grown more characteristically Finnish. Here
and there were small lakes, the outposts of the
thousand, the ten thousand, that lay calm and
majestic somewhere beyond. We were in Finland
now beyond a doubt.

But C. G. has a surprise for me—for me who have
never been in this part of the world before — have
never even seen Imatra. We shall be at a station
called St. Andrea soon, he tells me, and then I
shall see something which will interest me. What?
I am to wait; it shall burst upon my sight.

It does. It bursts upon my sight in all the calm beauty of its wide, white, gleaming, rippling majesty— the Voksa. At this distant spot, dedicated to the first Englishman probably who ever set foot in Finland, St. Henry,[1] my delighted English eyes catch their first glimpse of the ideal river—a river any Englishman would love at first sight. And what a spot for the fisherman! As I live, there is one at it down there. I can see him from the train whipping merrily at the rapids beneath the railway bridge! Instantly all the apathy of the long, slow journey is swallowed up in the enthusiasm of the angler; I feel inclined to wave my cap from the window and cry, like Xenophon's men, "Thalatta, thalatta!" Happy Bishop Henry, friend of Eric IX. of Sweden, who, about 1120, an Englishman, though Bishop of Upsala, brought Bible and sword and conquered and converted this pleasant land for his master,

[1] Finland has been a Christian country since the early part of the twelfth century, when Eric IX. of Sweden, accompanied by Henry, Bishop of Upsala, an Englishman, planted Christianity together with the Swedish flag in the hitherto heathen province. In the thirteenth century another English divine, Bishop Thomas, did his best to teach the Finns to shake off the Swedish yoke and become subject to the Pope alone, but in this he failed. The Finns have been Protestants since about 1530.

and became patron saint thereof. St. Andrea is
delightfully situated indeed. I wonder whether our
canonised countryman who gave his name to it
was ever here? St. Andrea sounds and reads
more like St. Andrew than St. Henry, but I may
explain that Henrys are always Andrews in Russia,
just as William is changed to Basil, Edward to
Dmitry, Bernard to Boris, and so on, because where
names do not exist in the Saints' calendar, substitutes
have had to be found. In the case of Henry, the
Finns appear to have followed the example of their
neighbours, and to have changed Henry into Andrea.
St. Andrew himself is connected with Russia, but
in no way, I believe, with Finland. This saint is
said to have travelled, preaching the Gospel, from
the Holy Land to Byzantium, and thence along the
Black Sea to the Danube, crossing that river and
reaching eventually the Dnieper. Here he went up
country as far as the spot where Kief was afterwards
built, and in this place, before turning to retrace
his steps to Byzantium, he uttered a long prophecy
as to the size and importance of the city which
should one day stand in that site, and which should
be dedicated to the faith which he had then come
to preach. So much for the Saints Andrew and

Henry, either of whom may claim, as far as names go, the honour of affording one to the remote Finnish village close to which the beautiful Voksa is first seen by the tourist.

Thence to Imatra is not far, and from Imatra to Varpa-Saari is a short drive of three miles or so, past the renowned "falls," about which I shall have more to say later. My friend and I accomplish this distance luxuriously in a spring cart, the commissariat following in a second vehicle. The roads in Finland are not like the roads in Russia. The Finnish roads are civilised, and may be driven upon without fatal results.

It was past eleven now, of a glorious July night, and in the white northern twilight, which is nearly daylight, we cantered up to the riverside and drew up at the spot where a landing stage has been made, communicating by means of an overhead wire over the Voksa with the island in mid-stream. The house is upon the island, and from the wire, at the island end, depends a bell. A tug at our end sets this bell clanging and a dog barking, destroying the calm majesty of the night in an instant, and causing dogs in all directions, far and near, to respond to the canine voice from mid-river in sleepy, querulous accents, as though barking were a terrible bore, but must be done out of conscientious motives. While we wait for the boat which is to take us across we hear ourselves hailed in English from some point hidden in the midnight mystery of the river, and when our eyes have located the sound we discover two boats swimming silently side by side, looking all one piece with the water, mystic, wonderful! It is J. H. and E. H., who have driven over from their lovely summer home a few miles below Imatra for a night's fishing in the Varpa waters. Slowly the two boats approach—it seems a sin to murder the marvel of the stillness by speaking—like two swans they swim towards us in the white twilight. Are we awake, and is all this really happening, or are these the creatures of a sleep-picture, and the witchery of the midnight Voksa a mere dream of unreal delight? The winding of two reels and C. G.'s hearty enquiry as to "what sport" has been enjoyed by these two midnight fishers put to flight all ideas of the unreality of things, and in a very few minutes we are each seated in a boat and crossing the gleaming, rippling, hurrying Voksa towards the little island which is to be our home for the next three days. As we reach the landing-stage at the island we find a sleepy Finn fisherman just preparing a boat, in response to our bell-summons, to take us across; but our friends have saved him this trouble. They land us, and away they float again, the two light craft moving noiselessly over the broad river propelled by the fisherman-Finn in the bows, and in the dim and mysterious distance we can hear the soft *crake, crake* of their reels as the lines are let out once more after having been wound in in compliment to ourselves. Before we are out of hearing there is a *whirr*, and we know that the phantom of one of them has found a billet.

Then up through leafy paths to the house, with only the murmur of water audible, but that from every side; with here a gleam and there a gleam between the trees, and everything else silence and shady darkness and mystery, and one's very soul feeling half numbed with the wonder of being in such a place and at such a time.

As for the house, it is the ideal of what a fishing lodge should be, with its racks for rods outside and in; its glorious roomy balcony dining-room, its large central sitting-room and its half-dozen or more of most excellent bedrooms, each commanding a more fascinating view over trees and river than its

next neighbour, and each with the perpetual sing-
song of the gentle mother Voksa to sing the tired
angler to sleep with her eternal lullaby.

And now, as C. G. most appropriately observes, a
little supper. The night and the place and the
circumstances are about as full of poetry as such
things can be; my very soul seems steeped in
mysticism, and the witchery of the surroundings has
made a poet of me to my very backbone; but—well,
they did not give us time to eat at Wiborg, nor at
St. Andrea, nor anywhere else, and the very word
"supper" is sufficient to send poetry to the winds
and to convert the poet into the ravening wolf until
the leeway of the appetite has been made up.
Luckily there is plenty to eat and it is ready to hand.
Julia, the Finn cook, a neat, clean-looking person who
cannot speak or understand a single word of Russian
or anything else but Finnish—Julia has baked some
quite delicious bread; and there is Finnish butter—
none of your "Dosset" this!—and C. G.'s baskets
contain town-bought dainties of the very best: it
is pleasant to sit and enjoy such a supper with the
white gleam of the midnight Voksa visible to us
wherever we choose to peep for it between the
ghostly trees that would screen it from us; and

with the soft babble of her waters for ever in our ears, as though they were constantly telling of the wonders in trout and silver grayling that lurk and hide from us in the secret depths beneath ; as though each wavelet had such a secret to tell us and were murmuring to us as it passed, " Down below—just here—oh, such a trout! oh, such a trout! Quick, or he will be off and away ! "

There can be no question of sleeping this night. We must fix up our rods and choose our phantom minnows, and go out in boats that are phantoms also, like those ghostly fellows, J. and E. H., there, who can be seen occasionally passing slowly across the white water in the distance, silent, mysterious, intent upon their spinning, two phantoms, in phantom boats and with phantom boatmen, fishing with phantom minnows, rightly so-called—all phantoms together ! What matter if we catch anything or nothing ? We must go, if it be only to steep our souls in the wonderful silence and beauty of this July night on the water, and to drink in the intoxicating delight and novelty of the whole thing.

And in an hour we are there, floating on Voksa's white bosom, propelled softly hither and thither as our boatmen think best ; for these men know where the huge silver Voksa and Saima trout most do congregate, and the charm and wonder of the river and of the night are nothing to them so long as some big ten or fifteen pounder can be induced to accept the invitation our cruel blue minnows hold out to them.   These superb fish are, so far as I can make out, of three kinds. First, great silvery fellows with bright red spots, for all the world like overgrown brothers of the little river trout.   Then there are darker coloured fish, of a golden brown hue, with spots less brightly accentuated, and, I think, larger heads.   Of these two kinds the former is the handsomer fish, but both are splendid specimens, and are caught up to twenty-four pounds in weight, C. G. having taken the record in this respect.   The third specimen I saw was a fish which I should have called a salmon, but, I believe, erroneously.   The Finns have a simple rule.   To them all fish over five pounds in weight are " Lochi," salmon (German, Lachs ; Russian, Lososino).   Now there are plenty of salmon in the Neva, and therefore in Lake Ladoga also ; and the reader might suppose that, since the Voksa flows into the Ladoga, there may be salmon in the Voksa just as well as in Ladoga itself.   So there may, in the lower parts of the river, but between Ladoga and Saima Lakes there is a barrier, known as

the Imatra Falls, which must surely be an insur-
mountable obstacle to the most enterprising of salmon.
The Voksa is a broad, generous, full-flowing river, of
three hundred yards in width, which is suddenly compelled at Imatra to compress itself into a narrow gorge
of scarcely twenty yards across, and to pass through
this as best it can for a distance of a couple of
hundred yards or so, after which it is free once more
to open itself out to its former wealth of elbow-room.
The reader may imagine with how much protest and
clamour the surprised and tortured waters of the proud
river perform this sudden act of self-compression.
Roaring and hissing with rage, they pile themselves
mountain high in an instant, and sweep down the
moderate incline in a furious phalanx of angry wave-
warriors, dashing from one rocky side of the gorge to
the other, diving, rearing, whirling, plunging, hurling
angry hisses of spray to this side and that, and at the
foot of the narrow torture-chamber standing up in
mighty water-columns and twisting round to face the
rock-walls that have confined them, as though they
half thought of turning again and rending them ere
they depart once more upon their course in unim-
peded freedom and gradually regained calm and
majesty. The very idea of any salmon mounting in

safety such a whirling, battling, irresistible fury of waters as Imatra is surely outrageous. There cannot be salmon above Imatra. The salmon-like lochi must be a salmon trout, or a lake trout, or some one of the non-seagoing families of *Salmonidæ*.

Full as the Voksa is of fish, and hard as my friend C. G. and I worked, both from the platforms with fly and from boat with phantoms of every shape and size likely to attract the monsters down in the depths beneath us, it was all in vain—or nearly in vain. We did, indeed, catch a few fish, but nothing very large, and hardly more than enough to keep us well supplied with toothsome, dainty fare for our own table. We offered those fish the choicest delicacies that London makers could produce; we tempted them with phantoms so fascinating that one would suppose any fish of decently discriminative powers would rise from its moist bed and come out, at night, to feed upon them as they lay on the table within the very house. We dangled these tempting morsels over the very spots where they were known to lie; but for two days did these Voksa monsters sulk and turn their faces steadfastly from us. There was thunder in the air; that, we concluded, was the mischief; perhaps during Sunday the storm would break. We would try them again on Monday, and meanwhile we would accept J. H.'s hospitable invitation and drive over to spend Sunday with him at his lovely home at Lappin-Haru (the Ridge, or the District, of the Lapps). Those Lapps who chose this spot for their habitation showed a wise discrimination and a taste for natural beauty of scene and site which one would scarcely look for in that unromantic tribe. Lappin-Haru overlooks the Voksa at one of its loveliest bends ; a truly noble river, flowing through dense forests and by the side of tidy, cultivated fields ; deep and majestic and silent at this corner, and bursting into rippling laughter at that ; a river that bears up the swimmer as buoyantly and as securely as the sea, so strong and so full and ample is the beautiful, bright, clear flood of it. My friend J. H.—the representative in St. Petersburg of a family as well known and as widely respected in Russia as it is in England—has built him a house in this corner of the Voksa Paradise, and a splendid house it is. And though in the very wilds of Finland, yet he is in communication with all centres of civilisation by means of the telephone ; indeed, you can even speak to him from the island club at Varpa-Saari, a dozen miles away ; while the Imatra trains stop for passengers within a mile of his front door. So quickly do the enlightened Finns avail themselves of the discoveries of science that the southern portion of their province is covered with a network of telephones, and no one in town or country dreams of being without this useful adjunct to civilised comfort.

Delightful indeed was it to come into a bit of England that Sunday morning at Lappin-Haru; delightful to hear English voices and to see English ladies and English children so far away from the madding crowd. And so Sunday passed very delightfully; and now Monday, our last day, has come round. I think it is at lunch this Monday afternoon that C. G. has an inspiration.

"I am going," he says, "to drive to Imatra and telephone over to Harraka for leave to fish there to-night." At this I laugh the laugh of the scornful, for it is well known that Harraka is the Paradise Lost of the English fishers, and that the present proprietors stand, figuratively, at the gate armed with the flaming sword of jealousy in order to keep out, with the utmost strictness, every would-be angler in their unique and incomparable waters.

Nevertheless, C. G. insists that he will try. "Who knows?" he says. "A kind and indulgent spirit may be animating for this day only the heart of Count

Arnoff!" (which is not the proprietor's real name);
"and, after all, he can but refuse."

This last proposition is só evidently true that I
scoff no more, but allow my sanguine C. G. to
proceed upon his way, though secretly remaining of
the opinion that Count Arnoff would sooner perish
than allow us upon his sacred waters.

Now, C. G. is undoubtedly personally fascinating,
but how he contrived to exercise his fascination
through the telephone I really cannot imagine; yet it
is certain that he returned home in a very short time,
and that, as I could see by the sunshine of his countenance long before the boat bore him to the landing stage on the island, where I awaited him, he had
been successful. The Count himself was away, but
his steward had taken upon himself to grant C. G.'s
request for an evening's fishing, and this very night
was to see us afloat in the magic basin of Harraka.
Paradise was to be regained, for one night only!

Oh! the care with which we dried and attended to
our lines and reels; the loving discrimination with
which we looked over phantom and totnes and
whisky-bobbie, and selected the most fascinating that
our tin reservoirs could supply. Oh! the anxiety
with which we watched the weather during the

G

afternoon, and the deep satisfaction with which we noted that all things tended towards the development of a fine fishing evening.

Then we took boat, at about eight o'clock, and rowed across to a spot where a trap awaited us—and such a trap!—and drove away through the drooping day towards the Count's wonderful water. The trap was a square iron cage on wheels, and the road —when it left the main track and branched off into the pine forest which jealously guards the upper reaches of the Voksa—was not a road at all, but a series of terrible abysses with no bottom excepting the native rock, which is granite in those parts, and painful to jolt against. Had the Count so arranged matters in order to keep intruders from his sacred precincts? We, at all events, were not deterred from pressing forward, and oh! the sight that rewarded us—a sight I shall never forget, and such as I had never thought to see. Try to picture it. When we reached Harraka and the basin or anteroom between Saima Lake and Voksa opened out before us, the entire surface of that basin of a third of a mile diameter was boiling and seething, and positively alive with leaping, gambolling monsters, so that it looked for all the world as though a shower of gigantic, long-shaped hailstones were falling over the entire surface of the water. There was not a square yard of the whole within which, if you watched it for a second or two, you would not see a mighty trout jump. Had it been possible to suddenly intercept a huge net between air and water you would have caught a million.

Even C. G., who has fished this marvellous basin in olden days, before Paradise was lost, has never seen anything like this. Our fingers, as we put up our rods, tremble with the mere excitement of seeing such a sight; we can hardly frame words of wonder and admiration. The feeling is almost awe——

But the two Finnish fishermen appointed to row us about shake their heads discouragingly. When the fish are playing in this way, they give us to understand, they will not take the bait. They are, it appears, not feeding at all, but merely enjoying life, and endeavouring to rid themselves of certain parasites which cling to them at this season. Probably in an hour or two they will feed. This is discouraging, but we intend to try all the same.

And for an hour we slowly float up and down and across the little lagoon, and the monster fish leap and play all round us, so that we might, if we pleased, touch them with our hands; they almost jump into the very boat at our feet, but neither minnow, nor fly, nor whisky - bobbie will tempt them.

We must leave the place at midnight, alas! for the Count's huge establishment — he has built a palace in this once beautiful place, beautiful in the fullest loveliness of prodigal nature — the Count's many servants and officers and stewards and clerks will not retire until we depart, and we cannot decently keep them all up later than twelve. Nevertheless, we will rest for half-an-hour, no more, and then try again for an hour or three-quarters of an hour; perhaps we may yet tempt at least one of these million monsters from his element. At present it is too tantalising to bear; we must turn our backs upon the seething basin and walk inland for the half-hour of enforced idleness—and then——

C. G. tells me that his fisherman has recognised him as an old friend, and declares that he, C. G., in the old club days, gave him, Mikki, a pair of trousers. C. G. does not remember the circumstance, but feels that the trousers were garments well bestowed, for Mikki will certainly take him to the best places by virtue of the gift. Cast your bread, says C. G., upon the waters, or in other words, freely distribute old pairs of trousers, and you shall reap the benefit of your liberality after many days.

Then we returned and settled ourselves once more in our luxurious, red-velvet cushioned boats, selected our biggest and most fascinating phantoms, and started. It was now past eleven o'clock. The fish had nearly finished their tantalising antics at the surface and had disappeared into the secret depths ; the swirling water was scarcely broken by a single leaping monster. Night had fallen at last : it was as still, as silent, as mysterious, as bewitching as a dream-river. You could hear the roar and turmoil of the Voksa breaking away in rapids at the far end of the basin, but here in the smooth water there was no sound—only a strong, silent draw of deep current towards the place where lake and river parted. Where were the fish? What had become of the thousands of sportive giants of half-an-hour ago? I tried to imagine them at the bottom, each lying behind stone or snag— lying with moving gill and bright silver body waving in the current, on the look-out for prey. Did they watch my blue phantom as it passed, and

half rush out at it, but hold back at the last
moment, noticing something which aroused suspicion in the cut of tail, or fin, or red marks on the
white belly? There is something fearfully sacri-
legious about all this. How dare I float with
impunity out here, at night, above these millions
of scaly beings, intent on their destruction and
fearing nothing for myself? What about the water-
spirits—the *Vodyannui* of Sclavonic folklore? This
is their own place : it is probably a sacred retreat
of theirs. At any moment they might——

Away go thoughts of water-folk and of everything else, for there is a great jerk. My heart
goes off at a hand gallop ; my rod instinctively
stands upright. Fifty yards away there is a rush
and the sudden flash of a silver streak of light—I
lower the point for an instant, an act of courtesy
always to be paid to a leaping fish—then there is
a whirr and a few moments of delirious, delicious
agitation. Yohann, my man, is making for the
land where the Count has built him a wonderful
granite embankment for the convenient landing of
fish; we reach it and I step out; but my captive
has not the smallest intention of giving in yet; he
is closer in now, but repeatedly he bolts away

and increases the distance again. Suddenly I perceive that C. G. is beside me: he, too, is playing
a fish—a big one he tells me. It is a race who
will requisition the huge landing-net first. Up and
down the embankment we go, and the fish are
leaping and struggling close in now; but C. G. gets
his home first, a beauty of nearly twenty pounds;
and mine, tired out, is ready to be landed as soon
as the net is free. A truly lovely fish, too, but
smaller than his by several pounds—no time to
weigh either of them now.

Back we go, and in three minutes both are on
land once more, and each is busy in the deliriously
fascinating occupation of battling with another giant.
Oh! this is life indeed. Better half-an-hour of
Harraka than a cycle of Cathay! Quick, C. G.;
land your fish and give me the net, and let us both
start again; this is too splendid to waste a minute!

And again we put forth our fatal phantoms, and
two more beauties are presently transferred from
the secret places of this wonder-tank to the hot
granite of the Count's quay—and then, alas! it is
midnight, and we must go. Seventy-five pounds,
in six fish, in little more than half-an-hour; it is
good enough, C. G. Furthermore, we are the richer

by more than these mere seventy-five pounds of trout-flesh, for we have seen a great sight to-night; we have been in Paradise; we have burst, this day, into the secret places of the trout people, the very sanctuary and central rendezvous of the tribe.

What should we have caught had we been able to continue our fishing on that marvellous night? Who can tell? If the fish are on the feed, really on the feed, in that wonderful basin, I believe you might catch any number while the appetite of the community lasted; there is no lack of them. No possible amount of angling could produce the smallest visible effect upon the numbers of the thousands we saw that night, when the basin boiled and splashed again with the play of them. A paradise indeed for anglers is this Finland paradise of the Voksa, and, alas! a paradise lost.

CHAPTER V

AFTER DUCKS ON LADOGA

ONCE upon a time when Autumn was holding sway, and Winter was within hail, a Russian friend, knowing my weakness for making acquaintance with every kind of creature to be seen in the Land of the Tsars, very kindly proposed to me to journey with him up the Neva to Schlüsselburg, or near it, where he owned a large house and much land; and there to embark in his steam-launch for a duck-shooting cruise on Lake Ladoga.

Duck-shooting from a steam-launch ! This would be quite a novel experience to me, and I jumped gladly at the proposal. But how were we going to get within range of ducks in a puffing and smoking steam-launch? I asked. Were they tame ducks?

"Tame ducks !" repeated my outraged host; "no, indeed; on the contrary, the ducks on Ladoga are the very wildest things in creation."

"Then how are we going to get at them in the

open?" I persisted, with true British pertinacity.
But my host only said, "Wait and see." His
manner was full of conviction; it was impossible to
doubt his good faith; clearly he was the proprietor of
a secret, which, in time, I too should learn! Delightful! I am for it; I shall see that there is something
new under heaven!

My friend Prohoroff is a capital fellow and a good
sportsman. I have shot with him over moor and
forest more than once, and found him possessed of
a chivalrous generosity and sportsmanlike nature rare
among the so-called sportsmen of his country. Prohoroff has a soul above family pot-shots at young
coveys huddled beneath their mother's wing; he
would scorn to break the egg of a grey hen in order
to add its unfledged contents to that of his game-
bag; that is not Prohoroff's style, which is robust,
and broad, and British. He lets his birds fly, does
Prohoroff, and misses them like a man; moreover, he
does not encourage his dog to catch the young game.
Prohoroff has rubbed shoulders with Britishers, and
has eaten of the tree of the knowledge of good and
evil in matters appertaining to fair dealing between
man and the brute creation. I shall be quite safe
in Prohoroff's hands.

From St. Petersburg to Schlüsselburg, up the
Neva, is a trip of some six or seven hours by the
deliberate steamer in which the journey is made;
it is, after all, the whole length of the Neva, from
source to sea. And a beautiful river it is, as far as
the stream itself is concerned. But the banks are
the reverse of interesting. Flat and dull, with here a
belt of pine forest, and there a tumble-down village—
all Russian villages present a tumble-down appearance
—and stubble and potatoes and waste land: there
is not much to look at, and no towns of any size and
importance are passed. But the water is beautiful
—clear and white, and, at this season—early October
—well stocked with salmon on the wander between
lake and sea. These may be caught, rarely, with a
minnow, *one* has been taken with a fly, I have heard,
but only one in the memory of man. For the rest,
the fishermen who ply for them with big nets worked
by a windlass from wooden jetties, appear to make
good hauls, and the quality of the fish is excellent.
I should dearly love to stop and have a cast or
two for one of them; but this is impossible. Prohoroff tells me that one of the favourite pastimes
of St. Petersburgers, with a taste for gentle gambling,
is to be conveyed out to one of these fishing stations,

and to speculate in "hauls" before the event. The cost of a "haul" about to be made and of course absolutely fortuitous as to its results, is from three to five roubles—six to ten shillings. The speculator may find himself possessor of salmon enough, as the result of but one cast, to feed a regiment for a week, or—if not one of the favoured of Fortune —may purchase a dozen "hauls" of the net and go away empty-handed. If so, he is sure to see, as he floats dejectedly away, a vast quantity of fish landed at the very next haul after his departure ; he will see their silver sides gleaming in the sun from a distance, and he will give his opinion as to the reliability of the goddess who holds the scales.

But here we are at Schlüsselburg, and here is Prohoroff's house—a huge, rambling structure with bedrooms like barracks, but unprovided with the commonest of comforts, excepting beds, and having no apparatus for washing. Russians are quite free from that insular faddiness as to cold water which is a characteristic of us Britishers ; they see no necessity for, and no virtue in, a washing-stand. As for a cold bath—*proh pudor!* What a dirty race they must be, think the Muscovites, who require a bath every morning ! There was once a *savant*

who gave the following definition of water : " A colour-
less liquid which turns black when the human hands
are placed in it." Was this learned man a joker?
I cannot think a *savant* would so demean himself;
he must have been of Russian extraction and perfectly serious. However, I have lived long enough
to learn the virtue of the saying, "*À la guerre,
comme à la guerre !*" Therefore, in a foreign land,
and in a strange house, when there are no facilities
for washing, I philosophically go unwashed until an
opportunity offers to repair the omission. So I went
to bed and wished for day.

In the morning a servant brought in a brown
pudding dish and a tumbler of water. I sat down, in
order to reflect calmly upon the possible uses of these
articles. Was I expected to seat myself in the dish and
pour the contents of the tumbler over me? I rejected
the idea. Eventually I placed the pudding dish upon
a chair, armed myself with the tumbler—and, by rigid
economy, and the exercise of superhuman patience,
succeeded in getting my face and neck wet and the
palms of both hands damp. Enough; I am washed
—now for breakfast and the ducks of Ladoga !

When we sallied forth to embark upon the steam-
launch and arrived at the water's edge, I did not

see the vessel, and inquired of Prohoroff where it
was. This was my good host's moment of triumph.
" Why, there, just in front of your nose!" he said,
laughing loudly and delightedly; "can't you see it?"
He pointed to what I had imagined was a grove of
young pine cover fringing a small island or promon-
tory. Then I understood the mystery, and was glad
that good-natured Prohoroff had succeeded so well
in bringing off his great surprise. It was indeed the
steam-launch; but so covered and hidden by pine
boughs, and small pine trees fastened to the boat's side
upright from the water's edge, that it really looked, as
I have intimated, for all the world like a pine-grown
island. Undoubtedly it was well done, and the ducks
might easily be deluded by it, even as I had been.

The skipper and the engineer were both aboard,
grinning with delight from behind the cover. My
host's successful deception was regarded by them as
a compliment to themselves, for they had built up
the fir-grove; consequently their joy was unfeigned.
These good fellows were armed with old muzzle-
loading English guns, always capped and at full
cock, and always held aimed, it seemed, at my head;
Prohoroff and I had our more modern weapons and
lots of cartridges; the party meant business!

Steam was up, however, and we must lose no more time, but be off towards the lake. Past the old Swedish castle we glide and the English cotton mills, and now we are in Ladoga, and hastening, a moving island, towards the middle of the great lake, to the waters wherein the big ducks most do congregate. Very soon Prohoroff sights the first duck community—a hundred of them—peacefully floating and diving a quarter of a mile away. "Ease her!" is the word; then, "Easy ahead;" and slowly and cautiously we glide forward towards our hitherto unsuspecting quarry. It is an exciting moment. I do not know the name of this duck now before us; but he is a huge black fellow, a diver, with white feathers in his wings. And now two hundred yards have been covered, and still we creep on unobserved. Then a very old duck lifts her head and looks at us. "My dears," says she, "did you notice an island about here? I didn't." One or two younger members of the family glance casually at us, their mouths full of food. One says the island has been there all the time; the other rudely enquires who on earth cares whether the old lady noticed the island or not; the island is certainly there now!

After this, the old lady settles down to her
usual morning avocations, until the island is within
a hundred yards, or less, of the party. Then she
gives us another and a longer look—her neck very
straight and long, and her face at right angles to
our advance—the one eye which is thus deputed
to scan us looking concerned and agitated. "I'll
tell you what it is, my dears," says she, "I don't
like that island; the current is setting the other
way, and yet we are nearer to it than we were.
I'm off, for one!" and in the twinkling of an eye
her black head has dipped beneath the surface;
her white-flecked tail for an instant shows itself,
then disappears, and Grandmother Duck is next
seen fifty yards further away. Fortunately for us,
her example is followed by one or two very old
stagers only—perhaps they have seen this game
played before; but the youngsters are not going
to listen to the fears and fancies of the old fogies.
What youngster ever did? Consequently, in another minute, judgment, swift and sure, has over-
taken them. Four barrelsful of flame and lead
belch out upon them as they float, two more as
they rise, and seven or eight young unbelievers
are lying dead upon the water, or endeavouring

madly, broken winged and in touch with grim
death, to dive out of range. All are picked up,
by degrees. Meanwhile, the community is wheeling around over our heads high in air; they see
us now, plainly enough, ensconced behind our
pine-tree ambuscade, and are forming their own
conclusions as to the morality of our proceedings.
Having settled this point, and, we trust, compli-
mented the old lady, their grandmother, upon her
sagacity, they fly away, and are no more seen.
They will exercise a wise caution with regard to
islands henceforth.

And so the day passes; with each duck community it is the same tale. There are a few
wise ducks and many unwise, and the deck of
our launch is strewn with the bodies of these
latter; great northern divers—who look as though
no foolishness could possibly, under any circumstances, find napping that stern wisdom which sits
for ever in the expression of their most serious
countenances—and divers and ducks of every sort
and kind, and to which my unlearned pen can
give no certain names. Some of these proved very
delicious when they afterwards made their positively
last appearance in public; some were very much the

H

reverse, though that sporting skipper and the can-
nonading engineer (who once nearly blew my head
off in the excitement of the chase!) liked them
all equally well. And so ended what was, to me,
a novel and delightful experience. It was one of
many days to which my soul cries out "encore!"
and cries in vain, for Destiny says, "Oh no! your
cake is eaten! you must wait your chance at next
baking day!"

CHAPTER VI

ABOUT BEARS: BY ONE OF THEM

I

I COME of what those conceited creatures, the humans, would probably call humble parentage. In other words, I belong to the great Ursine family: I am a bear. I may as well say at once, in order that there may be no misunderstandings between the humans and myself, in case my life story should ever come into their hands, that I do not in the slightest degree share their opinion as to the relative position in the scale of existence occupied respectively by them and by me. Indeed, if they will excuse my saying so, in my humble judgment I am at least as good as they are, and perhaps a little better. For instance, to compare us physically, I am taller than many, and broader, stronger, braver, fleeter, more majestic than the best of them. A human is a mere toy in my hands, as I have proved

over and over again—why, there was old Ivan the
keeper, only last month, he—but I am digressing.
Ha ha! I can't help laughing, though, when I
recall poor Ivan's face as I hugged him—my! how
his tongue did stick out!

Again, if we are compared intellectually, I very
much doubt whether we bears are so inferior as
my friends the humans suppose. We do not talk
their language—true! but, do they talk ours? I
think not. On the other hand, we *understand* theirs
—while they are ignorant altogether of ours!

As for their sciences, their education, their 'ologies
(which they think so much of), their arts, their wars,
their politics, their freedom—freedom! ha ha! it is
not *our* notion of freedom!—do all these things
render them the happier? What has all this "civilisation," so called, done for them? Are they freer
than I am? Do they get more to eat and drink, and
pay less for their victuals?

Well, well! I must not continue in this strain,
airing my pet ideas instead of proceeding with what
I intended to be a mere record of my own personal
career; I could say much in support of the opinion
expressed at the beginning of this chapter: namely,
that we bears are just as good, if not a little better,

than the human race; but then, after all, I shall
never succeed in convincing the conceited—the *most*
conceited of all creatures—man, of his inferiority:
as for my ursine readers;—well, we know what we
know!

My earliest recollections are among the most painful of all those scenes of my life which have impressed
themselves upon my memory; for they are connected
with the murder of my dear mother—the base and
barbarous murder of as good and indulgent a mother
as ever brought into the world and nourished a
promising little Bruin family, for such, I think, my
small brothers and sisters and I may fairly be called.
I will record the shocking circumstances of our great
domestic tragedy exactly as they occurred. My
earliest recollections are of life in a dark and confined space in which my two brothers and my two
sisters and I had but little room for our juvenile
recreations. I remember a dear old mother who
divided her time in sleeping, and admonishing and
educating us. We were born in this place, she told
us; it was called a "*berloga*," and was the den
she had prepared for herself as a shelter during the
long months of a cold and cruel Russian winter.
It was not cold inside this den of ours, on the

contrary it was very warm indeed. We had been born in December, and between that month and March we had had plenty of time to grow—we little ones—so that the *berloga*, which had been amply large enough for my mother alone, had become what I may describe as a tight fit for the six of us. It was lucky, mother used to say, that father was not with us at the time. He was away—she did not seem to know where, exactly, but she had arranged to meet him near a certain village, whose name she mentioned, some time in spring. I remember our mother used often to say, "*Do* let me go to sleep now, my dears; when you are older you will understand how difficult it is to keep awake in the winter time after the fatigues of a long season!" and, indeed, the good soul used frequently to fall fast asleep in the very midst of our lesson time—much to our joy, for we were always ready for a game of romps in that heyday time of childhood. Mother would have slept the whole winter but for us brats, she used to tell us! Well, one day about the end of March, when the other children and I were busily engaged in rolling over one another, and pretending to worry each other's ears, which was a favourite game of ours, we heard a terrible noise outside. Up to this time we had never heard any sound at all excepting such as we made ourselves. There were shouts and barking of dogs, and a creature—whom I afterwards discovered to be a human— was knocking at the sides of our house with a long pole—we could see all this through a small peephole which we kept open. We also saw other human creatures standing near. These last held in their hands steel sticks clubbed at one end, and were looking straight into the mouth of the den. Mother was fast asleep and we were obliged to awake her, for we felt alarmed at the aspect of these human creatures, puny beings though they seemed when compared with our beloved parent, who was so very much larger and stronger than they.

Mother started up and rubbed her eyes: "What is it, you tiresome children?" she asked. Just at this moment she caught sight of the man who, with his pole, was pushing and striking at the snowed-up mouth of the *berloga*. Immediately mother's face and form changed. I had never seen her look as she now did. Her beautiful brown coat stood out and her ears went back. Red blood came into her eyes, and her claws stretched out to their full length. She growled savagely, and for a moment or two glared at the human disturber of her peace as though she would every instant rush out and tear him limb from limb. At last she spoke to us: "Children," she said, "we are in great danger, and I know not what best to do: you are so young to take care of yourselves!"

"Take care of ourselves, mother?" we said —"what do you mean! you are not going to leave us?"

"Not if I can help it, dears," said my mother, licking and caressing us each in turn, as she spoke: "but do you see the sticks which yonder men hold in their hands? those are called guns; they are terrible things, and spit fire and smoke at us bears. But for them, I should fall upon these human miscreants and we should sup upon their flesh—which is very good eating, and some bears prefer it to a vegetable diet. As it is, I shall spring first at this· man with the pole—he cannot hurt me. Then I shall attack the others; but, dear children, it is very dangerous, for the contest is unequal; those fire-sticks may kill me before I reach them. If they do, you must all stay as still as mice in here—perhaps they will not see you. Should they see you, you must run for it; keep behind the trees, and don't run across the snow patches, of which there are still some about, for that will leaves traces of the direction you have taken, and you may be followed. If you escape, find some lair for yourselves and keep together for warmth. Eat what you can find. And now, dear children, we must part : if I escape with my life I shall soon return and find you ; if not, good-bye—don't forget your mother and all her advice ! "

With these words our dear mother suddenly sprang out of the *berloga*, and in an instant had knocked down the human who was the nearest to us—him with the pole. Then without waiting a second she hurled herself upon the other two creatures, those which held the fire-sticks, or guns. Instantly there was a terrific noise, like a clap of thunder, but shorter and louder; followed by a second and a third. But mother had reached the nearer of the two humans and had risen on her hind feet with such a roar that even we, her children, were startled and frightened. She seemed to reach and claw at him—oh! how majestic and grand she looked compared with her puny antagonist. Then she and he fell over together, and I saw the second creature point his fire-stick at them as they rolled on the ground; it spat out its fire again, and mother rose and disappeared among the trees! Dear, brave mother! what a glorious fight she made of it—and she had escaped after all, then! good, brave mother! Very soon we saw the pole-man rise and rub his head, and he and the third man creature went together to look at the second, who was lying as mother had left him, upon the ground. They did not seem to be able to mend him, however, for he still lay on and took no notice of them. But all this time a horrid little white creature who was with them, a thing called a dog, had been poking around our den with its tail tucked tightly between its hind legs—an ugly and silly habit of these creatures when they feel alarmed. He was sniffing about the mouth of the lair, and suddenly—entering a foot or two further than he had ventured before—caught sight of one of my sisters. He instantly turned and ran out of the *berloga* as fast as he could lay his wretched thin legs to the ground, barking and yelping, and my silly little sister, unable to resist the temptation, must needs run after him. Immediately there was another explosion from the man with the fire-stick, and poor little Katia, my sister, rolled over and over and then lay quite still—dead; murdered!

"Here! Ivan!" cried the man, "go into the *berloga* and see if there are more of the little brutes—try and catch one or two alive for the Zoo!"

It was all up! Ivan came blundering into our house, groping about with his hands, for it was too dark to see anything. We all lay still, for we were too small to hurt him. and we hoped to escape. But his hand came in contact with little Mishka's coat and Ivan held on tight, in spite of poor Mishka's struggles and snarls and bites. The rest of us, not wishing to lose our freedom, rushed out of the lair, leaving Mishka in Ivan's hands, a captive. As we darted out and made for the shelter of the trees, remembering mother's advice, the dreadful fire-stick spat out its fire and smoke at us, but none of us were hurt by it, and Vainka, Natasha, and I got safely away and huddled ourselves together inside the trunk of an old dead pine tree. Here we stayed for hours, not daring to move for fear of being found by the cruel humans and their fire-sticks. When it began to grow dark we ventured out and crept back to the *berloga*. There was no sign of the humans; poor dead Katia had been taken away and little prisoner Mishka also; but where was mother? We wandered about calling for her in all directions; at last—just as we were giving up the search for the night—Natasha heard a sound which she said she was sure was our dear mother crying. Then we all listened and heard it, and proceeding in the direction from which it seemed to come, we found poor dear mother lying stretched upon the ground, bleeding and weak. She had three horrible wounds, all given by those detestable fire-spitting sticks called guns, and her life-blood was fast oozing from them.

"I am dying, my children," she said—"are you all safe?" She looked around at us, with her poor glazing eyes, and noticed that some were missing.

"Where are Katia and Mishka?" she asked. We were obliged to tell the sad truth.

Again we saw that dreadful look of savage hatred come over mother's face. For a few moments she could say nothing; then at last she muttered:

"Promise me, children, that throughout your lives you will hate and fight mankind, wherever you meet his detested offspring! promise me this, and I shall die happy!"

We all promised faithfully to do as she wished. These were dear mother's last words to us, and a few moments later she died and her soul flew away to those happy hunting-grounds where, as we bears are taught to believe, it is our part to handle the fire-sticks, and that of the human beings to be hunted !

Thus we lost our dear mother, together with a small sister and brother whom we could better spare. Considering the circumstances of our deprivation, by means of the foulest murder, of a parent's care and authority, and of our last promise to a beloved and dying mother, is it to be wondered at that I can never cherish any other feeling towards that arch-enemy of my family—*man*, than hatred, and that of the deepest? My brother Mishka, from whom I hear occasionally, in a manner utterly unsuspected by his " Keepers " in the Zoological Gardens at St. Petersburg, frequently does his best to persuade me to modify my opinion of and conduct towards mankind. He says the humans are not nearly so bad as one thinks, and that he has a very good time in his perpetual *berloga* (from which the poor fellow cannot escape), and gets plenty of victuals of the best quality. He says he likes children the best— they are so very generous with their buns and cakes. Ha ha ! I agree with him about the youngsters ! I like the children best, too ! they are so deliciously

tender and flaky.   I have enjoyed several, and sin-
cerely hope I have not tasted my last.

But I must proceed with my narrative.   This then
was to be the pivot upon which my future career
was to turn : hatred of and animosity towards the
human race.   If I could at any time injure their
persons or damage their property it should be
done; I had vowed it; that very night as we three
children lay huddled and trembling, poor orphans
of a murdered mother, within our desolate *berloga*,
we all vowed it.   Man was henceforth our enemy.

We were all reduced to great straits just at this
time, for a living.   Poor little creatures that we were,
it puzzles me now, when I think of it, how we
managed to pull through that dreadful period.   The
fact of the matter is, we were obliged to eat all sorts
of things which we should otherwise have left alone ;
it was now April, and we contrived to live upon the
young leaves and grass blades and shoots of various
trees and bushes, together with--I blush to record it
—field-mice, squirrels, an occasional hare, and sometimes a partridge or grey hen, when one could be found
obligingly sitting on a nestful of eggs and dreaming
of the joys of maternity.   We ate the eggs also.

So we dragged along until July came.   But each day

life became easier and more enjoyable, for the rye and oats soon began to grow tall in the fields surrounding the villages ; the bees were up and about, and furnished us with the perfectly delicious results of their labours; and the woods gradually filled themselves with berries and luxuries of all sorts. When the oats were ripe we fared magnificently.

One day we met a splendid specimen of our family whom we soon discovered to be none other than our father—the consort of our dear mother, now deceased. He received us fairly well ; but my veneration for the paternal relative suffered a rude shock when he informed my brother and sister and myself that, with every desire to be a good father to us, he could not permit us to trespass upon a certain oat-field which he declared did not contain any more than he absolutely required for his own subsistence. He made some sympathetic remarks as to mother's death, with his mouth full of delicious ripe oats, and then bade farewell of us (meaning *us* to go—he evidently had no intention of leaving the field !), remarking, cordially enough, that he would always be glad to see us, and to hear of any favourable feeding-grounds we might come across, if large enough for all, "but never mind your old

father if rations are scarce!" he added. I never
saw my parent again. Very shortly after the day
upon which he warned us off that oat-field, which
— by the way — *we* had discovered, he actually
permitted himself to be driven away from its
precincts by a mere peasant-human armed with
an axe. I fancy my father must be a very
inferior person compared with my good brave
mother. *She* would have behaved very differently
towards that peasant—we should undoubtedly have
had him for supper: oats, peasant, and honey; a
supper of three courses fit for the gods. But for
a member of the family of Ursidæ to be ignomini-
ously chased away from an oat-field by a peasant
—oh! dear me—disgraceful! disgraceful!

II

Well, it was a grand time for us, that first summer.
How we grew and fattened! By the early part of
the autumn, we were really quite respectable-sized
members of the community. About this time we
lost our brother Vainka. It was an exciting thing,
rather, and I will note down the story in full. It
was like this.

We were all three busily engaged in breakfasting among the tall stems of a rye-field, near a village, when we observed several human children playing about in an adjoining belt of pasture-land. There were no grown men present, so far as we were aware, and we determined to amuse ourselves, and at the same time to piously observe the injunctions of our dear mother deceased, by doing our best to frighten the brats out of their wits, and, if possible, injure them besides ; we were too small, as yet, to do them any very serious harm ; in fact, they were rather bigger, I think, than we.

So we crept towards them, hidden from view by the beautiful thick rye-stalks, until we were close to the edge of the pasture-field. Then, at a signal from Natasha, we all three pounced out upon them, growling and open-mouthed. Oh dear, oh dear ! it was a funny sight to see those children ! The silly creatures were too startled to move until we were upon them. They stood staring and shrieking, with eyes and mouth open, and turned to run only when it was too late. How we laughed as we rolled them over and over in the grass and scratched their faces, and tore their dresses off their backs ! and how they screamed ! The whole

I

population of the village rushed out to see what all the noise was about, big men and women with axes and long things called scythes, and then we thought it was time to retire among our rye-stalks. There we hid ourselves and laughed, and ate the delicious cool, juicy grasses, and the luscious rye-grains, until we could eat and laugh no more, and determined to make a move into the woods, in order to have a good drink in a moss pool we knew of and then lie down a bit and sleep off the excitement. But to our horror we found that those mean wretches, the humans belonging to the village, were waiting for us outside the cover. They had sneaked up and surrounded us, and were sitting silently all along the edge of the field, armed with their axes and scythes and nets; luckily they had no fire-sticks !

"Well, Vainka was, as it happened, the first to step out from among the rye-stalks, and he was immediately confronted by two women and a man who ran after him—one getting in front and one on each side. While they were busy with him, however, Natasha and I escaped unnoticed and were able to watch the pursuit of poor Vainka from a position of safety. One of the women had a crawfish net with a long wooden handle. This creature kept calling to the others, "Don't kill him, don't kill him! we'll take him alive!" The others seemed to agree, for they closed in upon poor little Vainka and placed the crawfish net tightly over his head and face, so that, though he fought fiercely and bravely for liberty, he was quite powerless to hurt them. Then they led him away to the village and we saw him no more.

I have seen him often since, however, for his "master" (!) still lives in this village and brings him down from town at certain seasons. Vainka goes to town (St. Petersburg) in order to amuse the people by dancing on his hind legs, pretending to wrestle with his master, and other foolery, and with —I blush to record it—with a ring ·through his nostrils, to which a chain is attached. Poor dear old Vainka—his spirit is completely broken; he has actually learned to tolerate human-kind, and declares that they only require to be known in order to be appreciated, and that he does not think he could exist now without the applause which his performances call forth from the vulgar brutes of humans who have degraded him. Ugh! it is shameful! He has twice escaped from the village and

joined me—but I will, I think, relate these episodes
in full, in their proper place in this narrative; for
my ursine friends may learn much by a careful
consideration of the events, and I should not like
to deprive them of the advantage of considering this
matter in the light of a thorough and intimate knowledge of the circumstances. Meanwhile, I must relate the sad story of how Natasha and I separated
—after, alas! a quarrel. It was after our first winter
alone—without mother and the rest, I mean. Natasha
and I spent that winter together, in one *berloga*, for
warmth. It was a very uneventful time, for we were
not disturbed from November to April, and slept
steadily on through all those months. It was then
that we realised how dreadfully we must have worried
poor dear mother in the preceding year by keeping
her awake during that long period when we bears feel
as though it were impossible, whatever happened, to
rouse ourselves, and would almost sooner die than
move. But to continue : when spring came and we
sallied forth from our winter quarters, we were both
so hungry that positively we could almost have eaten
one another. Just outside a village close by, as we
were prowling around, hoping to find some sort of
food, Natasha taking one side of the village and I

the other, I had made my half round without success and was awaiting my sister with some degree of impatience, when I saw a dog issue from one of the huts and trot away across a field. The next instant I heard a yelping and observed Natasha in full pursuit, and scarcely a yard away from the dog's tail. Then they both disappeared behind a hedge, and for a moment the yelping was redoubled, and then ceased altogether. I hurried along to join and congratulate Natasha, as well as to take my share in a dinner which I felt that I required very badly, when suddenly I met Natasha returning.

"Well, where's the dog?" I said—feeling, I know not why, a strange sinking at the heart.

"What dog?" said Natasha, drooping her head a little and averting her face.

"Why, the dog you were hunting a moment ago!" I said.

"Oh, it escaped," said Natasha, who had some whitish fur, which was not her own, sticking to the corner of her mouth..

"Oh—you *nearly* caught it, I see!" said I.

"Yes, I very nearly caught it," said my sister, her voice dying away to nothing at the end of the sentence.

Well—I believed her, for we had never, as yet, deceived one another to any great extent.

Half an hour afterwards, as we were roaming the woods looking for something solid to eat, I suddenly missed Natasha. I called for her and searched the wood, but all in vain. I therefore left the forest and retraced my steps towards the open fields close to the village. There, after considerable hunting and much waste of time and temper, I at last came upon my sister, who was just polishing off the last remnants of the carcase of a dog. I fell upon her without a word, for she had deceived me and was unworthy of courtesy at my hands. Up to this time I had always been polite and kind and—in its best sense—brotherly towards Natasha; therefore she was astonished and indignant when I attacked her. I must confess I punished her savagely, for I was very angry and very hungry as well; indeed, I did not leave her alone until I had pretty nearly worried the breath out of her body. When she picked herself up from the grass she made off immediately, without making any remark either of abuse or excuse, and, as I have never set eyes on her since that morning, I conclude that she emigrated to a distant part of the country. I cannot say I was sorry, for

I should never have regained that confidence in her which her deceitful conduct on this occasion entirely destroyed, and the relations between us would have been so strained as to render life unpleasant.

So there was an end of family life for me—as a bachelor, of course. My father—well, the less said about my poor old selfish pater, the better. My mother, bless her, dead; my sister Katia dead also; Mishka and Vainka both prisoners, one at the Zoo, in St. Petersburg, the other in a village not far away from my own domain; and Natasha, as I have explained, an exile—a discredited fugitive from her native woods!

Soon after Natasha's disappearance, however, at least in the autumn of the same year, just before I had chosen the spot in which I should winter, something happened which filled me with true joy and thankfulness: for I have a tender heart in spite of what I have just recorded of my conduct towards Natasha.

I was wandering about the forest feeling very weary, and longing for the first fall of snow to herald in the approaching winter and allow of my retiring for the season. Hearing a noise behind me—a puffing, grunting noise which seemed to indicate

the presence of one of my own species,—I turned
quickly round to see who this could possibly be ;
and, if a stranger, to warn him that he was trespassing
upon land which already belonged to me by the sacred
rights summed up in the ancient Roman law which
all bears excepting extremely large ones still recognise
as binding : "*beati possidentes.*" What was my delight
to see my dear old brother Vainka puffing and blowing after me as fast as his poor old legs and lungs
—both sadly out of condition,—could bring him.
He had a ring through his nose, and from this
there dangled a piece of chain, and from the end
of the chain a torn portion of a halter.

We rushed towards one another :

" Why, Vainka ! " I exclaimed : "where in fortune's name do *you* come from, and how did you
escape ? "

" It's a long story ! " said Vainka—"never mind
the details—here I am ! I bit through the rope,
as you see, and escaped from the barn at night
by breaking down the door : now let's have some
food ! when we are in the *berloga*, which I suppose
will be to-morrow—I hope so, for I'm dead tired "
(here he yawned twice and I followed suit)—" I'll
tell you all about it."

I gave him a capital dinner considering the time of year, including some honey—of which I knew of a good store, and showed him the spot I had chosen for the *berloga*, which he quite approved of.

During the course of conversation, Vainka informed me that he had grown quite fond of his "master," and would not care to do him an injury; but at the same time he wished to mention that there were six young sheep grazing in the field behind the house he (Vainka) inhabited, and that he should imagine these sheep would make a delightful meal for any one liking mutton. Personally, he said, he would rather not touch them, and he hoped, for his master's sake, that no one else would; but that they were in such and such a field, and the humans never left the house before 6 A.M. A really good feed, he remarked, was considered by some people to be an advantage just before retiring for a sleep of several months.

He was perfectly right. Those young sheep were quite delicious ; and while we gaily consumed them for dinner next day old Vainka gave me many hints as to the exact disposal, by humans, of their time,— hints which have ever since been extremely useful to me in various ways. Did I mention that Vainka consumed his share of the two sheep which found their way to our larder? well, he did—anyhow; and enjoyed them very much, but was deeply put out (after he had dined) to remember that the mutton had belonged to his master.   He would not, he said, for anything have touched it had he recalled that fact in time.

.That day the snow came, and, after performing those maze-like evolutions in which our family invariably indulge at this time of year, and which are designed to bewilder any human being who might wander our way and wish to track us, with sinister purpose, to our lair, we lay down, and overcome by fatigue and—well, mutton—fell asleep almost immediately.   I had endeavoured, but in vain, to remove the badge of servitude and disgrace which poor Vainka was condemned to wear in the shape of the ring and chain, but could do nothing with it— Vainka had been obliged to settle down with the cruel, detestable thing still attached to his nose—bah!

The next thing either of us was conscious of was a knocking at the sides of our snowy, or icy house. The noise immediately aroused us, for it recalled a similar sound which we had good cause to remember, and carried us back to that dreadful day when our poor mother had been done to death, together with little Katia. On peeping through the hole we soon perceived that we were besieged by two men—both of whom were peasants. One of these held a fire-stick, and the sight of it put my heart all of a quake; for I confess, though I fear nothing else in the world, I am terribly frightened of that dreadful, death-spitting stick, called gun. But Vainka touched my shoulder: "The one with the gun," he whispered, "is my master: what's to be done?"

I didn't know. Then Vainka rose to the emergency and did that for which I shall always feel reverently and admiringly grateful to him. He undertook to see me safely out of the difficulty by giving himself up.

"They'll never dream that *you* are here as well as I," he said; "all you have to do is to stay snugly inside and let me go out: they won't shoot me; I am too valuable to them!"

I protested that this sacrifice was too noble; that I could not permit such self-abnegation on my account!

"Self-abnegation?" said Vainka; "nonsense! it's nothing of the sort. I declare to you that I would rather go back to the humans than earn my living in the woods; I came away because I pined for the winter sleep for which my nature yearns—I should have had to work, with them; *now*, I have had my rest and am as fresh as a daisy!"

I really believe the good fellow meant it. At all events, since I should certainly be killed or wounded if I went out and he would as certainly only be captured, it was clearly better that he should go than I; for he might always escape again; while I, if once killed, should appear upon the scene no more. So I embraced my dear Vainka, thanked him heartily for saving my life at the expense of his liberty (at which he smiled and said he didn't believe in liberty), and let him go—lying very close myself, and watching the development of circumstances through the peephole.

I must say that, in spite of all my hatred for mankind, I was a little softened towards Vainka's friends, on this occasion, by the events which now took place.

Vainka broke through the wall of our *berloga* and deliberately stepped out. The man with the pole quickly got out of the way, while the other raised his gun. For an instant I was in dread lest he should not recognise my dear brother in time, and was on the point of rushing forth to strike him dead before he should have slaughtered poor confiding Vainka,

when, luckily for us all (for I should not have been
in time), he dropped his arm, raised his hand to
shade his eyes, stared, and broke into a roar of
laughter : "Why!" he cried, "strike me blind if
it isn't dear old Mishka himself!" (The humans,
for reasons best known to themselves, call us all
" Mishka.")

· With these words, he rushed up to Vainka, caught
hold of the chain (the wrench to V.'s nose must
have been exceedingly painful!) put both arms round
my brother's neck, and commenced to kiss and to
hug him in the most comical manner. He really
appeared to be quite fond of Vainka, and Vainka
himself seemed almost as glad to greet *him*. Then
the peasant took some lumps of the cooked rye, which
my brother says is so delicious (and which, I may
mention, I believe in my heart to be one of the
chief causes of Vainka's marvellous attachment to
the debased life he leads!), and fed his new-found
and long-lost friend. Vainka dropped a large piece
of it on the ground, and I imagine the good fellow
meant it for me; but the frugal peasant picked it
up and pocketed it, so that I was not able to taste
the vaunted stuff—bah! I'm sure it isn't up to July
oats or honey, or even baby — which is delicious

when one happens to be of a carnivorous turn of
mind, as one is sometimes.

Then they all went away and left me, never
dreaming—as Vainka rightly anticipated—that another
bear lay concealed within the *berloga*, and that Master
Mishka, as they called him, was but my guest.   Ha !
ha ! I should have liked to have dashed out and
smashed them both—the men, I mean, when their
backs were turned ! I burned to do it—but discretion
gained the day : there was that accursed fire-stick to
be reckoned with : I have been told that guns can
be made to spit their fire in an instant even when a
man has been knocked down and is lying upon the
ground.   So I refrained and stayed where I was, and
in a while fell asleep once more, sleeping safely and
comfortably until April, when I left the den and went
out once again upon my travels.

I had one other visit from Vainka, a few months
later.

I had been hunting near his village, when of a
sudden I became aware of Master V. approaching
me through a thin birch spinney which lay between me and the fields around the hamlet.   He
looked very dejected — not at all as one would
expect a bear to look who had just regained

his liberty! He brightened up a little when he saw me.

"Is anything the matter, brother?" I inquired, as I went to meet him.

"Nothing whatever," he said, "excepting that, curiously enough, I do not feel inclined to escape, and yet here I am, in the act of escaping!"

"But how can that be?" I said; "in the first place you *must* be glad to escape—no bear of any self-respect could help feeling glad; and besides, how could you possibly escape against your will?"

"Well," he said, "perhaps I have no self-respect; anyhow I only came because they left the door of the stable wide open and my chain was off at the time. All I had to do was to walk out, and now I wish I hadn't! This is just the time when little Masha brings me my lunch of delicious bread" (that's the cooked rye I mentioned), "and—and— upon my word I think I shall go back—what's the use of being free—I am no longer fitted for a wild life."

And sure enough the poor-spirited creature, whose once keen, free spirit had been entirely deadened by contact with the humans and their debasing life, would have made off then and there!

But I stopped him. "You shall do nothing of
the kind, my friend!" I said firmly. "You shall
come into the woods with me and have a good
time, and when you've enjoyed a run and some
fresh air and natural food, you shall do as you
like! Come on!" So I got him away, and for
three days we had the grandest fun in the world.
He cheered up and agreed to join me in a little
hunting close to a neighbouring village—he would
do nothing near his own. We killed two dogs, a
young cow, and some sheep, old Vainka thoroughly
entering into the spirit of the fun, and even enjoying
the wild fury of the humans, who could not find
us—there being no snow.

But after three days of freedom and real life
Vainka grew home-sick. He yawned frequently,
and said how sad little Masha would be without
him, and wondered what she was doing now—and
now, and whether his master—whom, in spite of
his solemn vows to our mother, he had evidently
learned to love—was quite well—and so on. He
became so melancholy and maudlin, that I perceived it was no use fighting against destiny, and
I recommended him to be off to his dancing and
skipping and his Masha and his confounded man-

worship—and away he went—poor fellow! as clear a case of a good bear gone wrong as it has ever been my lot to come across.

III

The foregoing episode is a narrative of my last visit from Vainka. I have seen the poor old fellow now and again and communicated with him by signs, the nature of which my ursine readers will at once comprehend, but which—in case any artful human should happen to decipher these memoirs—I will not describe in detail. Both Vainka and Mishka are—much as I deplore the fact—now quite gone over to the enemy; they are, both of them, more man than bear, and this in spite of the tragic and bloody reasons which they, in common with myself, should cherish in their deepest hearts for loathing the very creatures whom they have learned to love—bah! it is unnatural, it is unbear-like, it is sickening.

I, for my part, have kept my vow as made to our murdered mother. I think I may fairly boast that this is so. Perhaps if I relate one or two of my principal adventures with mankind, my readers will do me the justice to admit that I have done my

K

best. I hope they will do *themselves* the justice to follow my example. Mankind should be suppressed, wherever found.

The first human being I successfully attacked and killed was a grown man, a peasant; the second was a baby. The latter was delicious, and I can safely recommend such of my relatives as have adhered, hitherto, to vegetarian principles, to relax them in favour, at least, of this dish.

Babies are not always easily procured; but a little excitement adds, I consider, zest to the pursuit. I may say at once that babies, in spite of the terrible noise which they are undoubtedly capable of producing, are perfectly harmless. They may be found occasionally lying on the grass close to rye or oat fields in which human beings are busy cutting down the food which naturally belongs to us, not to them. This is an act of burglary, and is punishable with singular propriety; because while these thieving humans are intent upon depriving us of our property it is the easiest matter in the world to creep up and make oneself master of *theirs*, in the shape of the babies which they leave in the adjoining field, ostensibly to take care of the food and drink which is packed in baskets for their dinner—though I must say it is just like human stupidity to place a helpless thing like a baby in charge of valuable property. I have never yet seen one raise a hand to protect its mother's dinner. But, as usual, I am wandering from my immediate subject, which is—a description of my first man.

It was towards evening one summer day, and I was wandering slowly through the wood. I was not in the best of humours, for a field of oats upon which I had been supporting myself for several days was this afternoon in the hands of the "reapers," as they call themselves: *thieves*, as I call them! I had come there for my dinner and found the gang of humans busy at the oats with scythe and reaping-hook. What could I do? there was nothing to be done, excepting to show my teeth and bristle up my coat at them—and since they did not see me that was not of much practical use! So I went away again, cross and revengeful, and as I roamed about the woods, fuming and hungry, whom should I meet of a sudden but a tall peasant, wearing an axe in his belt but otherwise unarmed.

For an instant we both stopped, surprised and startled. Then, full of the hatred for his kind which I always felt but which had received an additional

stimulus in the oatfield this afternoon, I raised myself upon my hind feet and caught hold of him.
He tried to reach his axe, but I had gripped his
arm and he could not. His face was a study : he
had become very pale and his eyes were protruding :
froth came from his mouth together with spluttering
words—bad language, of course ; those disgusting
peasant creatures never open their lips without using
language such as a bear would be shocked to employ.
I leant upon him, bending my whole weight forward,
growling fiercely, and reaching for his throat with
my teeth. I felt a strong lust for blood, and my
rage increased with every second. I knew that I
must kill this man, and that he could not escape
me or injure me. My fury knew no bounds ; I
seemed to hate him all the more for being in my
power, and I bore him pitilessly down to the earth—
I was far heavier than he. Then I seized his throat
in my teeth and his head with my claws and enjoyed
myself. How he kicked and struggled for a few
seconds – only a few—I wish it had been more !—
then he lay perfectly still, and I knew that I had
slain my first man. I was not anxious to eat him :
I had not as yet learned that human flesh is good,
especially that of babies ; therefore I mauled him

savagely for several minutes in order to make sure there should be no mistake about his incapacity for future mischief and treachery, which is all that his kind live for—and then I left him to the crows. But as I raised myself from his body I muttered to myself, "There, mother! Though thousands of exe- cutions could never avenge your assassination, here lies one, at least, of the hated family which murdered you!" I felt more or less appeased after the pious act of filial vengeance which I have just recorded, and ate my supper that night with a light heart— the supper consisting of some of the very oats which the peasants had thought to deprive me of! The silly creatures had cut the oats and tied them in bundles, which was extremely convenient for me, and saved me the trouble of picking the ears of grain for myself.

As for my first baby meal, that was a very simple affair: the small creature was lying, rolling about, in the grass while her mother (I suppose they have mothers, such as they are) was reaping together with a host of other humans in the adjoining field. The forest was the common boundary of the two fields, and all I had to do was to creep a few yards from the wood, take the goods the gods provided, and retire to

enjoy them.   I did this with entire success, catching
hold of the imp with one arm and hobbling along on
three feet.   But that baby made such a terrific cater-
wauling that positively I nearly dropped him out of
pure anxiety for the drums of my ears.   His mother
rushed out from among the oat stalks and ran after
me, though she did not see me, in the direction of the
baby's cries, but she soon returned: I think one of
her companions called to her that it was only the
child, was gone and that her dinner was all right,
wrapped up in a red pocket handkerchief. Well, that
baby was the most delightful thing I had ever tasted;
and I then and there determined that this dainty
should form an item of my diet whenever obtainable.
It is in season all the year round; but difficult to
obtain at any time except summer.   -

I must just add to the above narrative, that as I lay
enjoying my dinner within the pine forest, scarcely fifty
yards from those peasants, I could distinctly overhear
their remarks as to the disappearance of the young
human at that moment forming the staple item of my
dinner.   It appeared that I was not suspected.   The
whole odium of the affair was laid upon certain people
who, however disreputable and disagreeable they may
be (and they certainly are *both*), were at all events

innocent of this "crime." I mean those impostors and cads, the wolves. Many of my most successful enterprises in and about villages have been laid to the charge of wolves: so be it! this cannot injure me. True, I should like to have the credit of certain of my exploits! those in which mankind have been destroyed, especially ; but it is very amusing when you have successfully robbed an enemy, to hear some one else blamed and vengeance vowed upon persons who have had nothing whatever to do with the affair. So it was in the matter of my first baby. Not a man, woman, or child present but endeavoured to console the weeping mother by vowing vengeance upon the thieving "wolf," for she really did weep, though, as I have already declared, I did not touch her dinner but only a useless, squealing baby. That she did not really regret the loss of the tiny creature was abundantly proved by her own assertions at the time ; for she several times repeated that it was, after all, "better so ;" that the baby would never be hungry again (that it certainly would not!), or feel pain or worry of any sort, with more to the same effect, and all, of course, perfectly true. For all that, she cried steadily on, as she worked, and many of the other women cried also, though they all agreed as to the fact that things were better as they were, and repeated this a hundred times. Of course things were better as they were. What better or worthier thing could a human baby do than provide a dinner for one of the Ursidæ? All I desired was that they should so thoroughly feel the force of the truism, as to bring me another tender morsel without delay. This, however, they did not do. On the contrary, they brought dogs instead of babies, and I felt that, though dog is tasty enough when nothing better is obtainable, I would transfer my custom, for the present, to another parish.

And now I propose to dismiss for a while the disagreeable subject of the human race, and to give my readers a glimpse into some of the dangers and difficulties which I have at different times of my life encountered while living the free and, on the whole, happy life of the woods.

I have incidentally referred to certain persons for whom I have the supremest contempt, as for animals of an altogether inferior rank in the scale of life : that is, inferior to our own ; I would not go so far as to say that they are not superior to humans, for the latter, when without their detestable fire-sticks, are contemptibly weak and defenceless : their teeth are ridiculously inefficient, and as for their claws

—well, they have none, so far as I can ascertain. The creatures I refer to are *wolves*, as they call themselves. These are the very plebeians of the forest. They are hated by every resident, great or small; for they are mean and cowardly creatures, hunting in companies of three or four—they dare not show themselves singly—and sometimes in packs of a dozen or more. A wolf, if unaccompanied by his friends, would probably run away from a hare, and hide himself from a little red fox. They are thieves of the first water, besides, and have no respect whatever for the rights of property. Many a time have I left a portion of some choice repast which I was not capable of consuming at one sitting, expecting to find and enjoy the remains on the following night. What I actually found was a few white bones and the vision of two grey tails stuffed tightly between four hind legs just in the act of disappearing into the cover—ugh ! they are cads — *cads*, that is just the word, the only word for them.

Well, one fine evening, about September a year or two ago, as I was strolling through the wood thinking of—well, I'll tell you all about that presently— enough that I was thinking of *someone* and feeling rather love-sick and depressed — when I suddenly heard a cantering noise behind me, and turning round I beheld seven very large wolves coming up on my scent. The instant that I turned round the whole party stopped, sat down on their haunches, and stared at me. They looked hungry and wicked, but would not meet my eye. I darted at the nearest, but in a moment he and his companions had disappeared—in the marvellous way which these cowards understand so well. Oh ho! I thought, if you are afraid to stand up to me you will certainly not dare to pursue me! So I made off towards that portion of the forest in which I generally took my night's rest. But I was mistaken in my conclusions, for no sooner was I well on my way, than the cantering sound recommenced, and the wolves were after me again. It was useless to stop and attack them, for they are too active to be caught in this way; I therefore decided to push along and take no notice. But before many minutes had elapsed, the leading wolf began to set up that loathsome howling of theirs, and was immediately imitated by the rest. I hate noise, so I hurried on, hoping to shake them off—for I had not as yet realised that these plebeians were actually organising a pursuit with the ultimate object of tiring me out and pulling me down. After all it takes some little while for the very idea of such an unexampled insult as this to take root in the patrician mind: *me* to be pursued and pulled down by wolves! the thing was outrageous, impossible! But I confess I was somewhat disconcerted when I realised that the wolves were howling with a purpose; for in a very few minutes I was aware of new arrivals among my pursuers: grey forms with bright, hungry eyes, appeared in the moonlight to right and left of me; one or two cantered on ahead—it was really growing a little exciting. I stopped once more and turned to survey the pack and count the new arrivals. As if by magic each wolf stopped dead and sat down, some concealing themselves behind trees, others looking away; none ventured to assume a threatening aspect. As far as I could ascertain there were now nearly twenty wolves present: the situation was not altogether a pleasant one. Then I played a successful little ruse upon them. I turned as though to fly, taking a few rapid strides forward; then I suddenly stopped, and, as I had expected, the leader shot up to my side before he could control the impetus which he had already gained.

Well—I had him in a moment, and I have reason
to believe his own mother would not have recognised him a minute or two afterwards, for I made
a very complete wreck of him, and left him literally
torn to pieces. During the operation, which did
not occupy me very long, his companions had
totally disappeared : there was neither sound nor
sight of them. But, shall I be believed? no sooner
did I leave him and continue my journey than
the unnatural creatures, instantly reappearing from
every side, fell upon their mangled brother and consumed his body, quarrelling and snarling and fighting over him like so many devils, which I believe
they are under an assumed name !

I thought, for awhile, that I had shaken off the
thieving brutes, but this was not the case. I soon
found that they were after me once more, howling
and snarling, every devil's son of them ! I own that
at this point I suddenly lost heart and, to use a
familiar expression, took to my heels. I make this
confession in all humility and with shame. Why I
lost heart I cannot explain. I have mentioned the depression of spirits from which I was suffering this night,
and I can only suppose that it was the pandemonium
of noise made by my pursuers which, acting upon a

state of mind already somewhat enfeebled by the depression referred to, had relaxed my nerve-power and caused me to disgrace myself in the manner indicated.

So I fled, I own it with shame; I fled at the top of my speed, pursued by the howling pack of miserable plebs, which dared not come very close, but followed me some ten yards behind and at each side, trusting to my bulk and weight, which they hoped would prove so cumbrous that I should be unable to run far without collapsing into a defenceless condition of breathlessness and weakness, when they would, they imagined, pull me down.

Well, so far as the breathlessness was concerned they proved perfectly right. Not being accustomed to much running, I was naturally out of condition; and consequently before I had run many miles I felt that this sort of thing could not continue: I must devise some scheme by which to put to flight or to evade the enemy. Then this idea suddenly struck me: Why not climb a tree? Wolves are notoriously incapable of climbing (after all, what *can* a wolf do?). I should thus at least gain time enough to recover my breath and consider my position.

No sooner thought of than done. I had not enjoyed much climbing of late, so that I anticipated some little trouble and exertion in reaching the required altitude; therefore I pushed along until I saw a tree which looked easy to climb; then I ran to its foot, stopped, and turned round.

As before, the wolves instantly paused and sat down; while some, as usual, disappeared. I immediately commenced the ascent of my tree refuge. But no sooner did the wolves realise that this was my intention than they seemed to gather courage from the prospect of losing me, and with redoubled howls and noise they surrounded the tree and actually dared to grab at my hind legs as I swarmed up the trunk. I sustained one or two nasty bites during that degrading moment, but those bites did for me what perhaps nothing else would have done. They restored me to myself, and in addition inspired me with so terrible and righteous a fury (and when we bears *do* lose our tempers we certainly are *properly* angry!) that in an instant I was down and among my pursuers—tearing, hugging, crushing!— oh, when I remember that triumphant moment of crushing bones and ripping flesh my heart fills with the emotion of pride and thankfulness to reflect that I was born a bear and no other meaner creature! True, I have never seen a lion, or tiger—both of which animals, tradition says, are capable of slaying a bear; but with all deference to tradition I prefer to think otherwise. I am told that lions and tigers are both *cats*—cats !! I have seen, and I may add *eaten*, many cats, and howsoever large and fierce these traditional members of the family may be, I beg leave to state that, speaking for the Ursidæ generally, we shall be delighted to see any number of lions, or tigers, or any other form of cats in these parts, and to try conclusions with them. My brother Mishka has seen, in the distance, specimens of the creatures referred to in his home at the Zoological Gardens, and does not think much of them, though, he says, they are large. Well, size is nothing; a cow is big enough, in all conscience, but I have never had the slightest difficulty in negotiating a cow, however large.

But to continue: it was a real pleasure to me— though I have seldom been so angry—to rend and crush those too enterprising wolves who had presumed to attack my person. When I had done with them, three lay stiff and stark, while two others were limping and howling somewhere out of sight among the bushes. As for me, I had a scratch or two, but nothing to matter. I need hardly say that I was not molested again, as I deliberately climbed that tree and settled myself for the rest of the night in a cosy corner among the branches. But no sooner was I out of their reach than a dozen wolves came howling around the trunk and leaping up in pretended anxiety to get at me. They were but playing a part in order to deceive one another, of course; but this is the way of wolves, who have no dignity and self-respect. Had I shown so much as one tooth they would have instantly disappeared!

IV

So the night passed away, in perfect comfort for me and with quite as much actual repose as could be expected, having regard to the pandemonium going on below, where the wolves quarrelled and fought over the bodies of their relatives, entirely consuming them among themselves in a wonderfully short space of time. I was much amused to watch their dealings with the wounded heroes who turned up to claim a share in the feast. Not being in a condition to fight for the disgusting food, they were themselves promptly set upon, slain by their un-wounded brethren, and eaten with the greatest gusto.

Whether my besiegers were satiated with the feast

I had thus provided for them, or whether—like all malefactors—they were afraid of the daylight, I know not; but it is certain that soon after the last bone had been picked, and just as the began to show signs in the east of his intentions with regard to another day, they all departed. Had they remained I should have attacked them, presently; and they would have run like sheep!

Wolves, as I have already remarked, are dreadful cowards. I shall scarcely be believed, perhaps, but it is a positive fact, that I have seen three of them sitting in the snow around a dying man who was unarmed and perfectly helpless, waiting until he should have breathed his last breath before they dared pounce upon him. I came upon the party accidentally. The man had lost himself in the snow and was slowly dying of fatigue and cold and hunger. It was rather amusing, for it must have been a considerable trial to him to have those wolves sitting there, and to know that they did but await his death or stupor. Now, I had no great desire to eat that man : I don't care much for tough, grown-up humans; but I gave him a touch sufficient to knock the breath out of his body, and ate him all the same. I always take the opportunity to pay off old scores; and here was a double one.

L

However, taking one thing with another, I am really not quite sure that I do not dislike wolves even more than men : I certainly despise them more. A man will, as a rule, stand up to an enemy, even to a superior creature like myself ; whereas a wolf will never fight until he is wounded so badly that he cannot run away. Since my little adventure with the pack of wolves I have never felt the slightest vestige of respect for their class. I cannot forget the sickening spectacle of those cowardly humbugs jumping up around the tree in which I sat, as though they were anxious to get at me—bah !

Now I am going to tell of the most terrible adventure I ever met with, and one which very nearly proved the last experience for me this side of the grave.

It was autumn—the autumn of the year before last. I had had a splendid season : the crops had been good all over my district, which is a pretty large one. Oats, rye, wheat, and buckwheat were to be had in any quantity and no one to eat them excepting myself and of course, those thieves the humans who invariably dispute possession with me, and hasten to cut down any field of ripe grain which I have claimed as my own by virtue of having the first feed off it.

Well, I was as fat and strong as I had ever been, stronger; and I felt gloriously well—ready for anything. I had enjoyed my usual sumptuous breakfast, and was now indulging in a siesta within a dense portion of the forest which lay at a distance of about three miles from one of my villages. I was lying in a charming spot. Pines rustled above my head, peopled with tree partridges and fieldfares. Beautiful purple bilberries grew around me in profusion, and heather too; and close at hand was a small pool of water at the foot of a tree. There was always water in this spot in the driest season. If none appeared on the surface, all I had to do was to tread the moss for a minute or two and I soon had the cool liquid flowing about my feet. It was a hot day, one of the last we should see, for this was what, Vainka says, the humans call "old woman's summer," which comes after the real summer and lasts but a few days. Perhaps I was asleep: I may have been taking forty winks, for about this time we bears begin to do a trifle of yawning and napping at odd moments, in preparation for the winter function; but suddenly a truly awe-inspiring noise startled the delicious silence of the forest and brought me out of the land of dreams and upon my feet in a moment. The noise was

produced by humans or devils, that much was certain.   I could recognise human voices ; but there were
strange sounds besides, like rattles and gongs and
bell-ringings, which seemed to come from all sides
at once.   I stood still, irresolute, for upon my word
I did not know what to do.   Had the humans orga-
nised a chase after me ?   Impossible, for they could
not know my whereabouts without snow . to show
them my tracks.   What could it all mean ?   I
quickly concluded that whatever might be the object
of these humans in making so barbarous a din, that
object was at all events not my destruction, or
capture ; there was no thought of me in the matter.
Presently the dreaded sound of exploding fire-sticks
reached my ears.   I am not ashamed to confess that
this particular noise always causes me to lose my
head for awhile.   Before it rang out I had already
determined to remain quietly hidden where I then
was and allow the storm to go by ; but at the
banging of the guns my deliberate resolves—together
with my good sense and my presence of mind—were,
for the time, cast to the four winds.   I jumped up
and careered wildly from end to end of the wood.
This gradually sobered me, and at the same time
I discovered in which precise direction the real

danger lay. There were shouts and din from three sides, while from the fourth side came no sound at all, excepting the occasional bang of a gun. It therefore became clear to me that this was a deliberate attempt to so frighten any animals which might be within the limits of the four sides which were lined by everybody's enemy, man, as to cause them to run towards the only side where safety appeared to lie, and which was in effect the only dangerous quarter. This plan must of a surety have been the invention of the devil, who is, of course, a man, for it is full of the most diabolical cunning. It was pitiful to see numbers of silly hares and even a red fox—who certainly ought to have known better!—rushing past me to their destruction. No sooner did a hare run by towards the corner whence no shoutings came, than, a moment later, I would hear the bang of a gun and I knew that the poor innocent creature had been done to death by a concealed human. Birds flew over my head —I do not know their names, for we do not associate with birds excepting in so far as to pull one off its nest now and again, about luncheon time; but there were birds of all sizes; and each one, as it reached the concealed lane of armed humanity,

was greeted with an explosion and fell dead: it
was always the same story—blood, blood; blood;
the arch-enemy man was there to kill anything he
could lay hands upon.

Meanwhile, my position became uncomfortable;
for I soon discovered that the shouting creatures
were fast approaching me, closing in their circle;
still, no one had any idea, as yet, that I was
in the ring. I determined to convey the knowledge of my presence with some emphasis, but to
keep out of reach of the accursed fire-sticks. So I
crept through the thickest of the brushwood in
the direction of the shouts. As I came nearer I
perceived that the noise proceeded from a line of
men—peasants, women, and even children, which
last were furnished with rattles and drums and
small trumpets. These were stationed about twenty
paces apart one from another, and I saw at once
that by rushing between two of these I should
easily escape. I felt that such a proceeding was
altogether beneath my dignity; but then I hate a
scene and publicity of any sort, and I did not
wish to become the centre of a shouting, swearing
(for these humans occasionally demean themselves
by using very disgraceful language), and perhaps

hatchet-wielding mob, with the possibility of a fire ball into the bargain. So I waited until the peasants approached my ambush, and then selected the pair between which I should make my rush. I chose a quiet-looking old she-human and a small boy who was making the most terrible noise with a tin trumpet. Now all these creatures had been making noise enough, in all conscience, before; but when I suddenly showed my somewhat bulky person in their midst the noise instantly became doubly, nay, ten times as loud as it was before, each creature shrieking out my name with imprecations and personalities of every kind, in execrable taste. Well, the din and the abuse and all aggravated me to such an extent that I did a very foolish thing: I lost my temper, as we bears are rather too apt to do, and hurled myself at the boy nearest me. Just as I caught and crunched him, the stupid old woman next to him, who turned out to be his mother, flung herself at me and, by beating me with a stick she carried, endeavoured to force me to drop the child, whom I suppose she required for some purpose of her own. Her stupidity and the coarseness of her language enraged me still more, and—giving the cub a last scrunch (I heard his

bones go !)—I rushed at his idiotic parent and mauled
her nicely. But by this time half a hundred of
the yelling creatures had surrounded me and were
punching at me with every kind of stick, throwing
tin cans and rattles at me, and doing everything
they could to induce me to let go of the old
woman—though what they could want with an old
creature like that I cannot imagine ! But my blood
was up, and I preferred to have my will with her
first; so I tore and crunched her until she ceased
to scold and swear, and lay as still as the boy; then
I looked around and paused, for I began to think I
had better be making off into the thick cover: I
had had enough of the din and publicity. But just
at this moment something happened to me. I did
not realise at first what it was, but I know now.
In a word, I suddenly fell head over heels, my legs
giving way under me for no apparent reason. But
as I raised myself I became aware of a slight pain
in the thick part of my hind leg, which increased
and seemed to numb my limb. Looking over my
shoulder I saw the cause of this : a man stood
near with a smoking fire-stick in his hand : I had
been shot. Oh ! if I could have got at that human,
how I should have crunched his bones and gripped

his throat with my strong teeth till the life went out of him ! I rose to my full height as I came near and threw myself upon him. At the same moment there was a crash from his fire-stick, I staggered forward towards him and fell again ; my strength was failing —I must fly for the time, and hide myself while I had the power—quick !—was I wounded to death, like mother, I wondered, as I stepped blindly away. I knew not whither my steps were tending ; I was but half conscious—still I rushed madly forwards—the pain was excruciating ; there was another place that hurt me, one of my shoulders, besides my leg,—on and on I fled ; the shouts were far away behind me now and the cover was thick—now the sounds had died away altogether ; a little farther and I might lie down and rest—but oh ! the pain—it was maddening. Then, through my dimming eyes I perceived a pool of water in mid-forest, and staggering forward I fell prone into the midst of it, and for some little while remembered no more.

When I became conscious I was still lying in the shallow pool, which was red with my blood. But my pain was less ; in fact, beyond being exceedingly stiff I did not at this time feel my wounds to any great extent. What I did feel was the most bitter hatred towards human beings and their most accursed weapons, and a consuming desire for revenge upon the tribe. I had always hated man : I hated him tenfold now : I think it was this passion for vengeance which kept me alive through that dreadful time of suffering and privation. I could barely crawl for several weeks, and it was with the greatest difficulty that I managed to obtain sufficient food to support me. Ah me! it was a trying time! But for the proximity of a village I know not how I should have lived. The wolves —who were not within a hundred miles—got all the credit, or abuse, for my depredations. I am glad to say that by the end of the autumn season that village was the poorer by two small children —who foolishly went mushroom hunting in the woods one Sunday afternoon, and were prevented by "the wolves" from returning home to their tea (an exceedingly welcome contribution, these, to my impoverished larder)—besides sundry dogs and other comestibles which kindly wandered my way at meal times.

I have already hinted that at one period of my life I—even I—have fallen, like weaker persons, beneath the spell of the tender passion. Now that all this is long since over and done with I cannot help laughing to think how I can have been so foolish as to permit myself to indulge in such feeble frivolity as love. I declare, I hardly like to confess it, but it is nevertheless true that during the time of my bedazzlement, or whatever you like to call it, I was actually in the habit of hunting for the benefit of another and of watching while the object of my adoration consumed provisions which *I* had found. How completely does one's nature change during the undignified process of befoolment which some member of the opposite and greatly inferior sex—goodness only knows how! —exercises over a creature infinitely her superior! How, at such a time, all that is excellent deteriorates into that which is weak and despicable and unworthy! Here was I, perhaps the biggest and bravest of my grand race—ever independent and intolerant of interference—suddenly bewitched into the most slavish, inoffensive, insignificant person that ever disgraced the family of Ursidæ. I am glad to say—indeed, it is a great comfort to me to be able to reflect—that the spell which was cast over me did not enslave me for any great length of time; and I like to think that but for my wounds and the condition of collapse into which they brought me, I might never have fallen so low. Ha ha! what a despicable, mean-spirited creature I was, to be sure, at that time. Let me explain how it all happened. The day, or two days after my dreadful experience at the hands of the doubly accursed human brute who twice wounded me with his fire-weapon, I lay dozing restlessly beneath a tall pine in the forest. As I reclined, dreaming uncomfortable dreams and conscious all the while of severe pain and of the worse than pain of fevered veins and parched throat, I suddenly became aware of a delicious sensation of relief in the region of one of my wounds. A feeling of soothing rest began to take the place of the racking pain of a few moments before; at the same time I was conscious of a sound close to my ear—a sort of crooning, inarticulate murmur of sympathy which fell very delightfully upon my suffering senses. I scarcely had sufficient energy to open my eyes, but with an effort I did so, and then I beheld a sight which—at that moment of weakness and consequent softness—filled me with an emotion to which I had hitherto been a stranger.

Stretched upon the earth beside me, softly licking my wound and crooning as she did so, was the most beautiful creature (she certainly was beautiful, I admit that much even now, though I must also admit that I was an abject fool to allow myself to be captivated by mere good looks) that ever eye beheld. Her fur was the darkest of browns, and had not a spot or taint of mange to disfigure it. Her claws and teeth were perfect—as good as my own, and that is saying not a little! She was large and strong, beyond the size and strength of most persons of her sex. Her eyes looked languishing and gentle, but their expression was belied by the formation of her snout, which was slightly upturned—an unfailing indication of ferocity of disposition amongst us Ursidæ. She was, as I have said, licking my wounds; I shall never forget the delicious sensation of peace and ease from pain that her action thus instilled into my being. I did not dare betray the fact that I was awake, lest she should cease to caress me. I felt that I could lie on thus for ever, contentedly, and let her soothe me, if she would, into a sleep that had no end. As a matter of fact she did lull me to sleep, a delicious, long restful sleep from which I awoke, after several hours, a different bear. She had disappeared, when I opened my eyes,

and at the first instant I feared that I might
have merely dreamed of the beautiful ministering
creature; at which thought—so weak and ill was
I—I declare I actually whined aloud! But she
soon returned, and then, seeing that I was awake,
rushed to my side once more, and licked and
caressed me with a thousand blandishments. . . .
Ah me! well, well; perhaps I should. never have
recovered at all but for her! I must in justice
confess that she helped me very much through the
trying time of my illness, and I believe she was .
very fond of me. I allowed her to share in all the
good things that she or I found or caught, and I
am bound to say she made very free with the ripe
oats in my fields, and enjoyed a good half of
every dog and baby that fell to our lot. I am
glad to say that I taught her to appreciate (inter-
nally) the human race : baby is now (if she is still
alive) her favourite dish, and she will go miles to
surprise and choke a human of any description ;
so that, if only for this reason, my period of fool-
ing and softness was not altogether time wasted.
We plighted our troth, of course, and were bear and
·wife for the time being—until nearly hibernating-
time, in fact; but before November we had

quarrelled and parted. As my health and strength returned I became increasingly conscious of the degradation of my present mode of life. That I should permit any one, even so beautiful a creature as she undoubtedly was, to feed in my pastures and treat me as an equal, was a standing disgrace to my bearhood, and I felt that this shocking condition of things must cease. I had hoped to bring about an understanding with my wife without the use of violence; but when she continued .to assert her right to share with me that which was mine after I had pointed out to her that love had had his season and that there was now a distinction between the words *thine* and *mine* which during my infatuation I had been unable to discern, why—to my regret—I was obliged to despatch her about her business with, as the saying goes, a flea in her ear! She made a good fight of it—ha ha! I declare, I never loved her so well as that day! Never shall I forget the ugly look in her eyes and the wicked curl of her turn-up snout as she limped away from the field of battle. She certainly looked about as deliciously ferocious as I ever saw a member of our somewhat quick-tempered family, and as for her language—oh! dear me—it was enough to cause a blight, and I was quite glad that it was not the season for such a disaster.

Thus ended my one and only experience of the inglorious delights of love : it was quite enough for me!

Well, my narrative is drawing to a close now. I have had many adventures, sufficient to keep my tongue employed for many a long day, if I were to tell them all; but I think I really must, before finishing my autobiography, relate one little incident which has kept me in merriment for months : indeed, however low my spirits may fall at any time, it is sufficient for me to recall this little episode and I feel at once that life is, after all, worth living in spite of its ups and downs, which would just about balance one another but for the occasional gleams of mirth which shine in upon our dreary existence and enable the balance, on the whole, to kick the beam on the up side. This is how it happened. I was wandering about the woods one night in April, shortly after my winter sleep. I was more than hungry, I was ravenous. Consequently, when my nostrils were suddenly assailed by the delicious odour of what I quickly recognised as dead horse, I felt that I had wandered for once into luck's way.

There is something very soothing about horse when one is famished, and I made such a meal that night as I have seldom eaten before or since. Towards morning I left the banqueting-place resolved to revisit it on the following night. Now comes the fun. Sauntering merrily along next evening I had approached within a short distance of my feasting-ground, quite ready—in spite of yesterday's somewhat generous repast—to repeat the delightful experience, when my faithful nostrils apprised me of the presence of an enemy. Besides the strong—very strong—smell of dead horse, there was another scent in the air, that of a human being. Fifty yards or so from me lay the remains of the horse: I could just make out its outlines in the darkness; but peer about as I would I could not discern the presence of a man. However, I always prefer to trust to my nose rather than to my eyes, and therefore, convinced that a human being either had been, recently, on the spot or was even now present within a short distance of me, I decided to keep very quiet and listen and watch. I may explain that I was well concealed from the sight of any human, supposing that one of these creatures should be busy over my supper. I had not thought that raw

M

horse was an article much valued by men as a deli-
cacy—indeed, my dear brother once told me that his
"master" never ate any flesh which had not been
previously *burned* (disgusting idea!)—but it was likely
enough that the greedy and ill-natured creatures
would be glad enough to eat anything whatever if by
doing so they successfully deprived a fellow-creature
of the food.

How long I lay and waited thus I cannot say,
but it was a weary time and I grew very tired of
it, and, naturally enough, horribly hungry and pro-
portionately wrathful. Yet the longer I waited the
more certain I became not only that a human had
been about the place but that he was actually
there now. My ursidine readers will perhaps wonder
—knowing by this time something of my character
and sentiments towards the human race—that I did
not stake all upon an attack. To such I would reply
that I am no fool even in my moments of blind but
righteous ferocity, and this human might be armed
with a fire-stick. Besides, I could not detect the
sound of eating: what then could he be about? men
have no sense of smell, therefore he could not be
aware that I was near at hand: he was, clearly, not
on the look-out for me. If not on the look-out for

me he might possibly be without his fire-stick—
grand Bruin! if so—well, to say "a man without his
fire-stick" is another way of saying "a meal": I
should have two courses for my supper to-night—
man with horse to follow—glorious! The idea re-
vived me and caused my hunger to grow so keen
that I could no longer resist running the risk of
approaching, cautiously, a little closer in order to
have a good survey around.

So I crept noiselessly towards the open space
where lay my last night's repast and commenced
to peer about; but strain my eyes as I would I
could see nothing. Suddenly a soft sound broke
the silence. It was like a grunt, or a deep breath;
I remembered that I had heard a young peasant
whom I found asleep under a tree (and subsequently
ate) make a similar sound. Could the human be
asleep? The noise appeared to proceed from
among the pine boughs over my head, and I now
peered about with redoubled diligence in the direction whence it came. After a while, I saw him—
at least I saw a dark and motionless mass up in
the branches of a tree some twenty paces away.
Now what in the name of all that is wonderful did
the creature mean by choosing such a place to pass

the night in? I had seen a man in a tree before this (I have chased many a one up—they always forget that I can follow!), but I never yet saw a human fast asleep among the branches. Then, of a sudden, the true explanation of the mystery occurred to me. This creature had placed the dead horse where I had found it with the deliberate intention of using it as a bait to attract me. Having thus, as it were, invited me to supper, he intended to lie in wait for me and basely slay me from his ambush up in the tree as I feasted below. Oh! the vile, human, petty meanness of the device; the hideous perfidy to be enacted under the mask of hospitality—bah! it sickens me to think of it.

However, it appeared that the tables were about to be turned upon my friend. I was not long making up my mind as to a plan of attack; he had his fire-stick with him, of course, so I must be careful. He was grunting away merrily, and as fast asleep as though it were mid-winter, and the tree his *berloga!* Well, I crept cautiously along until I reached the foot of his pine tree: I could see him plainly now sitting up in the fork of the lowest branches; his head was sunk forward on his chest and he held his fire-weapon in one hand, one

end of it resting against his foot—ha, ha! I can
see him now, fool that he was—dreaming there in
a fool's paradise : he little knew whom he had to
deal with, or he would have remained wide enough
awake, I warrant him!

Then I commenced to climb very carefully and
silently. But, cautious as I was, I suppose I must
have made some sound, for when I was within a
foot or two of his perch, the human suddenly awoke
with a start, and stared out into the open space
where the dead horse lay. Even then he did not
see me. It was a critical moment. Just then he
lowered his foot—I suppose it was stiff and required
stretching. Luckily for me it came close to my paw
and I clutched at it. In doing so I lost my hold
of the tree trunk, without, however, letting go of
the human creature's foot. Never in all my life did
I hear anything so piercing as the yell that human
gave as he and I fell to the earth together. To
make matters still more startling the fire-stick spat
out its fire at the same moment, dropping out of
his hand as it did so. The flame did not touch
me, luckily, though for a moment I was deafened
and scared, as well as blinded, by the discharge.
I am proud to say, however, that I did not loose my

grip, and as we touched the earth together, I was upon him, and squeezing his deceitful, perfidious life out of his body before he well knew what had happened.

Oh! it was glorious! To think that a crafty human being should have taken the trouble to cater for me, lie in wait for me—gun and all—actually beguile me within easy range of his fire-spitter, and then fall asleep as I lay absolutely at his mercy there—well, it was too rich for words! My supper that night was superlative—two courses—for even man tastes delicious when stolen, so to say, in this manner! Upon my word I find it difficult to say which was the more delicious; the only drawback to it was that I could positively scarcely eat for laughing. Well, well; I laid the rest of the sleepy individual beside the remains of the horse which he had provided for my entertainment, intending to finish him on the morrow; but, unfortunately, his friends found him, and carried him away—I cannot say what they wanted him for: I only hope he was not wasted; and so ended the very merriest adventure I ever experienced. It has proved an unfailing source of mirth to me from that day to this, and I am exceedingly grateful to the sportsman who so obligingly fell asleep and furnished me with an unex-

pected second course, instead of, as he had anticipated, procuring for himself a valuable bear-skin ; for
—shall I be believed ?—these insolent creatures, if by
perfidy or stratagem they manage to do one of us to
death, actually presume to wear our fur over their own
unworthy carcases, being entirely without any natural
covering to protect them from the cold.

But there ! I must not allow my tongue to wag any
longer ; I am getting old, I suppose, and garrulous,
but I do love to fight over again those countless
battles with my enemies, which have made of me
the far-renowned champion that I am. Up to now
my teeth are as sharp, my arms as powerful, and
my heart as sound as in the days of my youth ; but
there will come a time, I suppose, when teeth and
claws will become blunt, and sight dim ; when a
grouse rising suddenly from the thicket will startle
me, and a hare crossing my path will make my heart
to beat—ah, well ! when that time arrives, may the
end come soon, for I could never bear to support a
feeble existence ! When I feel that I am no longer a
match for my enemies, I am determined what to do :
I shall seek out a human who is armed. With his
fire-stick he shall free my soul from my body ; but
with my last strength I shall grip his throat and tear

his life from him, so that our two souls shall journey together to those happy hunting-grounds where *we* are to handle the fire-weapon, and the men to do the running: I shall like to have a human soul handy to start upon as soon as I arrive in those blessed regions; and oh! if I happen to meet my dear mother, how she will enjoy taking a share in the hunt!

However, I am all right here for the present, and life is pleasant enough while one's teeth are sharp!

CHAPTER VII

THE FOLK-LORE OF THE MOUJIK

THE Russian peasant, or moujik, is an individual who has never received his fair share of respect and admiration from us in this country. We know all about his faults: his laziness, his drunkenness, his uncleanliness, his superstition, his persistent wanderings from the narrow ways of truth and honesty; but few of us are prepared to concede to him certain excellent qualities which he undoubtedly possesses: strong religious feeling, unquestioning obedience towards those in authority over him, filial love and reverence towards his father, the Tsar, devotion to his country, reverence for age, the most pious veneration for the memory of his fathers; patience, docility, courage, strangely developed humour, hospitality, and a host of virtues and lovable qualities which only those who know him intimately are able to detect and appreciate. In the matter of their belief in and dealings with

those Beings with which they have peopled the
spiritual world, the Slavs are probably the most
superstitious of all the European families, or at
least they have clung with more pertinacity than
any of their neighbours to the old-world traditions and beliefs which were the common property,
centuries ago, of all. During these centuries the
Church, hand-in-hand with education and civilisation, has done its best to stamp out and destroy
the innumerable relics of purely Pagan and Christianised Pagan traditions which abound in the
country; but neither priest nor schoolmaster, nor
yet the common-sense of the community, have
made much appreciable headway against the ineradi-
cable superstition of the Russian moujik :—and the
air, the forests, the waters, the very houses are as
full of their spiritual inhabitants to-day as they ever
were in the days when men looked to the elements
and the forces of nature for the gods whom they must
worship, and before whose irresistible power they
realised their own insignificance. When St. Vladimir,
in the zeal of his recent conversion to Christianity,
cast into the waters of the Dnieper at Kief the huge
wooden, silver-headed, golden-bearded idol of Perun
the Thunderer, and in baptizing his twelve sons set

an example which was quickly followed by the rest of the population of his grand duchy, he was very far from convincing his people that thunderings in the future were to be regarded as merely impersonal manifestations of the forces of nature. It might not be Perun who thundered, they argued—and since Perun had gone to the bottom of the Dnieper this was probably the case—but if it were not Perun it clearly must be some one else, for the thunder could not roar by itself! Elijah fitted into the gap very neatly. Did not the Church teach that Elijah the prophet went up in a chariot to heaven? The thundering then was undoubtedly the rumbling of Elijah's chariot-wheels, and that, to this day, is the explanation which any Russian peasant will give if asked to account for the noise of the thunder. This is one of many examples of the manner in which Pagan beliefs have survived in Christianised forms. In certain parts of Russia, however, even the name of Perun or Perkun is still preserved in con-nection with the roar of the thunder. When the familiar rumbling and crashing noise is heard over-head, the peasants in some of the Baltic provinces still remark, "There is Perun thundering again!"

Hand-in-hand with the worship, in Russian Pagan

days, of the elements and the forces of nature, went the adoration of the dead; and while Perun and his fellow deities of that age have practically become extinct, or have been Christianised out of all recognition, the superstitious regard of the Russian peasant for the spirits of his departed ancestors has withstood the attacks of time as well as the teachings of Christianity, and is as marked now in some of the remoter districts of the empire as it ever was in the days of heathenism. Sometimes it is actually the spirits of the *rodítyelui*, or forefathers, themselves, who are cherished and invoked by the peasants; sometimes the *rodítyelui* have become merged in the personality of the *domovoy*, or house-spirit, of whom I shall presently have much to say. It is a comparatively common belief that the soul, after leaving the body, remains for a period of six weeks about the house, or at all events in the neighbourhood of its old home, watching the mourning of its relatives, and seeing that its memory is receiving at their hands fitting veneration. During the time that the body remains in the house the soul sits upon the upper portion of the coffin. As it has a long journey to perform before reaching its final home, money is frequently placed in the coffin in order

that the departed spirit may be enabled to de-
fray possible charges for being ferried across rivers
and seas; food is also provided, to sustain the
rodítyel·upon his way, together with small ladders
made of dough, in seven rungs, for scaling the
seven heavens.   In case the steep should be
slippery and difficult to climb, the parings from
the nails of the dead man, if these should have
been cut shortly before death, are placed close to
the folded hands—the talons of some bird of prey
being occasionally added, in order to render the
business of climbing as easy as possible to the
traveller.   The coffin itself is sometimes made in
the shape of a boat, in order that if Charon or his
representative should refuse to convey the traveller
across the dark river, or should charge an ex-
orbitant price for so doing, the latter may be
independent of the services of the ferryman.   All
these ancient customs are observed in the letter
in many of the remoter villages throughout the
empire; but it is doubtful whether the significance
of the observances is realised by the peasants who
thus perpetuate the ancient traditional customs of
their forefathers, as handed down to them, probably, without explanation.   It is certain that the

belief is very general that numbers of *rodityelui*,
i.e., the spirits of the fathers of the family, still
reside in and watch over the establishments of their
posterity not yet quit of the infirmities of the flesh.
These spirits are supposed to have their abode in
the wall behind the *ikon*, and food for their use is
occasionally placed on certain days close to the holy
picture. The spirits may, very rarely, be seen in the
form of a fly, sipping sugar-water or honey from a
plate ; or in the guise of a sparrow or other small bird,
gobbling up crumbs upon the window-sill. In the
case of a witch, the soul may occasionally take an
airing during the lifetime of the hag, choosing the
time when the latter is asleep to assume the form of
a moth, which issues from the mouth of the witch and
flutters about the room. This offers an excellent
opportunity to get rid of the *vyedma* altogether.
To this end all that has to be done is to conceal
the mouth of the hag, so that the moth, when it
returns to the body, cannot find its way home
again. Repulsed in this fashion, the moth-soul
easily becomes discouraged, and giving up the idea
of returning to its prison-house, flies out of the
window and disappears, and the witch is no more.
It should be mentioned with regard to the *rodityelui*

who live behind the *ikon*, that when the time approaches for a member of the family to be gathered to his fathers the spirits gently tap-tap within the wall, as a signal to the living members of the household that it is necessary for one of them to come and join his friends behind the *ikon*. This is, of course, the "death-watch," as we know it: and the wonder is that the entire household does not succumb to the terror which must be caused to a family in which the little tapping creature responsible for these summonses to the next world may have taken up its abode.

As for the *domovoy*, or house-spirit, it seems uncertain whether this strongly marked individuality is the embodiment, in one person, of the entire company of the *rodítyelui*, or a separate and distinct personality. He is named, together with the spirits of the air, water, and forests, as one of those who accompanied the evil one on the expulsion of the latter from heaven, and as such he would appear to be a distinct individual. But, on the other hand, there exist certain ceremonies in connection with the *domovóy*, and to which I shall refer again later on, which seem to associate him with the spirits of the departed. However this may be, it is quite certain

that the *domovoy* is a recognised and permanent
inhabitant of every peasant household throughout
Russia, and it is doubtful whether there exists from
end to end of the realm a single such household
which would venture to express a doubt of his
personal existence among them. Nevertheless, he
is rarely seen, though his appearance is accurately
known according to the particular notions with regard
to that appearance as held in the different portions
of the empire. In these he is variously described as
a tiny old man—he is always a man, not a woman,
and always old—no larger than a five-year-old child;
as very tall and large; as having long hair; as hairy
all over, even to the palms of his hands and the
soles of his feet; and as having the extremely disagreeable habit of passing his hands over the faces
of sleepers. If his touch is soft and warm all will
go well for some time with the establishment over
which he presides; but if, on the contrary, his hand
is cold, like ice, and rough to the touch, then woe
will betide the sleeper or his household in the near
future. The *domovoy* lives within the *pechka*, or
stove, and is, when properly treated, benignantly
disposed towards the members of his own particular
family, protecting these from all harm and from the

evil machinations of the neighbours, with whose *domovoys* he is always at enmity, quarrels between himself and these latter being of very frequent occurrence, and resulting in great damage to the crockery and other wreckable property of both establishments. The natural consequence of this rivalry between the guardian spirits of neighbouring families is that the reputation of the *domovoy* outside his own family circle is always very bad; for only one's own *domovoy* is admittedly a benevolent spirit, every one else's is a demon. Thus the *domovoy* presents the unusual spectacle of a being who is an angel at home and a devil out of doors, in direct contradistinction to members of the human race, who are, as I have been informed, frequently angelic in the presence of strangers, though quite "the other thing" at home.

But in spite of this zeal on behalf of his own folks —zeal which so sadly often gets him into trouble with the neighbours—the *domovoy* must be kept in good humour by the members of his own family, or he is liable to show in whose company he was obliged to hurriedly leave the Realms of Light, which are asserted to have been his original habitation— in other words, he may become mischievous and

N

troublesome even at home. At such times he will
take to throwing the furniture about during the night,
breaking the crockery, ill-treating the domestic pets,
and so on. Under these circumstances it is best to
be bold and upbraid the invisible offender loudly,
when he will generally recognise the error of his ways,
and desist, on the following night, from throwing the
dog and the tea-cups about : ·he is generous enough
to cherish no malice or ill-will against those who
have thus been courageous enough to remonstrate
with him, which proves that the *domovoy*, in spite of
his antecedents, is more or less in a state of grace.
The tastes and peculiarities of the *domovoy* may with
advantage be studied by those desirous of ingrati-
ating themselves with him. Especially in the matter
of the colouring of his surroundings it is easy and
well worth while to study his idiosyncrasies, and
to carry out his ideas in this respect by adapting
the hue of the feathered and furred animals about
the establishment to his known tastes in that direction. The way to find out the favourite colour of
the *domovoy* is so very simple that it would be
almost an insult to the guardian spirit to neglect to
pay him this little compliment. All that need be
done is to hang a small piece of meat by a string

to a nail and to leave it (well out of range of the family nose, let us hope), for a month. At the expiration of that period it will be found to be covered with maggots, and the colour of these maggots is the favourite tint of the *domovoy*. If the cows and the horses, the cocks and the hens, are not of the particular colour indicated by the above test, they had better be sold at once, and others bought which correspond with the ideas of the *domovoy* in this respect.

The ceremony to be performed by a peasant family removing from one house to another is full of significance, and is, or was, universally recognised as a most important function. In this ceremony there seems to occur that confusion between the *domovoy* and the spirits of the departed to which I have already made allusion in the course of this chapter. The whole function centres in the stove, or rather in the embers burning within it. When the family have packed up and are ready to go, the old grandmother, if there be one, or the oldest woman of the establishment, carefully rakes up the red-hot embers still glowing within the stove at the moment of departure, depositing these in a pan which is then quickly covered up. That these embers are supposed to be

in some way connected with the spirits of the departed is evident, because the tradition specially en-
joins that the greatest care must be observed lest any
of them slip through the aperture and into the grate;
for if this calamity should happen, it would signify
that certain of the *rodityelui* had slipped through
the barrier and fallen into the fires of hell. When
the whole of the glowing coals have been raked out
and collected, the old woman carries the pan across
to the new house, chanting over and over again as
she goes, the words, "Welcome, little grandsire, to
the new home." Arrived at the house, the old
woman knocks three times upon the wall, and is
admitted. The whole family have assembled meanwhile and are ready to greet the old woman and
her pan and embers. "Welcome, little grandsire, to
the new home" is the cry, repeated over and over
again, while the embers are taken out one by one,
and placed, still alight, within the new stove. Thus
the *rodityelui* perform their "flitting," after which they
are as much at home in the new abode as they were
in the old haunts. I should mention, before leaving
the subject, that previously to the occupation of a
new house, a cock and hen are let loose in the living
room, which is not entered until after the cock

has crowed. No evil spirit can bear to hear a cock crow, and the rite is doubtless performed with a view to ridding the house of any evil spirits which may have previously taken possession of the edifice. *Domovoys* do not object to the crowing of cocks—another proof that the *domovoy* is in a state of grace.

Holy Church has stepped in and substituted for the ceremonies which I have just described, special services for those about to occupy new premises, and these Christian functions now largely take the place of the Pagan rites ; but the change of ceremony has not dethroned either the *domovoy* or the *rodítyelui*, who still reign, and will doubtless reign for the next thousand years, over the imagination of Ivan Ivanovitch, as the personal and permanent and undoubted guests and guardians of his establishment. There is a special *domovoy* in charge of the bath-house which forms a feature in every Russian village. This *domovoy* has a strong objection to the villagers bathing themselves late at night, specially if they do so without having first prayed aloud. It is not very clear what form his displeasure takes when his wishes in this connection are disregarded ; but it is known that he dislikes the practice of late

bathing. Probably it keeps him up. However, if
the moujik be impious enough to disregard his ob-
jections and to take a bath at an unseasonable hour
of the night, when all good moujiks, and *banniks*
also, should be asleep, a can of warm water and a
birch-rod-swisher should be left by the untimely
"ablutioner" in propitiation of the *bannik* (who is
the *domovoy* of the bath-house) thus kept from his
rest by the thoughtless and unselfish conduct of the
former. Whether the *bannik* ever utilises the opportunity thus offered him of enjoying a comfortable
scrub, tradition does not say. If the bath *domovoy*
is a good Russian, and has imbibed anything of the
nature of the moujik during his long connection
with that unsavoury member of society, probably
he does *not* use the warm water and the swish;
for he will not wash himself unless he is forced
to do so by circumstances over which he has no
control, such as popular opinion, or the customs
or the bye-laws of the village in which he has his
habitation.

I have already mentioned that when the Prince
of the Spirits of Evil descended from the abode of
light and took up his dwelling in the realms of darkness, which are his habitation to this very hour,

there accompanied him certain other spirits, inferiors and followers. Among these, according to Slavonic folk-lore, were the *vodyánnuie*, or water-spirits ; the *vozdúshnuie*, or spirits of the air ; and the *liéshuie*, or wood-demons. There were many others in his train—such as the *karliki*, or gnomes—beings of little or no interest in the everyday life of the peasant because they rarely interfere in human affairs, if they can avoid it, and have no special connection with humanity ; whereas the *domovuie*, as I have shown, and the water and wood spirits, as I intend now to describe, are constantly in contact with members of our race, either for good or for evil. Many of the followers of the Chief demon accompanied their leader into his new home and there remain with him to this day ; but it will be better to leave these bad characters where they are, and to concern ourselves solely with those whom common interests have brought into connection with our race. The spirits which I have named did indeed accompany their former leader as far as the portals of his new realm, the nether regions ; but they did not actually enter its confines, or if they did do so, did not stay longer than just so much time as was required to arrive at the conclusion that the

atmosphere of the place was not such as to suit
their private ideas of comfort—which did not take
them long—after which they quickly turned their
backs upon the front gates and made off as rapidly
as possible; the *liéshuie* hiding themselves in the
forests, the *karliki* burying themselves in the earth,
while the *vozdúshnuie* remained in the cool air—
finding it refreshing after the heated atmosphere to
which they had been lately introduced; and the
vodyánnuie, who had perhaps stayed a moment or
two longer beside their chief, or who were possibly
more sensitive to the discomfort of a warm tempera-
ture, plunged headlong into the water in order to
cool their parched frames, and have remained in the
pleasant depths ever since—taking over the management of all springs and rivers and pools upon the
surface of the dry land. These same *vodyánnuie*
are a tricky race of beings and require much propitiation at the hands of millers, fishermen, and
others who have dealings with them or with the
waters within their jurisdiction. Millers, especially,
require to be careful to keep in touch with the
vodyánnuie; for each mill-race possesses its own
particular water-spirit, and the miller will have no
luck, and deserve none, if he does not cast into

the race at least one black pig per annum as a gift to the spirit which has its habitation in his waters. The ordinary annual offering to the water-spirits is, however, a horse, whose legs have been previously tied together with red ribbons, and who has been smeared for the sacrifice with honey. A heavy stone is attached to the unfortunate animal's neck and he is thrown into a deep pool. The *vodyánnuie*, who have in all probability shown their displeasure for some time before the sacrifice by causing the river to overflow its banks, or the ice to carry away the bridge, having now received their rights as by custom established, at once settle down in peace and quietness for a whole year. But they are, as I have said, a tricky lot, and they must not be depended upon by bathers, or by peasants who would fain cool their horses' heated flanks in the deep pool after a hard day of work in the fields. The *vodyánnui* of the place may be of a malicious disposition, and though everything may have been done in order to secure his benevolent neutrality towards bathers, yet he is just as likely as not to pull down by the leg his very warmest admirer, or the horse of his most sincere follower.

Here, again, the Church, anxious to substitute for

the Pagan observances which I have mentioned in connection with the *vodyánnuie* her own orthodox functions, has ordained for the use of the faithful solemn services for the "blessing of the waters." These services are now performed twice each year all over Russia, and have largely ousted the ancient rites and sacrifices which were considered necessary in honour, or in propitiation of the water-spirits; but though the sacrificial observances are discontinued, the belief in the existence of the *vodyánnuie*, as active and malevolent beings whose dwelling-place is in the pools and streams, still retains its hold upon the minds of the people with much of its ancient intensity. Before quitting the subject of water-spirits, I should mention that the nymphs and mermaids of our own and universal folk-lore are represented in that of the Slavs by beings known as *rusalki*, an entirely distinct species from the surly and malicious *vodyánnuie*. The latter are of the male sex, while the *rusalki* are all females, and frequently very beautiful. They employ their good looks unfortunately to the ruin of our race, too frequently luring young men to their doom, by enticing them into the deep waters and there either tickling them to death or else drowning them; for the *rusalki* are of a mischievous and frivolous nature and have very little good feeling about them. Many of the *rusalki* are supposed to be the spirits of still-born or of unbaptized children, or of women who have committed suicide or who have been for some other reason deprived of the privilege of Christian burial. When a child dies unbaptized, its spirit is said to wander through the world for seven years, longing and entreating to be baptized. If any person sufficiently pure in spirit to discern the pleading soul-voice has the presence of mind, on hearing it, to pronounce the words, "I baptize thee ·in the Name of the Father, the Son, and the Holy Ghost," then the forlorn soul is satisfied and flits away to Paradise; but if the seven years go by and the soul remains unbaptized, it becomes a *rusalka*. Annual prayers are offered in Russian churches for the unbaptized, and if the wandering spirit is fortu-nate enough to be close at hand and to overhear the words of the priest during one of these services, its object is attained: it is considered to have come within actual range of the working of the baptismal rite, and Paradise is won for that soul. There are some who believe that the spirits of the unbaptized, in their wanderings through the world, assume the form of a cuckoo; and these make a point for this reason of baptizing every cuckoo they hear, or even of performing the rite in effigy if no living cuckoo should be available. The fishermen of the Caspian have a pretty legend with regard to the *rusalki*. They declare that these water-maidens are frequently greatly troubled as to the nature of the future state and their own probable destiny therein. The mer-maids, to give them a familiar name, are represented as occasionally appearing at the surface of the water to inquire whether the fishermen can tell them whether the end of the world is still far off?

The *rusalki* vary in size, as do all the spirit forms of Russian folk-lore. Sometimes they are spoken of as tiny beings floating in the cup of the water-lily; sometimes as huge female forms which haunt the cornfields and steal the grain of the peasants. When caught thus misbehaving themselves the *rusalki* are punished in effigy, straw figures, representing the robbers, being tossed about by companies of girls, who eventually cast them into the water. When this has been done the cornfield is safe from further plunderings at the hands of the beautiful but dis-honest water-maidens.

The *vozdúshnuie*, or spirits of the air, have but

little to do with man, their realm being outside his usual "beat." There are no doubt as many spirits dwelling in the air as inhabit the waters, woods, and houses, but until man shall have taken to journeying in balloons or shall have mastered the science of flying, it is probable that he will not be molested to any great extent by this branch of the spirit family. I will therefore pass on to consider the wood-goblins, whom I have left until the last, because, with the sole exception of the *domovoy*, the *liéshui* is by far the most important of the spirits who engage in dealings with mankind, as well as the most picturesque. In a country whose woods and forests cover thousands of miles of territory, it is only natural that the spirits whose home is in the fastnesses of those pine-grown regions should play a great part in the imagination of a poetic and superstitious people living beneath the shadow of the pine trees. The *liéshuie* are, without doubt, by nature evil spirits, or demons; but, like their brethren of the waters and of the air, they may be propitiated by the observance of certain rites and ceremonies, and by this means rendered friendly or at least neutral towards those who are desirous of living in their good graces—a most necessary condition of existence for those whose flocks and herds wander day-long in the wilds and moors and woodlands of the interior of Russia. The *liéshui* is, in the estimation of his friend Ivan Ivanovitch,· a shocking bad character. He is generally an old man, very hairy and wild in appearance, as might be expected. He is a terrible drunkard, and is frequently quite incapacitated and helpless after his bacchanalian excesses; on such occasions he is watched over and protected from the assaults of his enemies by his chief friend and henchman, the bear. But not only is he a drunkard, he is equally a slave to another vice, the indulgence of which seems to strike one as unexpectedly sophisticated in a denizen of the forest : he is a gambler and a card-player, speculating to a tremendous extent, and staking all his possessions frequently enough at a single *coup.* When the village *ochotnik*, or sportsman, finds to his annoyance that the hares, the blackcock, or the tree partridges within his district have become so scarce that it is no longer worth his while to tramp the woods after them, the apparently unaccountable circumstance is plain enough to his enlightened intelligence : the *liéshui* of the place has gambled them away to his next-door neighbour. The same explanation accounts for the migration of squirrels and birds from one part of the country to another—they are in the act of going over to swell the possessions of the fortunate *lieshui* who has won them from their former owner. I should mention, however, that clubs are never used in the packs of cards with which the *lieshuie* carry on their games of speculation, since these, to a certain extent, resemble the shape of a cross, an emblem which neither woodgoblins, nor any other evil spirit dares to look upon. But besides these gamblings with one another, and perhaps as the outcome of these very transactions and the ill-feeling and bad blood which operations of this kind so frequently engender, terrific encounters occasionally take place between the rival *lieshuie* of a district, when the forest is devastated for hundreds of yards around, the pines lying prone and uprooted in every conceivable position and in every direction, just as though a hurricane of wind had passed by and torn them up, hurling them right and left as it went. Many a time have I encountered such a scene of desolation in mid-forest, and have found the greatest difficulty in forcing a way through the chaos formed by this *lom*, as it is called. Ignorant as I was in those days of the true origin of these

patches of devastation, I used fondly to imagine
that the ruin I saw had indeed been wrought by
the agency of the tempest, though it was always
a puzzle to me to account for the limited sphere
in which the whirlwind had conducted its destructive
operations; the theory of a wood-goblin duel, of
course, satisfactorily accounts for the circumstance.
When a *liéshui* marries—for he does take to himself
a wife in his own good time—his bridal feasts and
processions create terrible disorder in the forest;
birds and beasts rush frightened and screaming
from the neighbourhood, trees are knocked down
and strewn about the ground, and the place becomes a pandemonium. It is not very apparent
whom this unprincipled goblin finds to marry him.
Perhaps the Erl-King has an unlimited supply of
those deceitful daughters of his! The peasants
naturally have much to do with the spirits whose
habitation is in the forests which surround their
dwellings, for their flocks and herds must wander
free over the outlying pasture-lands, and if the
goblin of the district has not been propitiated, the
position of such herds, entirely at the mercy of every
marauding wolf or bear, is wretched indeed. When
the favour of the *liéshui* has been gained over, then

neither bear nor wolf will be permitted by that all-powerful sylvan authority to injure cow or horse, let it wander where it will, even within the actual confines of the forest.   In these days there is a special church function, known as the "blessing of the herd," for use on the first occasion, in each spring, on which the village cattle are allowed to go forth to pasture, this service being designed to take the place of more ancient ceremonies for the propitiation of the wood-goblins.

Occasionally a peasant, after a walk in the woods, feels himself indisposed without any apparent reason for his indisposition.   When this is the case it may be assumed with practical certainty that he has crossed the path of a *liéshui*.   The sick man must immediately return to the wood, bearing an offering of bread, salt, and a clean napkin.   Over these goods he must pronounce a prayer, afterwards leaving them behind him for the use of the goblin, and returning to his home, when the sickness will quickly pass from him.   If any favour is to be asked of the *liéshui*, he may be invoked for this purpose by the following process: Cut down a number of young birches and place them in a circle, taking care that the tops all converge towards the centre.

o

Then stand in the middle, take the cross from your neck—every Russian wears this—and pocket it, and call out "Grandpapa!" The spirit will instantly appear. There is "another way," as the cookery books would say: Go into the wood on St. John's Eve and fell a tree, taking care that it falls towards the west. Stand on the stump, facing east, and look down at your toes; then invoke the *lieshui* thus: "Oh! grandfather, come, but not in the form of a grey wolf, nor of a black raven; but come in the shape I myself wear!" Whereupon the spirit appears immediately in the form of a human being, and, like a man, prepared to make a bargain, if favours are asked. The *lieshui* has quite a strong sense of the great modern principle of *quid pro quo*, and generally gets the best of it in his dealings with mankind.

Yet another peculiarity of the wood-goblin is his love for startling and frightening those whose business compels them to journey through his domain. He will take up a position among the boughs of a tree under which the traveller must pass, suddenly giving vent, on the approach of the latter, to all manner of terrifying sounds — loud frenzied laughter, barking, neighing, bellowing, howling as of a wolf, anything that will startle or alarm the intruder.

Undoubtedly the wood-goblin is the cause of a vast amount of trouble to poor Ivan Ivanovitch; and he is, therefore, far from occupying the snug place which his cousin, the *domovoy*, enjoys in the national imagination. On the other hand, he might be very much worse than he is, and he is undoubtedly, with all his faults and shocking vices, infinitely preferable to that mean and skulking and treacherous relative of his, the *vodyánnui*.

CHAPTER VIII

THE BEAR THAT DIED OF CURSES

The village folk of Spask were a good-natured lot, as most Russian villagers are, and old Tatiana Danilovna was a popular character in the community for many sufficient reasons. In the first place she was a widow with several children, whom she did her best to support without begging, which is in itself a great distinction for any widow in a Russian village; and Tatiana, her special talents and qualifications apart, had but her late husband's little allotment of land, the portion of one soul (and oh, what a drunken soul was Yashka Shagin, while still under bondage to the flesh!), wherewith to feed the whole five of her brats. But then, as I have just hinted, Tatiana had talents of her own, which enabled her to supplement the meagre income producible from her bit of the communal land, which, but for this fortunate provision of nature in her favour, would have been just about enough to starve upon handsomely. The fact of the matter is, old Tatiana was a *znaharka*. If the reader were to look out this word in the dictionary he would probably find the English equivalent given as "a sorceress"; but this is not exactly the meaning of the name, ·which is derived from the root *zna*, and signifies rather "a woman who knows her way about." This much old Tatiana certainly did know, as well as most people, although I am sorry to say that her education in the usual fields of even elementary learning had been entirely overlooked. As *znaharka* she did a considerable business, however, in all of the following useful departments of that avocation. She gave her blessing to couples about to be married; and bold indeed would that couple have been who presumed to approach the hymeneal altar without having previously insured themselves against the onslaughts of the evil eye by undergoing the ceremony indicated. Besides this she did a fairish bit of exorcising, for there were always plenty of evil spirits knocking about near Spask, and the priest of the nearest church could not always be got at very conveniently; besides her fee was, naturally, lower than that of his reverence, who could not be expected to come all that distance and bring a large *ikon* with him into the bargain, for nothing; also, the priest had to be refreshed, while Tatiana was frugal to a fault in her habits, and was far too wise a woman to go near the village beer-shop at any time for drinking purposes. She would use the resort as a convenient place for haranguing the assembled souls, indeed, and visited it also occasionally in a benevolent way, to haul some boosing moujik out of the den before he should have drunk his soul out of his body. Then, again, Tatiana was the *sage femme* of the district, and ushered into the world every little squalling moujik that was unfortunate enough to be born into this vale of tears and poverty. Lastly, for even the tale of Tatiana's accomplishments must end somewhere, she was the medico of the place. Tatiana did not attempt surgery, but she knew a number of incantations and charms, which, of course, are the same thing without the vivisection. Faith and Tatiana together effected many a cure in Spask; and it is marvellous, when one thinks of it, how very simple a matter will set right our suffering bodies if we only know how to "do the trick." Tatiana knew how to do the trick, and had herbs and potent decoctions which were able to remove every disease, unless, indeed, it was God's will that the patient should die, in which case, of course, neither Tatiana, nor Professor Virchow, nor any one else, would have kept the poor creature alive. When Providence was willing that the sick person should enjoy a further lease of life, then Tatiana and her herbs and her occasional blood-letting were safe things to resort to, as all Spask well knew, and were as sure as anything could be to pull the patient through with flying colours. She also dealt in charms for the use of lovers, mothers (or would-be mothers), hunters, farmers, &c. ; and could doctor horses and cows and dogs and poultry with wonderful success, always, of course, under the saving clause as to *force majeure*, in the way of interferences from Providence. I will merely add that Tatiana was dear to all children, whom she regaled with *prianniki* (biscuits) after a good stroke of business, and that the whole village feared as well as respected the old woman.

Such being Tatiana's position in the community, it is not surprising that the entire population of Spask were ready and willing to lend a hand whenever the word went round that the *znaharka* was about to mow her field of grass, or to dig up her potatoes, or whatever may have been the particular nature of the work to be done upon her bit of land. On the occasion which we have to consider to-day there was hay to be made, and as Tatiana's allotment adjoined others upon which a similar work had to be performed, nearly all the "souls," or ratepayers, of the village were present and busy with their scythes, while there was assuredly no single child in the place absent; all were there, tossing Tatiana's hay about ("tedding" is the word, I believe), and making themselves more or less useful and entirely happy over the job. The field was a large one, for it comprised the whole of the hay allotments of the souls of the community, about twenty-five in all; hence Tatiana's strip, which was but one twenty-fifth of the whole, was soon mown by so large a body of workers, who then passed on to the next strip, and thence to a third and a fourth, until all was mown. The field lay close up to the very edge of the pine forest, Tatiana's strip being actually the nearest to the wood, so that, as the work went on, the whole body of workers gradually drew further and further from the cover, until towards evening the busy, noisy crowd were at quite a considerable distance from the spot at the edge of the forest where work had commenced in early morning. On such occasions as mowing day at Spask there is no question of returning to the village during working hours ; for once in a way Ivan Ivanich sticks to business, and meals, as well as any little refreshers of a liquid nature, are partaken of upon the spot ; hunks of black bread tied up in red handkerchiefs, salted herrings in grimy bits of newspaper, and *kvass*, in dirty-looking bottles, forming the principal items of the food and drink brought by the moujiks to be consumed upon the ground. *Kvass* is a drink to which I should recommend every reader to give a very wide berth, for it is without exception the nastiest decoction that ever the perverted ingenuity of mankind invented, and is calculated to nauseate the toughest British palate to such an extent that the said Britisher will flee the country rather than taste the noxious stuff a second time.

On this occasion there was quite an array of red handkerchiefs left at the edge of the field, together with sundry loose hunks of black bread and other comestibles, and half-a-dozen tiny children of a non-perambulating age, which latter had been brought to the field by their mothers for the excellent reason that there was no one left in the village to look after them, and were now peacefully sleeping, like so many little bundles of rags, each under the tree selected by its parent for the office of shade-giver. Assuredly not one of the red-shirted souls so busily wielding their scythes, or of the gaily-kerchiefed women tossing and drying the grass, ever bethought herself of the possibility of danger to the little ones thus left a hundred or so of yards away: for who would hurt them? There were no gipsies to carry them away, or brigands—they had never heard of such gentry; it was perfectly safe, and nobody bothered his head about the babies. Therefore it came as a terrible shock to every person present when of a sudden some one raised the cry: "Medvyed, medvyed!" (a bear, a bear!) There was no mistake about it, it was indeed a bear, and a big one, too— "the tsar of the bears," as a moujik expressed it afterwards. The brute was apparently busy searching among the red handkerchiefs for something to eat, when first seen; but at the general shout or howl of fear and surprise which immediately arose from the whole body of peasants in the field, he raised his nose and deliberately scanned the assembled villagers, showing his teeth and growling unpleasantly.

The villagers were too frightened, at first, to either

move or utter a sound. The spectacle of a bear in their midst was too unusual in that portion of Russia in which Spask lay to be other than intensely horrifying. Spask did not even boast of an *ochotnik*, or hunter, among its inhabitants; the population, one and all, were as ignorant of the best course to pursue under the circumstances as though the foul fiend himself had suddenly appeared among them, and their tongues, as well as their arms, were absolutely paralysed with amazement and terror.

Meanwhile the bear, seeing that none seemed anxious to dispute his presence, turned his attention to the red bundles which contained the food whose good smell had probably attracted him, visiting several of these in turn and rolling them about in his attempts to get at their contents. Then he visited a bundle which contained a baby. The child was, fortunately, fast asleep; neither did it awake when Bruin rolled it over to sniff at it; if it had moved the consequences might perhaps have been fatal. But, as matters turned out, the child slept on, and the bear, satisfied that it was dead, left it. Then at length the spirit of the assembled population returned to them, and, as though with one accord, the entire crowd gave vent to a shriek of relief and rage; men began to finger their scythes and women their rakes, and the whole assembly moved a step or two towards the intruder. Then Bruin began to think that discretion was, perhaps, after all, the better part of valour, and, with a few savage snarls and grunts, he retired into the forest, stepping upon a sleeping baby as he withdrew, and causing the child to wake and scream with pain or fright. Then he disappeared among the dark pines, moaning and grunting so as to be heard for a considerable distance.

The villagers lost no time in rushing to the assistance of the screaming child, now that danger was over; when it was seen that the baby was quite uninjured, and, further, that the child was a relative and goddaughter of old Tatiana, whose bundle of black bread the bear had also honoured with particular attention. These facts amounted, in the minds of the good people of Spask, to a coincidence. Why had the brute thus chosen out the *znaharka* for special and deliberate insult? Undoubtedly he was an evil spirit, and these acts of hostility on his part directed against the chief local enemy of evil spirits must be regarded as something in the nature of a challenge. Tatiana's bread was all eaten or spoiled, and Tatiana's godchild still lay screaming, though unhurt, in her mother's arms. There was more in this than appeared on the surface.

All eyes were now upon the *znaharka*, for it was evident that something must be said or done under the circumstances; the reputation of the wise woman of the village was, in a way, at stake.

Tatiana did not disappoint her admirers. She first crossed herself, and then spat; then she fixed her eyes upon the spot where the bear's retreating form had last been seen, and commenced a speech, half a formula of exorcisation and half pure (or rather very impure) abuse, which certainly did the greatest credit both to her inventive faculties and to her knowledge of the intricacies of the Russian language as arranged specially for the use of vituperative peasants. If one fractional portion of the old woman's curse had taken effect upon its object, the rest of the days of that bear upon this earth would indeed have been days of blighting and misery both for himself and for those who called him son or cousin or husband; his female relatives especially came under condemnation, and most of all she who had brought him into the world; her fate was to be shocking indeed, so much so that I shrink from entering into the matter in detail for fear of wounding the feelings of my readers, who are not perhaps accustomed to the beauties of the Russian peasant's vocabulary, which is exceedingly rich in certain forms of speech. Tatiana's curse, however, produced a great effect upon her fellow villagers, who felt that it was all that the occasion demanded, and that they had for the present obtained satisfaction for the insults heaped upon them by the uninvited stranger; the baby was also, presumably, of this opinion, for it now stopped crying, and began to look about it with eyes full of the last few unshed tears, as though it expected to find the corpse of the bear lying some- where about as the immediate result of Tatiana's heroics. After this, the souls, accompanied by their female relatives and the children, returned to the village, where the rest of the evening was spent by the majority of the gentlemen in the refinements of *vodka*-drinking and wrangling at the beer-shop.

But, alas! shocking though the curse of Tatiana had sounded, and dire as the results ought to have been in the way of utter confusion and annihilation in this world and the next for that bear and all his relations, it soon appeared that somehow or other the malediction had missed its mark. The very next day the creature was seen by a villager who chanced to penetrate somewhat deep into the forest in search of mushrooms; and so far from being any the worse for the liberal cursing it had had, the bear had appeared—so the moujik declared—to be all the better, or rather fiercer for it; it had actually chased him for some little distance, and would have caught him if he had not, most providentially, reached a wide expanse of open ground which the bear had hesitated to cross in daylight.

This was serious news, and Tatiana was observed that morning, after hearing it, to grow very thoughtful; she made her hay diligently, but silently, exchanging neither word nor salutation with man, woman, or child during the whole of the day. The peasant women eyed the old *znaharka* with unquiet minds; was this evil spirit destined to prove more mighty than she, and to defy with impunity the very clearly expressed maledictions of their all-powerful *znaharka*? Surely not. It would be a bad day for Spask if the confidence which the village had so long reposed in the mystic powers of the sagacious Tatiana were now to be shaken! This was the very reflection which was disturbing the mind of the *znaharka* herself, with the corollary that it would be an un commonly bad thing for her business also. Things

however, went from bad to worse. Far from feeling
any ill effects from the curses of Tatiana, these seemed
to have inspired the offending animal with greater
courage and ferocity than had ever hitherto been the
portion of mortal bruin. He chased the villagers at
every opportunity: he entered the village at night and
stole—alas! poor *znaharka*!—Tatiana's own dog; he
grew bolder day by day, and at last his daring culminated in the pursuit and capture of a poor little
child. The unfortunate baby, for she was scarcely
more, had strayed beyond the edge of the wood while
her people were busy in the hayfield, had been
caught, carried away, and eaten. This was the climax.
Tatiana's reputation was tottering. Already several
sick persons had presumed to get well without her
assistance; another had done an even worse thing,
he had ridden over to the neighbouring *selo*, which
means the chief of a group of villages, in order to
consult the local *feldscher*, an insult to the medical
genius of Tatiana which had never before been
offered to that lady—who, to do her justice, little as
she knew about medicine or human bodies and their
ailments, nevertheless knew a great deal more than
her professional rival upon these subjects, for he was
as absolutely ignorant of one as he was of the other.

And now Tatiana began to feel her influence in the village, and therefore her very livelihood, slipping away, not gradually, but, if I may use the expression, with a run. If something did not happen to re-establish her reputation, and that very soon, both position and emoluments as wise-woman of the district would inevitably go by the board! Folks began to eye her askance when they met her; some even openly mocked at her as she passed, delighting to tell her each new tale of the appearance of the demon bear, that thrived on curses; in a word, the position became insupportable. The discredited wise-woman now took to roaming the woods, armed with her sickle, in hopes of meeting and, by some fortunate combination of circumstances in which cursing and cunning and violence were all to play a part, compassing the death of her arch-enemy, the ruiner of her position and prospects, the hated, the accursed, the demoniac bear. Strangely enough, Tatiana still believed in herself though the rest of the village had learned to doubt her powers, and she was not without hope that a second curse, if personally applied, might yet prove efficacious. All Tatiana's wanderings in the forest seemed, however, to be doomed to end in disappointment; the enemy would not show himself,

P

and matters were growing extremely critical when at last one afternoon the unexpected happened. As the old woman was busily employed washing her children's clothes in the river, on chancing to raise her head she espied for the first time since the memorable evening of her first abortive cursing, the very identical object of that curse and of very many others since lavished upon him in the secret recesses of her being—Bruin himself. The bear, unaware of her proximity, was standing at.the edge of the steepish bank which at that spot overhung the water, endeavouring to reach the stream for a drink. Unsuccessful in his efforts to effect this, the brute was softly whining and grunting, growing excited and passionate the while, as baulked bears will, over his failure to get at the water. Seeing that his whole attention was absorbed in the interest of the moment, Tatiana, who, brave as she was, had at first forgotten everything in the terror of this sudden *rencontre* with the savage brute, determined to seize the opportunity to escape. But when she had crept a very few paces away, a thought struck her. She was discredited and disgraced at the village ; her reputation, which meant her livelihood, had gone from her ; what was life worth to her under the circumstances ? Why not make one bold stroke for reputation and fortune, and succeed or perish in the attempt? Here was this bear busily engaged in balancing himself over the surface of the swift stream, endeavouring to get at the water which he could not possibly reach, but, bear-like, persisting in the attempt; now, why not creep quietly up, and—yes, she would do it! Tatiana stole softly behind her enemy—it was a matter of life and death, she quite understood that, so she was careful enough to make no sound—approached within a yard or two of the monster's broad stern, then, as he bent himself further than ever over the water, gave one loud shout and one big rush, and in an instant had thrown the whole weight of her body against that of the already almost overbalanced animal at the brink. The next moment *znaharka* and bear were both rising to the surface of the river Neva, beneath whose cool waters they had plunged in company. Old Tatiana could swim like a duck and soon struck out for the best landing place; the bear, like a sensible creature, following her lead. But the old woman, trained to swim in these waters from childhood, quickly outstripped her companion, and was ready, with her sickle in her hand, when that half-drowned individual arrived. The river was deep to the very bank, so that Tatiana had no great difficulty in beating off her enemy, who, placing two huge paws upon the edge of the bank, received a cut from the sickle upon each, which soon compelled him to snatch away those members with a roar of pain and rage.

Then commenced an unequal battle. The bear splashed about endeavouring to gain a footing; but whenever he came to the bank, there was Tatiana awaiting him with her deadly sickle, and in addition to many cuts over paw and forearm the unfortunate brute had soon to bewail sundry gashes over face and head, which first enraged and then stupefied him, the old woman accom panying her blows with volleys of abuse and im- precations which, I am convinced, must have made that bear feel exceedingly ashamed of him- self had he not had other matters to engage his attention at the moment!

The result of all this was a foregone conclusion. The poor brute could not land; his efforts to gain a foothold waxed feeble; his roars of pain and rage grew weaker, thinned themselves into pitiful whines and bubbling moans, and then died away altogether. His head went under water, reappeared once and a second time, and sank again. He was drowned.

Then the old *znaharka* crossed herself, spat towards her defunct enemy, and fainted.

An hour afterwards, as the Souls of Spask were engaged, *more suo*, in wrangling over their midday *vodka*, at the beer-house, to them entered the pale and dishevelled figure of the discredited wisewoman.

"Well, little mother," said one, "what are you asking for curses this afternoon? I'm told they are a drug in the market!"

Rude laughter followed this sally.

"Curses have gone up since the morning," said the old woman. "I have seen a vision——"

"If your visions are as nourishing as your maledictions," interrupted a second moujik, "you'd better feed the demon bear with them. He may thrive on them, and it will save our oats!"

"The bear is dead," said Tatiana "I have seen him in a vision. You will find his body at the shallow rapids near Gouriefka. My curse has fallen upon him. He will eat no more oats!"

With which solemn words Tatiana made an effective exit before her hearers had decided what to make of them.

When the dripping body of that ill-used bear
was brought in triumph to the village and laid in
the street in front of Tatiana's cottage, it would
be difficult to say which of two parties, all the
members of which talked at once, were the loudest
—those who applauded and extolled the marvellous
triumph of the *znaharka* over the powers of darkness, or those who raised their voices in denuncia-
tion upon the prostrate enemy of mankind. The
two parties changed places continually, those who
cursed the bear taking a turn at extolling the
woman of the hour, and *vice versâ*. Suffice it to
say that never was bear better cursed, and never
was praise more lavished upon human being. For
several years after this, if there was a wise woman
in all Russia whose blessings and cursings were
esteemed absolutely effective in all emergencies,
and carried their own steady market value for
miles around Spask, that woman was Tatiana.
Her cures were marvellous after this, for so great
was the faith reposed in her powers that she
might have saved her herbs and still the patients
would have recovered. As for the death of the
bear, St. Sergius, on whose name-day the brute
perished, got the credit of that, after deduction

had been made for the glory fairly earned by Tatiana, but for whose maledictions the good saint might never have been moved to interfere for the relief of the Spask peasantry. Tatiana knew exactly how much St. Sergius had to do with the killing of the bear; but, in her opinion, it paid her far better to pose as the successful curser than as the intrepid hunter, and no doubt she knew best about that, as about most things, being a *znaharka*.

Moreover, the bear, whether he died of curses or of cold water, provided an excellent fur to clothe Tatiana withal when winter frosts came on, for the widow's ancient mantle had worn out with her reputation.

CHAPTER IX

AMONG THE WOOD-GOBLINS

Summer was "a comin' in," and a certain serious matter began to weigh upon the mind of the peasants of Kushlefka, which is a prosperous village in a grain-growing district of Archangel; for its settlement could not much longer be delayed. The fact is, that early in the winter Kushlefka had been so unfortunate as to lose the services of its *pastuch*, or cowherd, death having carried off the old man during the slack time—when the cows were all at home, that is, and needed no one to look after them. But now that summer was at hand, and the cows would soon be wanting to be up and about, wandering over communal pasture and moorland in search of the fresh young blades of grass, it was very awkward to feel that there was no pastuch to personally conduct them in their wanderings, and that no single candidate had been near the place to apply for the post. None of the villagers would so much as think of accepting the office, for it was but a poorly-paid billet, and was generally held by some one unconnected with the place— some outsider who had wandered into the village in search of a job and was appointed pastuch for as long as he would keep the situation.

Hence when, one Sunday afternoon, as the assembly of the Heads of Families or Souls composing the Mir or Commune of Kushlefka were met to consider matters of local interest, and to settle certain business questions appertaining to their jurisdiction, it was considered rather a stroke of good luck for the community when a ragged moujik of middle age suddenly appeared at the door of the council-hall, doffed his cap and crossed himself towards the *ikon* in the corner of the room, made a bow to those present, grinned, scratched his head, and said :

" Good day, brothers ; don't leave me ! "

The reader must not suppose that the new-comer in thus addressing the Souls of Kushlefka was seized with a sudden misgiving that those gentlemen might all arise and depart just as he had arrived ; the Russian expression " Don't leave me ! " merely indicates a desire to be heard, and if possible assisted, and is a common mode for an inferior to commence a conversation with a superior.

"What do you want?" asked the starost, or president.

"Why—work," said the man; "some job—bread to eat—any kind of work will do for me." This seemed most providential, and the starost looked meaningly around at his lieutenants.

"What do you know—what can you do?" he asked.

"Better ask me what I *can't* do!" replied the new man; "I can do a bit of anything and everything!"

"You can drink *vodka*, *I* warrant!" said one of the Souls, "or you'd have pockets in your clothes and something inside them!" This was in rude allusion to the attire of the new-comer.

"Well, if you come to that, brother," said that ragged individual, "the moujik who doesn't take kindly to *vodka* is like a fish who can't swim; I can drink *vodka* as well as most—try me, if you don't believe it."

"Do you understand the duties of a pastuch?" the starost inquired. The man laughed scornfully.

"You give me a pastuch's pipe, starost, and I'll show you what I can do! I can blow the pipe so that not only the cows of my own village follow me home, but the cattle from the next village as well ! Why, all the *liéshuie* (wood-spirits) come flying up from miles around when I play, and settle on the trees like *riabchiks* (tree partridges) to listen ! Wolves come and fawn at my feet !   You won't find a pastuch like me in all Russia ! "

The fact is, the stranger was exceedingly anxious to obtain the situation of pastuch ; it was just the sort of loafing work to suit him ; hence his eloquence.

Now, when the patron of a situation is no less anxious to give away the office at his disposal than the candidate is to obtain it, there is not much need to waste words over the appointment ; accordingly, Radion Vasilitch was speedily engaged as the village pastuch, at a salary of four roubles per month, and entered at once upon his duties.

The appointment was made none too soon ; for the very next day was that on which the cattle were annually allowed to make their first excursion beyond their own yard gates. Radion appeared in full pastuch costume at earliest morn, and blew his long horn or pipe in a manner which proved that he was no novice in the accomplishment.   Out came the cows into the street, a noisy, happy herd, lowing and gambolling in exuberant but ungainly joy, for they were very naturally delighted to learn that their long captivity was over. Each house contributed its one or two or four cows to the herd as Radion passed trumpeting down the street, and at last the starost's house was reached.

"Starost!" shouted Radion, "aren't you going to do what is necessary for the safety of the herd before I take them into the woods?"

"What do you mean?" asked the chief Soul, who was standing in *déshabille* at his own yard gate, watching the pastuch and his charge.

"Why, about the wood-goblins. It is better to propitiate them—we always did so on the first day of the season at Kirilova!"

"This is not Kirilova, my brother," said the starost, "but Kushlefka. We have no wood-spirits here. A good pastuch is better than charms and ceremonies."

"Very well; but don't blame me if anything happens!" said Radion; and blowing a mighty blast upon his strident instrument, he accompanied his cows down the road. Presently the whole party branched off to the left across the ditch—the cows jumping it, most of them, in the inimitable manner of their tribe—struck across a patch of sandy common, reached a stretch of green pasture-land beyond, distributed themselves over this natural banqueting-hall in picturesque blotches of whites and reds and blacks, and so gradually passed out of sight and went their happy way until the evening. The villagers meanwhile would see no more of them, but left them in perfect confidence to the care of the pastuch, who received, or was to receive, the sum of four roubles per month for thus taking the cows "off their minds."

Radion performed his work with perfect success, and brought his herd home safely, in spite of the danger to be apprehended from *liéshuie* and their chosen agents for destruction, the wolves and bears.

Days passed, and still all went well. Radion's playing of the blatant cowhorn was all that he had described it, and his success as pastuch was complete. He occasionally brought back with him a hare which he had managed, somehow, to capture ; or a greyhen, whom he had discovered upon her nest with nine little cheeping blackcock beneath her. Radion had none of the chivalry of the sportsman, and thought nothing

of taking the "matka," or mother-bird, from her helpless fledglings, leaving them to starvation, or to the
foxes and the grey-hooded crows. The game thus
acquired he would distribute as gifts to those of the
wives of the moujiks who had the most cows, for
Radion's aim in life, as is the aim and object of every
true Russian peasant, was "*na chaiok*," or tea money,
so called because tea would be the very last thing
upon which any moujik would think of laying out
a gratuity. Radion hoped, then, for substantial *na
chaioks* at the end of the season from those whose
large property in cattle he had safeguarded successfully. But one fine evening, while the summer
was yet young and Radion still more or less of a
novelty in the village, a terrible thing happened, of
a sort to make those in the community who had
laughed at the superstitious pastuch and his fears of
the wood-goblins to look grave, and ask themselves
whether there was not, after all, more in this question
of old-time superstitions than appeared at first sight.
True, the villagers had never hitherto had any reason
to fear the *lièshuie*, or indeed to regard them as anything more than mere story-book beings, having no
existence save in the pages of nursery literature and
in the brains of loafers like Radion ; but now . . .

The facts of the matter were as follows. Radion brought home the herd of cows on a certain evening *one short*. The pastuch arrived from the pasture looking pale and haggard, escorted the herd as far as the village street, and himself turned aside into the house of the starost, whom he found lying asleep upon the top of his stove. Radion spent a considerable time bowing and crossing himself before the *ikon*, prostrating himself several times and touching with his forehead the bare boards of the floor. Then he turned his wild eyes towards the chief peasant of the village.

"Starost," he said, "a fearful thing has happened. The *lièshuie* are against us. We have offended the Spirits of the Forest, in whose service are the bears and the wolves. Let us propitiate them before it is too late, or a worse thing may happen!"

"Worse than what?" asked the starost. "It appears to me, my brother, that you are drunk."

"I may be a little drunk, brother Ivan Ivanitch," replied Radion, "but who would not take a little drop if he had been chased by two enormous wolves and laughed at by the king of the *lièshuie* himself?"

"Are you sure it was not a *bielaya kooropatka* (willow grouse)?" said the unbelieving starost. "Even sober men have ere now mistaken the cry of the *kooropatka* for the laugh of a wood-goblin."

"And what of the wolves, your charitableness, and the cow that is eaten up together with her bones and skin?" retorted the offended pastuch.

"What!" cried Ivan Ivanitch, starting to his feet; "not one of *my* cows, Radion Vasilitch?" The starost was serious enough now!

"Yes, Ivan Ivanitch; and the best cow in the village, and the fattest. Do you think the wolf-hunters of the *lieshuie* do not know which is the pick of the herd? As for me, though I blew my horn — yes, and cracked my long whip at them and shouted—all I could do was to attract their attention to myself instead of to the cow. Starost, I would not again go through that fearful chase for ten times four roubles a month. They pursued me to the foot of a tree, Ivan Ivanitch—it is a true word" (here Radion turned towards the *ikon* and crossed himself); "and had I not remembered to call upon the holy saint and equal to the Apostles, my patron, they would have eaten me as well as the cow Masha! As it was, from the top of a tree I saw the furious beasts fall upon poor Masha, tear her to pieces, and eat her entirely up, so that not a trace remained, while an invisible *liéshui* spirit laughed aloud until every particle was consumed. Then the wolves came licking their lips, to the foot of my tree, and, looking up at me, howled three times and vanished. It was with difficulty that I succeeded in reaching the village, for my knees have no strength, and my heart is as the heart of a lamb or of a sucking-pig after this terrible day."

The starost looked grave and troubled. That these wolves should have appeared after Radion's warning as to *liéshuie* was curious. That they should have selected his cow would surely indicate a deliberate intention on the part of the spirits— if, indeed, the spirits were at the bottom of the trouble—to accentuate the significance of their action; for they had eaten Masha, and that cow represented the starost; therefore the *liéshuie* had struck their blow at the starost, who, again, was the representative man of the community. This surely would mean that the spirits desired to demonstrate their displeasure with the community through their representative, the starost. A meet-

Q

ing of the Mir was held that very evening in order to discuss the situation, and a Soul was sent on horseback to the priest of the district, five miles away, to ask for guidance in the emergency which had arisen. Late at night the deputy returned to the village bearing a message from the priest. The message was extremely to the point, though very short, and ran thus : " Tell the starost and his moujiks and the pastuch that - they are a set of drivelling fools. The only spirits they have to keep clear of are *vodka* and cognac."

This was encouraging, if somewhat lacking in courtesy. But a difficulty arose. The pastuch professed to be so terrified with his experiences of the preceding day that he really could not bring himself to enter the woods again unless the usual ceremonies were first performed to protect the herd from the perils of the forest. However, a *na chaiok* of a rouble from the public funds proved a strong argument, and Radion was persuaded to convoy his cows as usual into their pastures.

All went well on this occasion and the day after, but on the evening of the third day another catastrophe happened. Radion returned *minus* two more of the cattle placed under his care—a second cow and the only bull of the herd. Radion himself was in a terrible state. He raved and laughed and cried and cursed like one demented. To the ordinary observer he would have appeared to be merely rather far gone in alcoholic poisoning; but this, of course, could not be the case: the *znaharka*, the wise woman of the village, said so. It was the simple and natural result of great terror, she explained. In all probability he had seen the *lièshuie* or, at least, their wolf-slaves, and the terror of it had maddened him.

This proved to be the case; for after a night's rest Radion was so far recovered that he gave a history of the events of the preceding day. These were, it appeared, almost a repetition of those of last week, excepting that, in addition to the horrors before experienced, a huge bear had come out of the forest, as well as the two wolves, and had eaten an entire cow to itself. After the meal it had climbed the tree upon which the affrighted Radion had taken refuge, seated itself beside him, growled and roared three times in his face, and climbed down again, tearing his trousers as it did so. Radion showed a long slit in the leg of his nether garments, which, of course, proved the truth of his story.

After this there could be no further shilly-shally-
ing.   The *znaharka* called upon the starost, and
spoke to that official very seriously upon the subject.
She knew, she explained, the details of the proper
function to be performed before a herd can be considered safe from interference by the *lieshuie*, and
would be pleased to take the management of the
affair into her hands.   Her fee was three roubles.
The cattle could not possibly be sent to pasture again
before this most necessary function had been performed.   No one would send their cows out under
the circumstances—how could they?   It was tempting Providence ; or, at all events, insulting the
wood-spirits, which came to the same thing.   Besides, the pastuch had declared he would not go
out again, and who was to take his place?

A meeting of the Mir was convened without
further delay, and it was determined to allow the
wise woman to proceed with her preparations.   On
the morrow, early in the morning, the ceremony
should be performed.   On this particular day the
cows remained at home.   Radion could not think
of risking his life a third time, and as for the
owners of the cows, there was hardly one who
would have been foolhardy enough to allow his

cattle to wander through the woods under present circumstances.

When the morrow came the *znaharka* was at hand as the herd moved down the street in order to watch which of the cows took the lead, for her first ceremony was dependent upon that circumstance. Having fixed upon the leader she tied a bit of red wool round its neck. This was a symbol that thus henceforth were the throats of the wild beasts bound, lest they should swallow the cows. Next the *znaharka* walked solemnly three times round the entire herd, locking and unlocking a padlock the while, in token that thus were the jaws of the grey wolves locked, lest they should rend the cattle. After the third time the padlock was finally locked and buried.

Then came a sort of liturgy which the wise woman pronounced standing in front of the herd, the meek animals being much surprised at the proceedings, and at the unusual delay in allowing them to get away to their pasture.

"Deaf man, canst thou hear us? No. Then pray God the grey wolf may not hear our cattle in the forest.

"Lame man, canst thou overtake us? Nay,

I cannot. Then pray God that the grey wolves overtake not these cows.

" Blind man, canst thou see us? No. Then pray God the grey wolf may not perceive our cattle in the woods."

This was the end of the function, and the poor cows, who had been somewhat impatiently whisking away the mosquitoes and horseflies for the last half hour, were at length allowed to proceed. Radion expressed himself satisfied and went after them ; he was no longer afraid of the wood-spirits, he declared; they were now powerless to harm him.

After this, matters went quietly enough at Kushlefka. Nothing happened to the herd or to the pastuch himself, for both were protected by the solemnities conducted as above by the *znaharka*. But the bull which had formed a meal for the two demon wolves on the occasion of their second attack upon the herd was still unreplaced, and it was necessary to buy one somewhere. The starost, therefore, allowed it to be known far and wide that Kushlefka was in need of a bull and open to offers.

In a few days bulls began to come in, bulls of

every kind; but for some little while the right bull
could not be found: one was too savage, another
too big, a third too small. A week went by and
still Kushlefka remained without the head and
ornament to its herd of cows. Then a most
curious and astonishing circumstance happened.
One morning, not long after the pastuch had set out
with his cattle for the day's wandering over moor
and grass-land, a man arrived from a village distant
some seven or eight miles through the forest,
accompanied by a bull whose appearance filled the
minds of those who witnessed its arrival with
astonishment and some awe. If they had not
already known that old Vasilice, the late lord of
the herd, was in his grave, or rather in the
stomachs of two grey demon-wolves of the forest,
they would have said that this new bull was
Vasilice *redivivus*. He was strangely like. From
the brown stocking on his off hind-leg to the one
black ear and browny-black patch on his nose—
big white body and all—he was the very image of
Vasilice. What made it the more astonishing was
that no sooner did the animal arrive in the village
street than he walked straight to the lodgings of
the late lamented Vasilice, and would take no

denial, but must needs be let into the yard, and thence to the cowshed, where he immediately sniffed about as one who knows the lie of the land, helping himself, presently, to hay and other delicacies which he found to hand, as though it were his own of right. In vain his owner tried to turn him out of shed and yard; he would not budge; indeed, he surveyed the man with a look of mild surprise, as who should say, "What on earth is the matter with *you*? Go back to Drevnik if you like, but as for me, I stay here!"

Deep was the astonishment of Kushlefka. This thing was a mystery. Could the bull be the spirit of the departed Vasilice? Some of the spectators spat on the ground, some crossed themselves; it depended upon how the thing suggested took them.

But stay; the starost has an idea. Vasilice used to have a faint mark of an old brand, a mere scar on the off hindquarter. Ivan Ivanitch entered the shed and made a close inspection of the animal.

When he came out his face was grave; but his glance was serene and high, as of one who has triumphed over mysteries, and has discerned light through the darkness.

"It is Vasilice," he said. "Where did you buy him, brother?"

"At Drevnik, your mercifulness," replied the seller.

"And from whom?"

"From a stranger, a pastuch, who drove him, with a fine cow, into Drevnik—oh—a fortnight ago nearly; he said he had been commissioned to sell the pair by a moujik in Koltusha, which your mercifulness knows is twenty miles away, and that——"

"Should you know the man again?" interrupted the starost.

"Certainly, for we drank together for half an hour at the *kabak*, after the bargain for the bull and cow. A ragged pastuch—lantern-jawed, and red-hair—and with a scrag beard——"

"Good," said the starost. "You shall have back the money you paid for Vasilice, and a three-rouble note for your trouble! Now leave him here and come back to-morrow with the cow. Brothers," he continued, "not a word to Radion about the bull Vasilice when he returns! I will settle with Radion to-morrow."

Then the starost paid a long visit to Yegor,

the *ochotnik* (sportsman) of the village, and made certain arrangements. Yegor was a great hunter and had slain many bears and wolves, making a good living by the sale of their skins.

.   .   .   .

On the following day, while Radion was loafing the morning away amid his cows, counting his ill-gotten gains and meditating as to how he should spend them as soon as he got safely out of Kush-lefka and back home again, he suddenly perceived something which sent his lazy blood, for once, coursing through his veins at a speed which made the beating of his heart a painful function. Issuing from the dark fringe of the forest, which lay but a short fifty yards away, came a procession alarming enough to frighten, out of his very wits, a man with five times the courage of Radion; first a bear —a big one—and at his heels two wolves. Behind the wolves came a wild shape—half human, but with the head of a bear. The procession moved slowly in Radion's direction, who, his limbs being fixed and rigid with terror, was entirely unable to move. Not so the herd. Snorting and bellowing, with tails up and heads down, every cow was in-stantly in motion, and galloping for dear life across the moor. Radion would have shrieked in the anguish of his fright, but his tongue clave to his palate, and he could utter no sound but a hoarse rattle. He tried to pray and to cross himself, but could not raise his arm.

By this time the awful procession had reached him and stood motionless around him. If Radion had not been half dead with fear he must have noticed something strange about the style of locomotion of the terrible beasts, as well as a certain fixedness of expression about the eyes of all four. But he was too far gone to observe anything. At last the figure, half man and half beast, spoke:

"Radion—Radion," it said sepulchrally, "liar! Where are the bull Vasilice and the cows Masha and Katia?"

Radion's dry lips moved, but he could utter never a word.

"Radion—liar!" the voice continued, "you have lied in the village to the dishonour of the *liéshuie*, of whom I am king. Where is the money you received for Vasilice and the two cows?" Radion's hand made a movement towards his wallet, but had not strength to carry itself so far.

"Radion—liar and thief," continued the king of

the *lieshuie* "you are doomed—you must die! Advance wolves, tear and destroy ; rend, bear!"

.But before the terrific animals could obey the injunctions of their leader, Radion's tongue had freed itself, and with a fearful yell the unfortunate pastuch fell senseless upon the heather.

Then that mercenary *lieshui* king relieved Radion of his wallet, after which he retired quickly into the forest followed by his three slaves, carrying their heads under their arms, the weather being hot.

When Radion returned to the village at night, his face was as the countenance of those who have been through great tribulation ; and when the herd awaited the sound of his horn next morning, and wandered aimlessly about the village street, headed by Vasilice *redivivus* (whom they were very glad to see back again among them), they were doomed to a sad disappointment ; for it was discovered that their faithful pastuch had departed, leaving no address.

CHAPTER X

AN UNBAPTIZED SPIRIT

I HAVE already referred to a pretty tradition still existing among the peasantry of the Slavonic families that the soul of a child who dies unbaptized must wander for seven years, beseeching, at the hands of each Christian person it sees, that precious privilege of which it has been deprived. If the little soul should fail, during its term of seven years, to find a Christian man or woman who will hear its cry and give it the baptism it craves, that soul must forfeit its soulship, and the being becomes a member of a lower race, assuming thenceforth the form and character of a river-spirit, and taking up its abode among the members of that frivolous and somewhat mischievous family.

.   .   .   .

There was grief in the house of Pavel Shirkof, a peasant of the village of Chudyesin, near Perm, beneath the shadow of the dark Urals. Pavel was unlike most of his kind, for his ideas of happiness

were not as theirs, bounded by the narrow limits
of the interior of the *kabak* or drinking-shop. Pavel
was gifted with an earnestness of disposition rare
enough among men of his standing; he took life
seriously, and had been a good husband to his wife.
He had married but a short year ago, and now, alas!
the buxom girl of twelve months since lay, a young
mother, sighing out the last moments of her stricken
life. Unattended by doctor or nurse, far from all
skilled assistance, and watched only by her terrified
and ignorant though loving husband, the poor wife
tossed upon her so-called bed, while her tiny child
lay helpless and neglected upon a nest of old potato-
sacks and coats and rags in the corner by the stove—
a thing of feeble, struggling existence, as near to its
end had Pavel known it, as it was to its beginning,
and this was but a matter of half-an-hour or so. The
baby lay and wailed unnoticed, for her poor father
had his dying wife to attend to, and the sick woman,
but half conscious, had not as yet caught that sound
so dear to every mother's ear—her own child's voice.
But suddenly she paused in the restless side-to-side
movements of her head upon the pillow, and appeared to listen.

"Pavel," she said, and her pale cheek flushed, "it

is the child. Let me see it before I die. Hold it near me. Let me take it in my arms!" Pavel brought the little wailing thing and laid it in the mother's arms, which scarcely had strength to clasp themselves round their precious burden.

A beautiful smile went, like a sunset, over poor dying Doonya's face—the last gleam before nightfall; then she looked anxiously at the tiny bundle at her breast. "Pavel, my poor man," she said, "the child has death in its face; it will accompany me into the Unknown; we shall both leave you together, my soul. God comfort you at this time of tribulation! But now you shall do her the only service you can ever render her. Fetch the good priest from Volkova; take Shoora, the best horse, and the lightest cart, and fetch him quickly, my Pavel, for the child must be baptized."

But Pavel refused to leave his wife in her present condition. The child must wait, he said; and in case of emergency any one could pronounce the baptismal formula. He would do it himself. Meanwhile, what was the child to him, body or soul, in comparison with his beloved Doonya?

A very few minutes after this the soul of Doonya passed peacefully away, and poor Pavel was a widower. In his anguish of mind during that saddest hour, he had no thought for the tiny bundle of sickly humanity lying neglected upon its bed of rags and sacking. No neighbours were at hand. All were at work in the fields. For none had known of poor Doonya's sudden and immediate need of their services. When at length Pavel remembered to look at the child, therefore, it was cold and dead, and might have been so for an hour for all he knew. Pavel was not so ignorant as to be unaware that the fate of a child dying unbaptized is most melancholy. He knew, as every Slavonic peasant knows, that the unbaptized soul, whether of child or grown person, is doomed to wander over earth and sea and air for seven long years, seeking for some one sufficiently pure of spirit to hear its spirit-voice appealing to be baptized. If such an one should hear it and pronounce the orthodox formula, all would be well with the soul, and it might depart in peace into those blessed realms where waiting souls, as Christians believe, rest until the great day of their resurrection. If, however, none should hear the wanderer (and, alas! how few are those qualified to catch the tone of a spirit-voice!), and the seven years should expire, then that poor unbaptized soul must lose its soulship, and descend among the mortal *rusalki*, or water-nymphs, to be a *rusalka* for the remainder of her life, cut off for ever from the blessed privileges of Christianity. Then Pavel was overcome with sudden remorse, and, in the hope that the soul of little Liuba (for so the parents had agreed to call her) was still within hearing, he pronounced aloud the words, "Liuba, I baptize thee in the name of the Father, and of the Son, and of the Holy Ghost." But, alas! it was too late. The little neglected soul had fled away in its distress and despair, and was already far from the place of its birth, wandering over sea and land, and crying aloud to every human being whom it saw: "Have pity, Christian brother (or sister). Hear my cry and baptize me, or my soulship is lost, lost!"

.   .   .   .

When the spirit of little Liuba first left the tiny body in which it had commenced its career, and fled away, it knew not whither to direct its flight. One central idea was all the consciousness it possessed as yet, and this was the knowledge—half

R

hope and half despair—which is given to each
infant unbaptized soul for its heritage, namely, that
it has been deprived by misfortune of something
which should have been its dearest possession, the
sweet privilege of Christian baptism, and that it must
wander and weep and entreat until such time as it
shall find a baptized Christian into whose own pure
soul the cry of the wandering spirit may enter ;
from him it may then receive the precious gift which
is its own by right, but of which it had been unfortunately deprived.

So Liuba's infant soul fled wailing over valley and
hill and sea, and was far away when her widowed
father pronounced the baptismal formula over the
poor little wasted body which had once been her
earthly tenement. Liuba knew nothing of the fate
predestinated for those whose seven years expire
and find them still without the pale of blessedness ;
all this she should learn in good time ; at present
she only knew that she must wander and chant
her monotonous sorrowful prayer that she might
be heard and baptized.

Red-shirted peasants were busy at work in the
fields, together with gaily-clad women and a few
children. It was the time of the cutting of the

corn, and there was much laughter and merriness, while each peasant did as much work as he felt was good for him, which was not much; the women worked harder than the men and sang in a light-hearted manner as they laboured. The men were glad to allow the women to work as hard as they were willing to; it saved them much trouble.

"Brothers and sisters—Christian people," wailed the child-spirit, "baptize me and save my soul alive!" But not one of all the chattering, toiling throng could hear the spirit-voice, for the sounds of the world were loud in their ears and no other voice could reach them by reason of the noises which deafened them. So Liuba left them and fled away over hill and dale, wailing and weeping, for she had experienced her first taste of failure and disappointment; and by-and-by she came to the banks of a large river, and here she rested herself upon the shore, strange and lost and lonely. It was a beautiful sunny morning in August, and little Liuba could not resist the charm of the sunshine and the sparkle of the clear water about her; she saw it with delight, and the rustle of the leaves and the songs and twittering of the happy birds amid the leaflets overhead filled her with wondrous joy and content. "How beautiful it all is," she cried; "if only it were to be always like this I should not so much mind my misfortune."

To Liuba's surprise, at the sound of her voice a very beautiful form suddenly appeared rising out of the water. The shape was that of a human girl, but indistinct, and with wavy outlines that quivered and shifted, instead of the fixed lines of a human body. Masses of golden flowing hair fell over bosom and shoulders and lay floating upon the ripples of the water, of which it seemed to form a part; and though it had proceeded from the stream and still lay upon the surface of the river, yet the hair was not wet and draggled but wavy and dry and lovely to look upon. Liuba looked at the new-comer with admiration and joy. "How beautiful you are!" she cried, "and you have heard my voice and will baptize me!"

The beautiful creature laughed aloud, and the sound of her voice was like the flowing of shallow waters over the rapids.

"Oh, no!" she cried, "I cannot baptize you, and I would not if I could! You must be very young or you would know that I am a river-spirit, a *rusalka*, such as you yourself will be one day, unless you find some one to baptize you, which is very unlikely. I can hear your voice for I am a spirit, but mortal men cannot distinguish your speech, and if they hear anything they say, 'Listen to the whispering of the wind in the tree-top!' or, 'Do you hear how the breeze sighs this evening among the reeds in the stream?' Do you not know that you have but seven years in which to perform your hopeless task, and that after that you are at liberty to come down among us here in the cool waters? It were far better to save yourself these years of disappointment and toiling and to become one of us at once."

But the soul of Liuba thirsted for baptism as the new-born plant longs for the touch of the sun-god, and she was not satisfied with the words of the *rusalka*.

"But who *are* you? and are you baptized? and what do you do down there in the cool waters?" she asked. The *rusalka* looked grave for an instant, and then quickly laughed once more.

"No," she said, "we are not baptized; we are spirits now, but when the world comes to an end and the rivers are poured out and dried up, we shall exist no longer. We are the Water Folk, and our ancestors fell with Lucifer from heaven; at which time we took up our abode here, instead of following our captain to his home. As for what we do, we dance and sport amid the shining stones and caves, and chase the brilliant fishes, and scare the greedy otters; we fascinate silly humans, and when they follow us into the waves we strangle them or torture them to death because we hate them."

"Why do you hate them?" asked Liuba.

"Because they have souls and we have none; you will know why in seven years. And now, good-bye till then, for my sisters await me yonder; they are ready for the dance, while I tarry chattering here." With these words the beautiful nymph seemed to fade from the sight, growing every instant more and more indistinct. Liuba saw her wave her arms and heard her silvery laugh, and then she quite disappeared. From the spot where she had stood upon the bank a tiny stream of crystal water trickled through the grass and flowers and found its way back to the parent river.

"How terrible!" said Liuba. "Oh, *how* I hope

I shall never be a *rusalka !*" and a great rush of
longing came over the little bankrupt soul for that
baptism of which it knew nothing save its own
great need and desire for the gift, and away she
floated once more over woods, meadows, and rivers,
wailing and crying, "Oh, who will baptize me,
baptize me! Christian men, have pity upon a soul
that wanders and weeps, and baptize me!"

But the merchant was too busy over his money-
making, or too preoccupied with his money-losing
to have a thought to spare for a lost soul. And
the ships riding upon the bosom of the sea, many
of which Liuba passed in her flight, were filled with
sailors who thought of their dear wives and children
at home on shore, and of the loved cliffs of their
native country, but not of the poor bereft spirit
passing in distress and beseeching over the deck
of their vessel. Now and again one would say to
his comrade, "What sound was that amid the
rigging like the sighing of wind and the whirring
of the wings of a bird that flies from land to land?"
and the other would reply: "I heard no sound,
and it is too dark to follow the flight of a bird to-
night." Even the worshippers in the churches
were unable to hear the spirit-voice; they were

busy praying for themselves or for their dear ones; some thought of worldly matters in spite of themselves, some were sad for their sins, some were full of petty jealousies because of the grand clothes of their fellow-worshippers, or of pride for their own; none heard the wailing spirit-voice, and Liuba, the saddest soul in all that churchful of souls, went weeping upon her journey, ever weeping and ever beseeching, but never obtaining that sweet gift for which she longed with a longing that increased with each day and with every disappointment.

Once, when she had wandered thus for months enough to make two whole years, Liuba met with an adventure. Passing over the streets of a large city she was surprised to hear a voice, which at first she took for an echo of hers, for it spoke the same words, and the tone was that of distress and entreaty, as sorrowful as her own. Then she saw that the sound proceeded from a little form like hers, which slowly and sadly winged its way through the dusky air, close above the roofs of the human habitations below, and ever as it went it chanted its melancholy refrain: "Christian men and women, hear my voice, and baptize me ere it is too late, and my soulship is lost, lost!" Liuba accosted the little wandering soul, which was, she found, sadder even than herself because it had less of hope. This soul was that of a little human boy who had died unbaptized nearly seven years ago. For six long years and as many months it had wandered, entreating for baptism and finding none that could hear its voice; now there remained but a few months wherein to gain the blessed privilege, and hope had grown faint and weak. Liuba's companion had been over the world, he said, and over it a second time; but all in vain—none would hear him. He had met many lost souls like himself, and all were sad and disappointed; and for some, he knew, the term had expired and they had fallen to the status of water-spirits. Some had taken the form of cuckoos, and in the shape of that bird had wandered over the world crying "cuckoo" instead of the usual entreaty for baptism, because there are many, he said, upon the earth, who believe that each unbaptized soul assumes the form and voice of this bird in order to be seen and heard by Christian men. Those who believe thus are in the habit of pronouncing the formula of baptism over each cuckoo whose voice they hear, in the hope of thus saving some lost human soul.*

" And are some saved in this way," asked Liuba.

"I have heard so from others," said the new-comer, "but I know not whether it is true. For myself, I have been content to preserve my own likeness and voice, for surely, surely some day, though the time is now short, I shall yet be heard and saved!"

So Liuba and her companion journeyed together henceforth, and together they chanted their mono-tonous song, which none of all the Christian men and women they saw might hear: "Brothers, Christians, hear us and baptize us, or our soulship is lost!"

Then there came a sad day when the elder wanderer knew that his time for hoping was past, and that his soulship was indeed lost for ever. By the bank of a lovely river he and Liuba parted, and Liuba wept bitterly, and said: "Farewell, poor lost brother, in pity and love I greet you a last time, and even as your lot is so shall mine be; for, alas, there remain but a few more years!" But the other said, "Nay, hope on, Liuba, for, perhaps, by

* This belief is far from uncommon.

the mercy of the Highest, you may yet be saved."
Then he drooped his wings and plunged beneath the
waters, and when the cool element touched him he
forgot for ever that he had belonged to a higher
race of beings, and went among the river-spirits, and
was with them and of them, and knew of nothing
better.

But Liuba wandered on and on, and wearied not
of wrestling with Christian men and women for
that which they alone could give her if they would.
Once—a year from the end of her term—she
passed through a church in which prayers were
continually offered for those who die unbaptized,
and in which the form of baptism is gone through
annually once for the benefit of these, in case one
should be within hearing; but the service was just
finished as Liuba passed over the church, and she
was too late to hear those longed-for words which
should give her the priceless boon she desired.
In another place she came where a certain good
man pronounced every morning and every evening
the baptismal formula, in case some poor wandering
soul should be passing within hearing and should
hear and live. But though she saw him, she knew
not of his benevolent daily action, and passed on

unaware; neither did he hear her spirit-voice, for
his soul was full of many worldly matters, and
when at evening he performed the pious rite which
was his daily custom, Liuba was far away.

And it happened that a few months before the
expiration of her time, Liuba passed once again by
that stream where, on her first day of wandering,
she had seen the river-spirit; and now again, as
she rested upon the bank of the stream, that
beautiful nymph-form rose, glistening and undula-
ting, from the waters, and waved her arms and
laughed and beckoned to Liuba, and said, "Aha!
little lost soul, a few more days or weeks and you
are ours. We shall be kind to you, never fear, and
you shall dance and sport your time away instead
of wandering and whining over land and sea, and
all for the sake of something which may not be
worth the finding! And you shall learn to capti-
vate the hated human beings who would not listen
to your voice, and you shall entice them down
and strangle them—strangle them!" But Liuba fled
away in horror and dread, and would not listen to
what the *rusalka* had to say. But her last few
months were at hand, and the poor wanderer
toiled on, beseeching and entreating wherever she

went, and weeping and wailing more pitifully as hope receded further and further.

. . . . . .

Far away in the east of Europe there is a great city which is full of large shops, and immense houses, and busy streets, and of rich and poor, and of good and evil, as is every other large city everywhere. It was Christmas eve, and the last hour of work had come for bank and shop and factory. After this there should be holiday-time for all. The factory hands poured in a great stream from the open doors of a cotton-mill—pale men and women, happy enough in the prospect of a day or two to be spent far away from the stuffiness and the heat and the toil of the mill. All chatted and laughed and made plans, and told one another of what they would do at Christmas and on Boxing Day. And many went away to dance and to sing and enjoy themselves; and some went to the inns and public-houses, and were rowdily happy in their own way; and many went to the brilliant shops and bought materials for their Christmas dinner or presents for their friends. And one man of all the crowd did not join those who were bent on merrymaking. Yet he, too, was full of plans of happiness for the season. He was not rich, this man, but he spent little, and the wages of the factory were good; and each year he contrived to save a sum of money in preparation for that which he had in his mind for Christmas time. He had brought his savings with him this evening—a fair sum for a man in his position—and with the money. he proceeded from shop to shop, buying here a pot of sweet flowers, there a book, here a doll, and there a toy, until his large basket was full and as heavy as he could carry. Then he went to the children's hospital, where for seven years his kind face had been well known; and here he was received with acclamation by the little suffering inmates, for they knew well the meaning of his appearance in company with the basket; and there were some who had been in that building, alas! for years, and had learned to consider the visit of this man and his basket as an established thing, as certain and as regular as Christmas itself. Many little hearts beat higher with joy when Paul Shirkof's round was finished and the basket was empty, and Paul's own heart was joyful and happy indeed as he returned to his home that night and knelt to say his Christmas prayer. His was no conventional prayer, nor did he pray in the words of any formula; but he thought of the Christ-child born as on this night in its helplessness and innocence, and he prayed for simplicity and for innocence, that his heart might be as the heart of a child, and his spirit pure, so that he might discern God in all His works.

And even as he prayed there was borne in upon him—though he could see nothing—as the sound of the voice of a tiny child, and it said—entreating and wailing—"Oh, Christian man, pity me; hear my voice—and baptize me, or my soulship is lost!"

And a great fear fell upon the man, so that he could scarcely frame words to ask:

"Who are you that address me?" Then the answer came: "An unbaptized soul—Liuba; baptize me before it is too late, and save me!"

And the man delayed no longer, but made the sign of the Cross and said, "I baptize thee in the name of the Father, and of the Son, and of the Holy Ghost, Amen." Then at the words the soul of Liuba rejoiced with a great joy, and departed, whither I know not; but this is certain, that it wandered no longer wailing over land and sea, for it was henceforth at rest for ever, and, by Divine mercy, in possession of that sweet privilege which for a while had been lost to it.

And the father knew not that he had baptized his own child's soul; but he shall know it one day, perhaps, when those who are pure in spirit shall see God.

CHAPTER XI

A WITCH! A WITCH!

In this year of grace, close to the end of the nineteenth century, many of the villages in the Tsar's dominions are almost up to date in the science of cholera-fighting, thanks to the energy of the Zemstvo, which is a species of County Council. They set apart, some of them, a hut or house as a hospital for suspicious cases; the villagers occasionally boil their drinking water; they drink their *vodka*—well, perhaps the merest trifle more discreetly, in times of scare, than in the piping days of health and security. I would not go so far as to say that they waste much water in personal ablutions, because I wish my readers to take me seriously; and as for the drainage and sanitation of the villages, there is none from end to end of the realm.

Nevertheless, matters are very much more satisfactory now than was the case forty or fifty years ago; when, at the appearance of the terrible scourge

s

of cholera, most of the inhabitants at once gave themselves up for lost, and, resolving to make the most of the short time remaining to them for indulgence in the pleasures of terrestrial existence, drank themselves into alcoholic coma every day, until the disease fastened itself upon their *vodka*-sodden bodies, and carried them away where no *vodka* is to be had for love or money.

Tirnova, in the government of Vologda, was one of the villages most sorely attacked by the cholera-fiend during the outbreak of 1861.

The peasants of this village had many and many a time received good advice from the priest of the nearest parish village, Shishkina, who, being a man of sense, had recommended them, before the outbreak (having driven over on purpose to warn them), to do their best to stave off the threatened attack of " the plague," as they called it, by prayer and personal cleanliness. But since the cholera had not as yet made its appearance in the place it was clearly unnecessary, the peasants decided, to put themselves out, and no notice was taken of the priest's warning. Now, however, that the plague had come, a deputation headed by the starost, or head-peasant, waited upon the priest in order to receive further counsel, for, as a matter of fact, they had forgotten all he told them. " Fools that you are and sons of dogs," said the good man, who well knew how the moujik must be addressed if it is desired that he should listen, "did I not tell you long ago to pray to the Almighty, first; and secondly, to clean your filthy houses and your own bodies with soap and hot water? Go home, and pray and wash!" At this, all present removed their caps and scratched their heads, implying thereby that there was a difficulty still unexplained.

"If," said the starost, stepping out to speak, "if it be the will of the Almighty that cholera should visit our village, then surely it would be impious to do anything, such as the cleansing of our houses, to keep it off? We can pray, of course, that it may please the Almighty to modify His will in this matter, and, no doubt, your reverence would come over with the large and holy *ikon* of St. Luke the Physician, with whom for intercessor we might hold a solemn procession; but——"

"Did not I tell you you were a set of brainless idiots?" said the priest; "the saints only help those who help themselves. Pray, by all means; but when you have done praying, go out and

wash yourselves, and your clothes, and your houses;
and don't afterwards drink yourselves into the likeness of swine at the beer-house—oh, it's no use
wagging your head at me, Matvéi Stepanitch; I
know you well enough! There, that's my advice;
now go!"

"And the *ikon?*" said the moujiks, giving their
matted locks a final scratching before departure.

"You shall have the *ikon*, and a special litany,
as soon as you have cleaned up the village, and
washed yourselves, but not before," said the firm
ecclesiastic, and with this ultimatum he slammed
the door in their faces.

The deputation felt that this was business-like and
savoured of authority, which is a thing the Russian
peasant invariably respects, especially if the authority
is abusive and has a loud voice, and does not mince
matters. They greatly approved of the strong language of their spiritual adviser, and of his vigorous
way of presenting his views; but the advice as to
cleanliness was extremely unpopular, while, as for his
allusion to the beer-shop—well, the "little father"
might have known better; he must be well aware
that life without *vodka* is an impossibility, cholera
or no cholera. Therefore the deputation pro-

ceeded straight to the village drinking-shop and there drank the priest's health times enough to secure *his* immunity from cholera anyhow, unless the fates persistently disregarded the vows of the pious intoxicated. Afterwards some of them took a bath in the streamlet which ran like a˙ silver ribbon through the village; being but eighteen inches deep or so, this rivulet could scarcely afford scope for the malice of a *vodyannui*, or water-demon, so they were safe enough; but they did not like the feel of the water, it was unfamiliar and uncanny, and gave them the shivers. Others patronised the bath-house and employed hot steam to take off as much of the outer coating of griminess as each considered safe or desirable; for there is nothing so certain to give one cold as the sudden leaving off of clothes or other coverings to which the body has become accustomed. As for prayers in church, the "little father's" remark was surely uncalled for; did not the women attend to this department, and was not the priest aware of the fact? They had, indeed, been. specially devout during the cholera scare, and the stands before the *ikons* in church were simply overburdened with candles devoted to the favourite

saints.   Was all this not enough to satisfy him?
He could hardly expect the moujiks themselves to
attend on ordinary Sundays !   After the toil of the
week (toil of which the women took *more* than
their full share, though no mention of the circumstance was made by their lords in council), surely
the men were entitled to a day of undisturbed rest !
It was a long walk to the church, five miles at
least, while the beer-shop was so very handy.   So
far as cleansing the houses was concerned, since
the priest seemed to desire it, the *babui* (women)
should be told to use their brooms a bit, for it was
just as well that the " little father " should come
over and bring his *ikon* with him, the big one ; and
the moujiks knew him well enough to be quite sure
that he would keep his word and come so soon
as they had made a fair show of performing their
part of the agreement.   The starost's house, where
the priest would put up for the afternoon, accordingly received such a cleaning as it had not enjoyed
for years ; but portions of the village which he would
not visit, or would see only when the procession
was half-way round its course, remained untouched
by broom or scrubbing-brush.

Thus did the moujiks of Tirnova observe the

counsels of their priest; their obedience went as far as their convenience, and no further. They succeeded, however, in making so good a show as to justify the pastor in coming over with the big *ikon* and holding the religious function proper to the occasion, namely, that designed to stay the ravages of the demon of cholera.

But, alas! the plague seemed to ignore all attempts to quash or turn it aside. In spite of processions and *ikons* and the chanting of priest and deacons, in spite of everything, the cholera raged on just as furiously as ever, if not more furiously.

It was at this critical stage of affairs that Marfa Kapústina came to the fore. Marfa was the *znaharka*, or "wise woman," of the place. Learned to a degree was Marfa in all manner of spells and incantations, and in the virtues of herbs and of charms; moreover, she was a firm believer in her own wisdom, and in the potency of the spells and mummeries of which she held the secret, though no whit the less an excellent churchwoman according to the orthodox faith of the country, in spite of her dealings with matters upon which Holy Church would certainly look with suspicion and dislike. The fact is, Marfa, like the great majority of her countrymen and women throughout rural Russia, was a little mixed as to what constituted religion and what was meant by "superstition," and where one ended and the other began. If she had been informed that some of those rites and ceremonies, the minutest details of which she carried in her memory for use in all emergencies, were nothing more nor less than mere survivals of the paganism which had flourished in Russia but a few centuries ago, she would have been immensely surprised, but not in the least convinced. Up to the present time, however, Marfa had enjoyed but little opportunity of demonstrating her talents and knowledge in all kinds of exorcisms and spells; indeed, she was far better known as one eminently skilful in the more mundane art of escorting little Christians into this world of trouble, and of looking after their mothers in the time of tribulation and sickness.

But now at last Marfa felt that the great opportunity of her life had arrived. Shortly after the painful fact became apparent to all in the village that the orthodox ceremonies for the "laying" of the cholera ghost had entirely failed in their object, the starost received a visit from the *znaharka*, who looked preoccupied and feverish.

"Matvéi Ivanitch," she began abruptly, "the cholera is very bad—worse than ever. Only last night Avdotia Timofeyevna and her child were carried away, and this morning Feodor Zaitzoff has followed them. Old Vainka, the *ooriadnik* (sub-policeman) is very bad too ! "

" It is God's will ! " said the starost.

"That is certain," the *znaharka* assented ; "but what, Matvéi Ivanitch, if it is also God's will that we should at least do our best to rid ourselves of the scourge He has permitted to fall upon our backs, or rather of the devils which have come among us ? Our *rodityelui* (forefathers) were accustomed to fight the plague-demon by means of certain ceremonies— simple ceremonies and very effectual. It is at least possible that the Almighty is angry that we neglect to employ those simple weapons which a little knowledge places in our hands." The wise woman paused.

"Well," said the starost, "go on. What are you referring to ? Were they Christian ceremonies that the *rodityelui* employed ? "

"Assuredly ! " said the *znaharka* ; "there were prayers, and an *ikon* was carried about."

"But the priest has already been amongst us with his *ikon*, and you see how much we have gained by it," observed the starost impatiently.

"The function was incomplete, Matvéi Ivanitch," the wise woman hastened to explain. "The prayers were good and the *ikon* was good, but there were other things, good also, omitted. There is but one individual within a thirty-mile ride who knows of the true ceremony, and that is myself. Pay me ten roubles from the funds and the ceremony shall be performed, and the plague, perhaps, shall be stayed —who knows?" The *znaharka* glanced at the sacred picture in the corner and crossed herself.

The starost, feeling unable to decide the question single-handed, resolved to convoke a special meeting of the Souls of the Village in order to give full consideration to the proposal of the wise woman. The gaps among the ranks of the Souls were already distressingly numerous; and the Souls being the heads of houses, this fact told a sad tale of families deprived of the bread-winner, stricken down and lost to the community by the terrible ravages of the cholera-demon. It was in itself a silent but sufficient *primâ facie* argument in favour of adopting the proposal of the *znaharka*.

Of the moujiks still remaining alive, however, some few were found presumptuous enough to laugh to scorn the very idea of holding a pagan function in order to complete that which the Christian ceremony had omitted or failed to perform! Better to keep the ten roubles, they said, for the relief of the widows and children of those who had already fallen victims to the plague. But the great majority were strongly in favour of adopting the *znaharka's* suggestion; it was at least a straw to grasp at, and certainly nothing could be more desperate than the situation of affairs in the village at the present moment. As for the ten roubles, it was pointed out by some that if "this sort of thing" were to continue much longer, there would be no one left alive to enjoy "the funds;" far wiser were it to spend the money in an endeavour to strike a blow at the insidious enemy, who threatened to depopulate the village within a measurable period of time!

Accordingly the *znaharka* was informed that her proposal was to be adopted, and Marfa was instructed to make her arrangements as quickly as possible, and to proceed with the function exactly as the *rodityelui* had been accustomed in former ages to perform it.

Marfa showed herself to be not only perfectly at home in the minutest details of the ceremony about to be gone through, but also determined to lose not a single moment in pushing forward the necessary preparations. The very next morning an order went out from the starost, at Marfa's request, that all the mankind of the village, young and old, should remain within doors until after the conclusion of the proceedings. They might lie on their stoves and sleep out the morning hours, if they chose ; but—for certain good reasons—they must not look out of the windows or watch the ceremony about to be performed. The girls and women of the community, on the other hand, as the actors and participants in the function, were instructed to assemble at an appointed place at an early hour. Each was to be clad in the scanty costume enjoined by tradition for the occasion— that is, in a short, thin shirt or chemise, and that only. Attired in this airy costume, all the females of the village, from the oldest to the youngest, assembled at the rendezvous at the appointed hour, when a procession was formed in the following order :—In front went the oldest woman in Tirnova carrying an *ikon*. Next to her

walked the *znaharka* herself, astride of a broom-
handle, and bearing under her arm a cock of a
black or dark colour. Behind the *znaharka* followed the rest of the girls and women, ranged in
pairs. A huge bonfire had previously been built
up and lighted at one end of the village street,
while a similar one blazed at the opposite extremity
of the village. The procession having marched towards the first of these bonfires, all solemnly walked
three times round it, chanting and praying, taking
the words from the *znaharka*, who knew the correct
liturgy by heart. After the completion of the third
circle, Marfa suddenly—as though struck with an
idea—clasped the cock in her two hands and with
it rushed down the street shrieking loudly, followed
and imitated by the rest of the women. As soon
as the second bonfire was reached the unfortunate
cock was thrown into the flames, while the procession marched three times round, singing and
praying as before. Lastly, the procession was
reformed and an entire circuit of the village was
made, the line of march passing outside of each
and every house; for no cholera-devil could afterwards cross the line thus determined.

As the army of wailing and chanting females

passed close to an outlying cottage a black cat
was unfortunate enough to select that moment for
rushing out of the yard and crossing the path of
the procession. Instantly the *znaharka* caught it,
and seizing it by the hind legs dashed its head
against a stone, killing it on the spot. This
incident delighted beyond measure the *znaharka*,
and through her the rest of the women, for, as
she quickly explained, within the mangy person of
the black cat, now deceased, had undoubtedly
been located the demon of cholera, which was
now, consequently, "done for" in so far as concerned the village of Tirnova, and no fresh case
of the plague would occur in the place from this
hour forward.

Then the entire company returned to their
homes and dressed themselves, and proudly informed their male relatives of the wonderful success
which had attended the mysteries in which they
had been engaged.

It was certainly a remarkable circumstance that,
from that day on, the cholera actually ceased its
ravages among the inhabitants of the village. Whether
the black cat deceased had really been the desperate
character which it was accused of being, or whether

faith in the methods of the *znaharka* had cast out fear, and with it the principal element of danger in a cholera epidemic, when, as every one knows, it is scare that carries off half the victims who succumb to the disease, or whether, again, the epidemic had already worn itself out and had taken all the victims it meant to claim, I know not; but, as a matter of fact, there perished no more moujiks on this occasion with the exception of one man, who, as it happened, had scoffed and derided the *znaharka* and her procession, and had even made rude remarks about the ladies in their airy costumes as they had passed his house full of their solemn undertaking. Probably this man was afterwards seized with doubt as to the wisdom of his conduct, then with panic, and lastly—as so frequently happens —took the plague out of sheer nervousness. However this may have been, all these things immensely added to the prestige of the *znaharka*, who now found herself famous, and in possession of a reputation which placed her upon a pinnacle far higher than that of any wise woman or wise man for miles around.

It must not be supposed that by the marvellous success of the pagan ceremony just described any sort of a blow was dealt to the orthodox beliefs of the villagers—nothing of the kind. The prestige of the priest may have suffered, but not the cause of religion. It was merely concluded by these simple-minded people that their *znaharka* knew the priest's business better than the *bátuishka* did himself, that was all!

For many a long day after these events belief in the *znaharka* was the supreme motive-power of the peasants of the district. If any cursing had to be done, Marfa was invited to do it. Had the evil eye fallen upon a moujik or woman of the place? Marfa defeated the sinister effects of that deplorable circumstance. Her benedictions were equally effective and in request; so were her spells, her charms, her incantations and mummeries of every kind. As the faith of the people in her powers was absolute, so her success was naturally marvellous in proportion, and for many a long year Marfa's reputation was unquestioned and her position assured. Nevertheless, a great reputation carries great responsibilities and great risks, and once a hole is found or picked in that flimsy material prestige, a rent is inevitable, and the fabric will easily and quickly go to rags and ruin! Even Marfa's

glory was destined to end at last, and the beginning
of the end came in the miscarriage of a certain
benediction. Young Vainka Shahgin, a peasant of
the village, had wooed and won the attractive
Masha Sotsky; or, perhaps, the friends of Vainka
had wooed the friends of Masha and won *them*.
Anyhow, the pair were married and had been duly
blessed by the *znaharka*, now an old woman; for
without her benediction no married couple in the
district would have dreamed of going forth to battle
with the world and its tribulations. But ever since
the *znaharka's* blessing had been accorded to this
particular union the pair had led a cat-and-dog
life. Vainka had taken to drinking immediately,
while Masha had proved herself a slovenly slattern
at home and the worst of housekeepers. No
children came to cement the union; the marriage
was a failure all round. It was rather hard on
Marfa that all this should be laid to her account;
but such is life! It was; and this was the first of
her serious misfires. Shortly after this there came
troubles with wolves. During the coldest period of
a certain very severe winter, those famished animals
became so tamed by starvation as to lose some of
their natural aversion to the near presence of man-

T

kind. They took to making daring raids upon the village of Tirnova during the gloom of night, carrying away dogs and other domestic creatures. Soon they waxed bolder still, and, arriving in force, succeeded in killing and getting safe away with a cow and two horses. The *znaharka*, after this climax, was requested to solemnly curse the offenders, which she promptly did, using the *ikon* and the prayers of the Church as well as certain traditional incantations of a pagan character.

But the wolves were none the worse for this mixed dose—on the contrary, they seemed to be all the better for it; the treatment did them good and improved their appetite. Where, up to this time, they had been content to steal a cat, they now carried off a grown pig; the horses and cows were invaded in their very stables and outhouses; things went from bad to worse. All the world recognised that the curses of the *znaharka* agreed with the wolves, they grew fat upon her maledictions and the Tirnova cattle: Marfa had made another lamentable failure!

Thus, gradually, the immense prestige of the old woman waned and drooped and disappeared. One thing after another failed with her. Now that faith

had gone, success went also. Those who, but yesterday, had believed in and honoured her, scoffed to-day
as she passed them; nor was this all. As failures
multiplied, ill-feeling towards her increased. Where
she had been feared and loved, she was now
ridiculed and hated. Men no longer accorded
to her her former honourable appellation of "the
wise woman"; they took to calling her *vyedma*
and *bába yagá*, both of which terms mean witch, or
sorceress, and carry a weight of abusive meaning, for
a witch is always malignant, while a *znaharka* is invariably a useful and benevolent member of society.

The idea once started that poor Marfa was a
vyedma, the unfortunate woman was—like the pro-
verbial dog to whom a bad name has been given—
practically already hanged. She rapidly grew in
the ill-favour of the inconstant villagers, by whom
she was accused of all manner of monstrosities of
which she was entirely innocent. There was no
misfortune or calamity that happened at this time
within the district but it was quickly laid to the
charge of Marfa. In a short while she was cursed
and hated by the entire population. At last
matters culminated in an accusation brought against
the poor woman by the pastuch, or cowherd, of the

community. The *znaharka*, this man declared, had taken to milking the cows of the villagers by means of witchcraft, while the animals were away at the pasture. There were two circumstances which lent colour to this statement. In the first place, the milking of cows by magical means was known to be a favourite accomplishment of *vyedmui*, who, from all times, have been addicted to this dishonest and wicked practice—a practice exercised by them not out of mere mischief, but for profit—for witches must live as well as any one else. In the second place, many of the cows had, of late, been unaccountably short of milk; good milkers, too, who had never hitherto disappointed their owners. Day after day these animals were found, at milking time, to be absolutely without their frothy produce. At a hastily convened meeting of the heads of houses the pastuch was instructed to watch the herd while at pasture, to watch carefully from a convenient spot, he himself remaining, if possible, unseen; and then to return and report. This the cowherd did, and with so much success that on the third day after he had received his instructions he returned from the pasture lands with full particulars as to how the *vyedma* Marfa had proceeded in order to effect the robbery of which she was accused. Her method proved to be an old and favourite device among witches. The herd described his experience thus: He had taken up a position, he said, in the topmost branches of a birch tree, whence he could see for miles around, while the herd browsed peacefully about the foot. At about midday he observed the *vyedma* (at whose name—for it had come to this—the pastuch and all his audience spat upon the ground in token of their disgust!), he observed, he said, the *vyedma* approaching from the direction of the village, bearing a basket which was full of empty bottles, each bottle having a separate compartment in the basket. She stopped in the middle of the communal grass-field, at a spot where lay the old plough which Ivan Tussoff had left there since last autumn to save himself the trouble of throwing it away. Then she raised her arms and waved her hands, and pronounced some incantations, the nature of which, being so far away, he could not hear, but which, he said, must have been very potent, for the entire herd, as with one accord, began to show signs of great restlessness and to low softly and mournfully. He himself also felt the effects, which were such as to give him a sensation of nervousness and great depression, and a creepy feeling all down his back, while he distinctly recognised a strong smell of sulphur filling the air. Then the *vyedma*, after more incantations, stuck what appeared to be a penknife into the woodwork of the old plough, when immediately drops of milk began to, first, drip from the knife, then to slowly trickle, and lastly to flow. Marfa placed her bottles one after the other beneath this singular milk-tap until all these were filled, then she departed, carrying the basket, as though it were a thing of no weight at all. When she had disappeared, the pastuch descended from his perch and tested some of the best of the cows. They proved to be as dry as bones; not a single drop of milk did their udders afford! The herdsman concluded his tale amid exclamations of horror and dismay. The peasants crossed themselves and spat. What need of further evidence? Undoubtedly there was a *vyedma* among them; suspicion must give place to certainty. Undoubtedly also it was the duty of those in authority in the village to rid themselves of the shame and horror of harbouring such a creature in their midst.

Russian peasants, when they have made up their

minds in times of excitement to any outrageous proceeding, rarely delay long before putting their ideas
into execution. Within an hour of the conclusion
of the meeting the unfortunate Marfa had been
arrested, accused, found guilty, sentenced, and
executed. The manner of her execution was in
accordance with the traditional end of convicted
witches: she was placed in a large wheat sack,
together with a dog, a cat, and a cock—all as
innocent of conscious offence as she was herself—
and thrown into the village pond, where the whole
company went down to the bottom together, as a
warning to other witches and evildoers, of which
poor Marfa was neither the one nor the other.

Two days after this tragedy a strange moujik
sauntered into the village of Tirnova and called
to see the starost, who, as it happened, was at
home and received him.

"Starost, brother," said the stranger, going straight
to business, "why do you send your pastuch with
milk to sell in our district? Have you no market
of your own that you must needs spoil ours by
overstocking it, and sending prices down for us?"

"Ah, my brother, forgive us this time," said the
starost; "it can never occur again. It was our

misfortune to harbour among us a *vyedma*, who stole the milk from us and no doubt sold it in your district. She is now at the bottom of the village pond, and will steal no more milk. May her purchasers escape poisoning if they have drunk the milk of the witch."

"Was your *vyedma*, then, in the likeness of a pastuch?" inquired the stranger.

"She must have assumed his likeness," said the starost, who felt, nevertheless, a spasm of uncomfortable surmise dart through his brain. "What was this pastuch like?"

The stranger described the Tirnova herdsman to the life. The starost, in spite of himself, now grew very grave with unpleasant reflections. When the strange moujik had departed he confided the story to a friend, who was, like the starost, immediately assailed by similar uncomfortable thoughts, which played havoc with the repose of his inmost soul. The pair decided to speak with the pastuch on this matter so soon as that functionary should have returned from the pasture. ·

But that wily herdsman never did return to Tirnova. When the herd trooped into the village street at night, its meekly lowing members were

without the guidance of their authorised protector.
Moreover, the herd was short of a good horse
which had belonged to the starost himself. Furthermore, when the proprietors of each cow came forward
to make the usual demand upon the udders of the
patient creatures, it was found that not one of them
had a single pint of milk to present to its lawful
and indignant owner.

Then those villagers realised that poor Marfa
had been a victim to the guile of the herdsman,
and they fished her up from the bottom of the
pond. But, alas! she was quite dead—both she
and her companions; and this it was agreed was
conclusive evidence that poor Marfa had been all
the while an innocent *znaharka* and not a witch.
Had she been a *vyedma* she might still have been
alive, for—the starost declared—she had only been
under water eight-and-forty hours, and a *vyedma*
must soak for fully ten days or a fortnight before
she can be got to drown.

As for the herdsman, the direct cause of the
flagrant miscarriage of justice which ended in the
drowning of poor old Marfa, he escaped scot free.

The Souls of Tirnova did, indeed, hold a specially
convened meeting in order to decide what steps

could or should be taken to find and bring the rascal to justice, but it was unanimously decided that it would save trouble to take no steps at all. This decision was arrived at partly as the result of the starost's eloquence, and partly because it was in perfect agreement with the disposition of the councillors, who, being Russian peasants, were naturally unwilling to take any unnecessary trouble or to do anything that could with equal ease be left undone.

As for the starost's speech, it was short but very much to the point. Here it is :

" Brothers," he said, " God is in heaven and the Tsar is far away; also Russia is very large and the pastuch is very small. How should we set about to find one little herdsman? "

Clearly the thing was ridiculous.

THE END

Printed by BALLANTYNE, HANSON & Co.
Edinburgh and London

MESSRS. LONGMANS, GREEN, & CO.'S
CLASSIFIED CATALOGUE

OF

WORKS IN GENERAL LITERATURE.

History, Politics, Polity, Political Memoirs, &c.

Abbott.—A HISTORY OF GREECE. By EVELYN ABBOTT, M.A., LL.D.
Part I.—From the Earliest Times to the Ionian Revolt. Crown 8vo., 10s. 6d.
Part II.—500-445 B.C. Cr. 8vo., 10s. 6d.

Acland and Ransome.—A HANDBOOK IN OUTLINE OF THE POLITICAL HISTORY OF ENGLAND TO 1894. Chronologically Arranged. By A. H. DYKE ACLAND, M.P., and CYRIL RANSOME, M.A. Cr. 8vo., 6s.

ANNUAL REGISTER (THE). A Review of Public Events at Home and Abroad, for the year 1894. 8vo., 18s.
Volumes of the ANNUAL REGISTER for the years 1863-1893 can still be had. 18s. each.

Armstrong.—ELIZABETH FARNESE ; The Termagant of Spain. By EDWARD ARMSTRONG, M.A. 8vo., 16s.

Arnold.—Works by T. ARNOLD, D.D., formerly Head Master of Rugby School.
INTRODUCTORY LECTURES ON MODERN HISTORY. 8vo., 7s. 6d.
MISCELLANEOUS WORKS. 8vo., 7s. 6d.

Bagwell.—IRELAND UNDER THE TUDORS. By RICHARD BAGWELL, LL.D. 3 vols. Vols. I. and II. From the first Invasion of the Northmen to the year 1578. 8vo., 32s. Vol. III. 1578-1603. 8vo., 18s.

Ball.—HISTORICAL REVIEW OF THE LEGISLATIVE SYSTEMS OPERATIVE IN IRELAND, from the Invasion of Henry the Second to the Union (1172-1800). By the Rt. Hon. J. T. BALL. 8vo., 6s.

Besant.—THE HISTORY OF LONDON. By WALTER BESANT. With 74 Illustrations. Crown 8vo., 1s. 9d. Or bound as a School Prize Book, 2s. 6d.

Brassey.—PAPERS AND ADDRESSES. By LORD BRASSEY.
NAVAL AND MARITIME, 1872-1893. 2 vols. Crown 8vo., 10s.
MERCANTILE MARINE AND NAVIGATION, 1871-1894. Crown 8vo., 5s.

Bright.—A HISTORY OF ENGLAND. By the Rev. J. FRANK BRIGHT, D.D.,
Period I. MEDIÆVAL MONARCHY: A.D. 449 to 1485. Crown 8vo., 4s. 6d.
Period II. PERSONAL MONARCHY: 1485 to 1688. Crown 8vo., 5s.
Period III. CONSTITUTIONAL MONARCHY: 1689 to 1837. Cr. 8vo., 7s. 6d.
Period IV. THE GROWTH OF DEMOCRACY: 1837 to 1880. Cr. 8vo., 6s.

Buckle.—HISTORY OF CIVILISATION IN ENGLAND AND FRANCE, SPAIN AND SCOTLAND. By HENRY THOMAS BUCKLE. 3 vols. Crown 8vo., 24s.

Burke.—A HISTORY OF SPAIN, from the Earliest Times to the Death of Ferdinand the Catholic. By ULICK RALPH BURKE, M.A. 2 vols. 8vo., 32s.

Chesney.—INDIAN POLITY: a View of the System of Administration in India. By General Sir GEORGE CHESNEY, K.C.B., M.P. With Map showing all the Administrative Divisions of British India. 8vo. 21s.

Creighton.—HISTORY OF THE PAPACY DURING THE REFORMATION. By MANDELL CREIGHTON, D.D., LL.D., Bishop of Peterborough. Vols. I. and II., 1378-1464, 32s. Vols. III. and IV., 1464-1518., 24s. Vol. V., 1517-1527, 8vo., 15s.

Curzon.—Works by the HON. GEORGE N. CURZON, M.P.
PROBLEMS OF THE FAR EAST: JAPAN, COREA, CHINA. With 2 Maps and 50 Illustrations. 8vo., 21s.
PERSIA AND THE PERSIAN QUESTION. With 9 Maps, 96 Illustrations, Appendices, and an Index. 2 vols. 8vo., 42s.

History, Politics, Polity, Political Memoirs, &c.—continued.

De Tocqueville.— DEMOCRACY IN AMERICA. By ALEXIS DE TOCQUE-VILLE. 2 vols. Crown 8vo., 16s.

Ewald.—Works by HEINRICH EWALD, Professor in the University of Göttingen.
THE ANTIQUITIES OF ISRAEL. 8vo., 12s. 6d.
THE HISTORY OF ISRAEL. 8 vols. 8vo. Vols. I. and II., 24s. Vols. III. and IV., 21s. Vol. V., 18s. Vol. VI., 16s. Vol. VII., 21s. Vol. VIII., 18s.

Fitzpatrick.—SECRET SERVICE UNDER PITT. By W. J. FITZPATRICK, F.S.A., Author of 'Correspondence of Daniel O'Connell'. 8vo., 7s. 6d.

Froude.—Works by JAMES A. FROUDE.
THE HISTORY OF ENGLAND, from the Fall of Wolsey to the Defeat of the Spanish Armada. 12 vols. Cr. 8vo., 3s. 6d. each.
THE DIVORCE OF CATHERINE OF ARAGON: the Story as told by the Imperial Ambassadors resident at the Court of Henry VIII. Crown 8vo., 6s.
THE SPANISH STORY OF THE ARMADA, and other Essays.
Silver Library Edition. Crown 8vo., 3s. 6d.
ENGLISH SEAMEN IN THE SIXTEENTH CENTURY. 8vo., 10s. 6d.
THE ENGLISH IN IRELAND IN THE EIGHTEENTH CENTURY.
Cabinet Edition. 3 vols. Cr. 8vo., 18s.
Silver Library Edition. 3 vols. Cr. 8vo., 10s. 6d.
ENGLISH SEAMEN IN THE SIXTEENTH CENTURY. Lectures delivered at Oxford, 1893-94. Crown 8vo., 6s.
SHORT STUDIES ON GREAT SUBJECTS.
Cabinet Edition. 4 vols. Cr. 8vo., 24s.
Silver Library Edition. 4 vols. Cr. 8vo., 3s. 6d. each.
CÆSAR: a Sketch. Cr. 8vo., 3s. 6d.

Gardiner.—Works by SAMUEL RAW-SON GARDINER, M.A., Hon. LL.D., Edinburgh.
HISTORY OF ENGLAND, from the Accession of James I. to the Outbreak of the Civil War, 1603-1642. 10 vols. Crown 8vo., 6s. each.
HISTORY OF THE GREAT CIVIL WAR, 1642-1649. 4 vols. Cr. 8vo., 6s. each.
HISTORY OF THE COMMONWEALTH AND THE PROTECTORATE, 1649-1660. Vol. I., 1649-1651. With 14 Maps. 8vo., 21s.

Gardiner.—Works by Samuel RAW-SON GARDINER, M.A., Hon. LL.D., Edinburgh—continued.
THE STUDENT'S HISTORY OF ENGLAND. With 378 Illustrations. Cr. 8vo., 12s.
Also in Three Volumes.
Vol. I. B.C. 55—A.D. 1509. With 173 Illustrations. Crown 8vo. 4s.
Vol. II. 1509-1689. With 96 Illustrations. Crown 8vo. 4s.
Vol. III. 1689-1885. With 109 Illustrations. Crown 8vo. 4s.

Greville.—A JOURNAL OF THE REIGNS OF KING GEORGE IV., KING WILLIAM IV., AND QUEEN VICTORIA. By CHARLES C. F. GREVILLE, formerly Clerk of the Council. 8 vols. Crown 8vo., 6s. each

Hearn.—THE GOVERNMENT OF ENGLAND: its Structure and its Development By W. EDWARD HEARN. 8vo., 16s.

Herbert.—THE DEFENCE OF PLEVNA, 1877. Written by One who took Part in it. By WILLIAM V. HERBERT. With Maps. 8vo., 18s.

Historic Towns.—Edited by E. A. FREEMAN, D.C.L., and Rev. WILLIAM HUNT, M.A. With Maps and Plans. Crown 8vo., 3s. 6d. each.
BRISTOL. By the Rev. W. HUNT.
CARLISLE. By MANDELL CREIGHTON, D.D., Bishop of Peterborough.
CINQUE PORTS. By MONTAGU BURROWS.
COLCHESTER. By Rev. E. L. CUTTS.
EXETER. By E. A. FREEMAN.
LONDON. By Rev. W. J. LOFTIE.
OXFORD. By Rev. C. W. BOASE.
WINCHESTER. By Rev. G. W. KITCHIN, D.D.
YORK. By Rev. JAMES RAINE.
NEW YORK. By THEODORE ROOSEVELT.
BOSTON (U.S.) By HENRY CABOT LODGE.

Joyce.—A SHORT HISTORY OF IRELAND, from the Earliest Times to 1608. By P. W. JOYCE, LL.D. Crown 8vo., 10s. 6d.

Lang.—ST. ANDREWS. By ANDREW LANG. With 8 Plates and 24 Illustrations in the Text, by T. HODGE. 8vo., 15s. net.

History, Politics, Polity, Political Memoirs, &c.—*continued.*

Lecky.—Works by WILLIAM EDWARD HARTPOLE LECKY.

HISTORY OF ENGLAND IN THE EIGHTEENTH CENTURY.

Library Edition. 8 vols. 8vo., £7 4s.

Cabinet Edition. ENGLAND. 7 vols. Cr. 8vo., 6s. each. IRELAND. 5 vols. Crown 8vo., 6s. each.

HISTORY OF EUROPEAN MORALS FROM AUGUSTUS TO CHARLEMAGNE. 2 vols. Crown 8vo., 16s.

HISTORY OF THE RISE AND INFLUENCE OF THE SPIRIT OF RATIONALISM IN EUROPE. 2 vols. Crown 8vo., 16s.

THE EMPIRE : its Value and its Growth. An Inaugural Address delivered at the Imperial Institute, November 20, 1893, under the Presidency of H. R.H. the Prince of Wales. Crown 8vo. 1s. 6d.

Macaulay.—Works by LORD MACAULAY.

COMPLETE WORKS.

Cabinet Edition. 16 vols. Post 8vo., £4 16s.

Library Edition. 8 vols. 8vo., £5 5s.

HISTORY OF ENGLAND FROM THE ACCESSION OF JAMES THE SECOND.

Popular Edition. 2 vols. Cr. 8vo., 5s.

Student's Edit. 2 vols. Cr. 8vo., 12s.

People's Edition. 4 vols. Cr. 8vo., 16s.

Cabinet Edition. 8 vols. Post 8vo., 48s.

Library Edition. 5 vols. 8vo., £4.

CRITICAL AND HISTORICAL ESSAYS, WITH LAYS OF ANCIENT ROME, in 1 volume.

Popular Edition. Crown 8vo., 2s. 6d.

Authorised Edition. Crown 8vo., 2s. 6d., or 3s. 6d., gilt edges.

Silver Library Edition. Crown 8vo., 3s. 6d.

CRITICAL AND HISTORICAL ESSAYS.

Student's Edition. 1 vol. Cr. 8vo., 6s.

People's Edition. 2 vols. Cr. 8vo., 8s.

Trevelyan Edit. 2 vols. Cr. 8vo., 9s.

Cabinet Edition. 4 vols. Post 8vo., 24s.

Library Edition. 3 vols. 8vo., 36s.

ESSAYS which may be had separately, price 6d. each sewed, 1s. e ach cloth.

Addison and Walpole.	Lord Clive.
Frederick the Great.	The Earl of Chatham(Two Essays).
Lord Bacon.	Ranke and Gladstone.
Croker's Boswell's Johnson.	Milton and Machiavelli.
Hallam's Constitutional History.	Lord Byron,and The Comic Dramatists of the Restoration.
Warren Hastings (3d. swd., 6d. cl.).	

Macaulay.—Works by LORD MACAULAY.—*continued.*

MISCELLANEOUS WRITINGS AND SPEECHES.

Popular Edition. Cr. 8vo., 2s. 6d.

Cabinet Edition. Including Indian Penal Code, Lays of Ancient Rome, and Miscellaneous Poems. 4 vols. Post 8vo., 24s.

MISCELLANEOUS WRITINGS.

People's Edit. 1 vol. Cr. 8vo., 4s. 6d.

Library Edition. 2 vols. 8vo., 21s.

SELECTIONS FROM THE WRITINGS OF LORD MACAULAY. Edited, with Occasional Notes, by the Right Hon. Sir G. O. Trevelyan, Bart. Crown 8vo., 6s.

May.—THE CONSTITUTIONAL HISTORY OF ENGLAND since the Accession of George III. 1760-1870. By Sir THOMAS ERSKINE MAY, K.C.B. (Lord Farnborough). 3 vols. Crown 8vo., 18s.

Merivale.—Works by the Very Rev. CHARLES MERIVALE, late Dean of Ely.

HISTORY OF THE ROMANS UNDER THE EMPIRE.

Cabinet Edition. 8 vols. Cr. 8vo., 48s.

Silver Library Edition. 8 vols. Cr. 8vo., 3s. 6d. each.

THE FALL OF THE ROMAN REPUBLIC: a Short History of the Last Century of the Commonwealth. 12mo., 7s. 6d.

Montague.—THE ELEMENTS OF ENGLISH CONSTITUTIONAL HISTORY, from the Earliest Time to the Present Day. By F. C. MONTAGUE, M.A. Crown 8vo., 3s. 6d.

Moore—THE AMERICAN CONGRESS : a History of National Legislation and Political Events, 1774-1895. By JOSEPH WEST MOORE. 8vo., 15s. net.

O'Brien.—IRISH IDEAS. REPRINTED ADDRESSES. By WILLIAM O'BRIEN, M.P. Cr. 8vo. 2s. 6d.

Prendergast.—IRELAND FROM THE RESTORATION TO THE REVOLUTION, 1660-1690. By JOHN P. PRENDERGAST, Author of 'The Cromwellian Settlement in Ireland'. 8vo., 5s.

Seebohm. — Works by FREDERICK SEEBOHM.

THE ENGLISH VILLAGE COMMUNITY Examined in its Relations to the Manorial and Tribal Systems, &c. By FREDERIC SEEBOHM. With 13 Maps and Plates. 8vo., 16s.

History, Politics, Polity, Political Memoirs, &c.—*continued.*

Seebohm.—Works by FREDERICK SEEBOHM—*continued.*

THE TRIBAL SYSTEM IN WALES : being Part of an Inquiry into the Structure and Methods of Tribal Society. With 3 Maps, 8vo., 12*s.*

Sharpe.—LONDON AND THE KINGDOM: a History derived mainly from the Archives at Guildhall in the custody of the Corporation of the City of London. By REGINALD R. SHARPE, D.C.L., Records Clerk in the Office of the Town Clerk of the City of London. 3 vols. 8vo. Vols. I. and II., 10*s.* 6*d.* each.

Sheppard.—MEMORIALS OF ST. JAMES'S PALACE. By the Rev. EDGAR SHEPPARD, M.A., Sub-Dean of the Chapels Royal. With 41 full-page Plates (8 photo-intaglio), and 32 Illustrations in the Text. 2 Vols. 8vo, 36*s.* net.

Smith.—CARTHAGE AND THE CARTHAGINIANS. By R. BOSWORTH SMITH, M.A., Assistant Master in Harrow School. With Maps, Plans, &c. Cr. 8vo., 3*s.* 6*d.*

Stephens.—A HISTORY OF THE FRENCH REVOLUTION. By H. MORSE STEPHENS, Balliol College, Oxford. 3 vols. 8vo. Vols. I. and II. 18*s.* each.

Stubbs.—HISTORY OF THE UNIVERSITY OF DUBLIN, from its Foundation to the End of the Eighteenth Century. By J. W. STUBBS. 8vo., 12*s.* 6*d.*.

Sutherland.—THE HISTORY OF AUSTRALIA AND NEW ZEALAND, from 1606 to 1890. By ALEXANDER SUTHERLAND, M.A., and GEORGE SUTHERLAND, M.A. Crown 8vo., 2*s.* 6*d.*

Todd.—PARLIAMENTARY GOVERNMENT IN THE BRITISH COLONIES. By ALPHEUS TODD, LL.D. 8vo., 30*s.* net.

Wakeman and Hassall.—ESSAYS INTRODUCTORY TO THE STUDY OF ENGLISH CONSTITUTIONAL HISTORY. Edited by HENRY OFFLEY WAKEMAN, M.A., and ARTHUR HASSALL, M.A. Crown 8vo., 6*s.*

Walpole.—Works by SPENCER WALPOLE.

HISTORY OF ENGLAND FROM THE CONCLUSION OF THE GREAT WAR IN 1815 TO 1858. 6 vols. Cr. 8vo., 6*s.* each.

THE LAND OF HOME RULE : being an Account of the History and Institutions of the Isle of Man. Cr. 8vo., 6*s.*

Wylie.—HISTORY OF ENGLAND UNDER HENRY IV. By JAMES HAMILTON WYLIE, M.A., one of H. M. Inspectors of Schools. 3 vols. Crown 8vo. Vol. I., 1399-1404, 10*s.* 6*d.* Vol. II. 15*s.* Vol. III. [*In preparation.*]

Biography, Personal Memoirs, &c.

Armstrong.—THE LIFE AND LETTERS OF EDMUND J. ARMSTRONG. Edited by G. F. ARMSTRONG. Fcp. 8vo., 7*s.* 6*d.*

Bacon.—LETTERS AND LIFE OF FRANCIS BACON, INCLUDING ALL HIS OCCASIONAL WORKS. Edited by J. SPEDDING. 7 vols. 8vo., £4 4*s.*

Bagehot.—BIOGRAPHICAL STUDIES. By WALTER BAGEHOT. Crown 8vo., 3*s.* 6*d.*

Boyd.—Works by A. K. H. BOYD, D.D., LL.D., Author of 'Recreations of a Country Parson,' &c.

TWENTY-FIVE YEARS OF ST. ANDREWS. 1865-1890. 2 vols. 8vo. Vol. I., 12*s.* Vol. II., 15*s.*

ST. ANDREWS AND ELSEWHERE : Glimpses of Some Gone and of Things Left. 8vo., 15*s.*

Carlyle.—THOMAS CARLYLE: a History of his Life. By J. ANTHONY FROUDE. 1795-1835. 2 vols. Crown 8vo., 7*s.* 1834-1881. 2 vols. Crown 8vo., 7*s.*

Erasmus.—LIFE AND LETTERS OF ERASMUS; a Series of Lectures delivered at Oxford. By JAMES ANTHONY FROUDE. Crown 8vo., 6*s.*

Fabert.—ABRAHAM FABERT : Governor of Sedan and Marshal of France. His Life and Times, 1599-1662. By GEORGE HOOPER. With a Portrait. 8vo., 10*s.* 6*d.*

Fox.—THE EARLY HISTORY OF CHARLES JAMES FOX. By the Right Hon. Sir G. O. TREVELYAN, Bart.
Library Edition. 8vo., 18*s.*
Cabinet Edition. Crown 8vo., 6*s.*

Hamilton.—LIFE OF SIR WILLIAM HAMILTON. By R. P. GRAVES. 3 vols. 15*s.* each. ADDENDUM. 8vo., 6*d.* sewed.

Havelock.—MEMOIRS OF SIR HENRY HAVELOCK, K.C.B. By JOHN CLARK MARSHMAN. Crown 8vo., 3*s.* 6*d.*

Luther.—LIFE OF LUTHER. By JULIUS KÖSTLIN. With Illustrations from Authentic Sources. Translated from the German. Crown 8vo., 7*s.* 6*d.*

Macaulay.—THE LIFE AND LETTERS OF LORD MACAULAY. By the Right Hon. Sir G. O. TREVELYAN, Bart.
Popular Edit. 1 vol. Cr. 8vo., 2*s.* 6*d.*
Student's Edition. 1 vol. Cr. 8vo., 6*s.*
Cabinet Edition. 2 vols. Post 8vo., 12*s.*
Library Edition. 2 vols. 8vo., 36*s.*

Biography, Personal Memoirs, &c.—*continued.*

Marbot.—THE MEMOIRS OF THE BARON DE MARBOT. Translated from the French by ARTHUR JOHN BUTLER, M.A. Crown 8vo., 7*s.* 6*d.*

Seebohm.—THE OXFORD REFORMERS —JOHN COLET, ERASMUS AND THOMAS MORE : a History of their Fellow-Work. By FREDERIC SEEBOHM. 8vo., 14*s.*

Shakespeare.—OUTLINES OF THE LIFE OF SHAKESPEARE. By J. O. HALLIWELL-PHILLIPPS. With numerous Illustrations and Fac-similes. 2 vols. Royal 8vo., £1 1*s.*

Shakespeare's TRUE LIFE. By JAS. WALTER. With 500 Illustrations by GERALD E. MOIRA. Imp. 8vo., 21*s.*

Stephen.—ESSAYS IN ECCLESIASTICAL BIOGRAPHY. By Sir JAMES STEPHEN. Crown 8vo., 7*s.* 6*d.*

Turgot.—THE LIFE AND WRITINGS OF TURGOT, Comptroller-General of France, 1774-1776. Edited for English Readers by W. WALKER STEPHENS. 8vo., 12*s.* 6*d.*

Verney.—MEMOIRS OF THE VERNEY FAMILY. Compiled from the Letters and Illustrated by the Portraits at Claydon House, Bucks.

Vols. I. and II. DURING THE CIVIL WAR. By FRANCES VERNEY. With 38 Portraits. Royal 8vo., 42*s.*

Vol. III. DURING THE COMMONWEALTH. 1650-1660. By MARGARET M. VERNEY. With 10 Portraits, &c. 8vo., 21*s.*

Walford.—TWELVE ENGLISH AUTHORESSES. By L. B. WALFORD. Cr. 8vo.,4*s.* 6*d.*

Wellington.—LIFE OF THE DUKE OF WELLINGTON. By the Rev. G. R. GLEIG, M.A. Crown 8vo., 3*s.* 6*d.*

Travel and Adventure, the Colonies, &c.

Arnold.—Works by Sir EDWIN ARNOLD, K.C.I.E.

SEAS AND LANDS. With 71 Illustrations. Cr. 8vo., 7*s.* 6*d.* Cheap Edition. Cr. 8vo., 3*s.* 6*d.*

WANDERING WORDS. With 45 Illustrations. 8vo., 18*s.*

AUSTRALIA AS IT IS, or Facts and Features, Sketches and Incidents of Australia and Australian Life, with Notices of New Zealand. By A CLERGYMAN, thirteen years resident in the interior of NewSouth Wales. Cr. 8vo., 5*s.*

Baker.—Works by Sir SAMUEL WHITE BAKER.

EIGHT YEARS IN CEYLON. With 6 Illustrations. Crown 8vo., 3*s.* 6*d.*

THE RIFLE AND THE HOUND IN CEYLON. 6 Illustrations. Cr. 8vo., 3*s.* 6*d.*

Bent.—Works by J. THEODORE BENT.

THE RUINED CITIES OF MASHONALAND : being a Record of Excavation and Exploration in 1891. With Map, 13 Plates, and 104 Illustrations in the Text. Crown 8vo., 3*s.* 6*d.*

THE SACRED CITY OF THE ETHIOPIANS: being a Record of Travel and Research in Abyssinia in 1893. With 8 Plates and 65 Illustrations in the Text. 8vo., 18*s.*

Brassey.—VOYAGES AND TRAVELS OF LORD BRASSEY, K.C.B., D.C.L., 1862-1894. Arranged and Edited by Captain S. EARDLEY-WILMOT. 2 vols. Cr. 8vo., 10*s.* [*Nearly ready.*

Brassey.—Works by the late LADY BRASSEY.

A VOYAGE IN THE 'SUNBEAM'; OUR HOME ON THE OCEAN FOR ELEVEN MONTHS.

Library Edition. With 8 Maps and Charts, and 118 Illustrations. 8vo., 21*s.*

Cabinet Edition. With Map and 66 Illustrations. Crown 8vo., 7*s.* 6*d.*

Silver Library Edition. With 66 Illustrations. Crown 8vo., 3*s.* 6*d.*

Popular Edition. With 60 Illustrations. 4to., 6*d.* sewed, 1*s.* cloth.

School Edition. With 37 Illustrations. Fcp., 2*s.* cloth, or 3*s.* white parchment.

SUNSHINE AND STORM IN THE EAST.

Library Edition. With 2 Maps and 141 Illustrations. 8vo., 21*s.*

Cabinet Edition. With 2 Maps and 114 Illustrations. Crown 8vo., 7*s.* 6*d.*

Popular Edition. With 103 Illustrations. 4to., 6*d.* sewed, 1*s.* cloth.

Travel and Adventure, the Colonies, &c.—*continued.*

Brassey.—Works by the late LADY BRASSEY—*continued.*

IN THE TRADES, THE TROPICS, AND THE 'ROARING FORTIES'. *Cabinet Edition.* With Map and 220 Illustrations. Crown 8vo., 7s. 6d. *Popular Edition.* With 183 Illustrations. 4to., 6d. sewed, 1s. cloth.

THREE VOYAGES IN THE 'SUNBEAM'. *Popular Edition.* 346 Illustrations. 4to., 2s. 6d.

THE LAST VOYAGE TO INDIA AND AUSTRALIA IN THE 'SUNBEAM'. With Charts and Maps, and 40 Illustrations in Monotone, and nearly 200 Illustrations in the Text. 8vo., 21s.

Brassey.—VOYAGES AND TRAVELS OF LORD BRASSEY, K.C.B., D.C.L., 1862-1894. Arranged and Edited by Captain S. EARDLEY-WILMOT. 2 vols. Crown 8vo., 10s.

Froude.—Works by JAMES A. FROUDE.

OCEANA : or England and her Colonies. With 9 Illustrations. Crown 8vo., 2s. boards, 2s. 6d. cloth.

THE ENGLISH IN THE WEST INDIES : or the Bow of Ulysses. With 9 Illustrations. Cr. 8vo., 2s. bds., 2s. 6d. cl.

Hapgood.—RUSSIAN RAMBLES. By ISABEL F. HAPGOOD. Crown 8vo., 6s.

CONTENTS :—Passports, Police, and Post-Office in Russia—The Névsky Prospékt—My Experience with the Russian Censor—Bargaining in Russia—Experiences—A Russian Summer Resort—A Stroll in Moscow with Count Tolstóy—Count Tolstóy at Home—A Russian Holy City—A Journey on the Volga—The Russian Kumys Cure—Moscow Memories—The Nízhni-Nóvgorod Fair and the Volga.

Howitt.—VISITS TO REMARKABLE PLACES, Old Halls, Battle-Fields, Scenes illustrative of Striking Passages in English History and Poetry. By WILLIAM HOWITT. With 80 Illustrations. Crown 8vo., 3s. 6d.

Knight.—Works by E. F. KNIGHT.

THE CRUISE OF THE 'ALERTE': the Narrative of a Search for Treasure on the Desert Island of Trinidad. 2 Maps and 23 Illustrations. Cr. 8vo., 3s. 6d.

WHERE THREE EMPIRES MEET: a Narrative of Recent Travel in Kashmir, Western Tibet, Baltistan, Ladak, Gilgit, and the adjoining Countries. With a Map and 54 Illustrations. Cr. 8vo., 3s. 6d.

Knight.—Works by E. F. KNIGHT—*continued.*

RHODESIA OF TO-DAY: a Description of the Present Condition and the Prospects of Matabeleland and Mashonaland. Crown 8vo., 2s. 6d.

Lees and Clutterbuck.—B. C. 1887: A RAMBLE IN BRITISH COLUMBIA. By J. A. LEES and W. J. CLUTTERBUCK. With Map and 75 Illustrations. Cr. 8vo., 3s. 6d.

Murdoch.—FROM EDINBURGH TO THE ANTARCTIC: An Artist's Notes and Sketches during the Dundee Antarctic Expedition of 1892-93. By W. G. BURN MURDOCH. With 2 Maps and numerous Illustrations. 8vo., 18s.

Nansen.—Works by Dr. FRIDTJOF NANSEN.

THE FIRST CROSSING OF GREENLAND. With numerous Illustrations and a Map. Crown 8vo., 3s. 6d.

ESKIMO LIFE. Translated by WILLIAM ARCHER. With 31 Illustrations. 8vo., 16s.

Peary.—MY ARCTIC JOURNAL: a Year among Ice-Fields and Eskimos. By JOSEPHINE DIEBITSCH-PEARY. With 19 Plates, 3 Sketch Maps, and 44 Illustrations in the Text. 8vo., 12s.

Smith.—CLIMBING IN THE BRITISH ISLES. By W. P. HASKETT SMITH. With Illustrations by ELLIS CARR.

Part I. ENGLAND. Fcp. 8vo., 3s. 6d.

Part II. WALES. [*In preparation.*

Part III. SCOTLAND. [*In preparation.*

Stephen. — THE PLAYGROUND OF EUROPE. By LESLIE STEPHEN, formerly President of the Alpine Club. New Edition, with Additions and 4 Illustrations. Crown 8vo., 6s. net.

THREE IN NORWAY. By Two of Them. With a Map and 59 Illustrations. Cr. 8vo., 2s. boards, 2s. 6d. cloth.

Sport and Pastime.
THE BADMINTON LIBRARY.
Edited by the DUKE OF BEAUFORT, K.G., assisted by ALFRED E. T. WATSON.

ARCHERY. By C. J. LONGMAN and Col. H. WALROND. With Contributions by Miss LEGH, Viscount DILLON, &c. With 195 Illustrations. Crown 8vo., 10s. 6d.

ATHLETICS AND FOOTBALL. By MONTAGUE SHEARMAN. With 51 Illlustrations. Crown 8vo., 10s. 6d.

BIG GAME SHOOTING. By C. PHILLIPPS-WOLLEY, F. C. SELOUS, ST. GEORGE LITTLEDALE, &c. With 150 Illustrations. 2 vols., 10s. 6d. each.

BOATING. By W. B. WOODGATE. With an Introduction by the Rev EDMOND WARRE, D.D., and a Chapter on ' Rowing at Eton,' by R. HARVEY MASON. With 49 Illustrations. Cr. 8vo., 10s. 6d.

COURSING AND FALCONRY. By HARDING COX and the Hon. GERALD LASCELLES. With 76 Illustrations. Crown 8vo., 10s. 6d.

CRICKET. By A. G. STEEL and the Hon. R. H. LYTTELTON. With Contributions by ANDREW LANG, R. A. H. MITCHELL, W. G. GRACE, and F. GALE. With 64 Illustrations. Cr. 8vo., 10s. 6d.

CYCLING. By VISCOUNT BURY (Earl of Albemarle), K.C.M.G., and G. LACY HILLIER. With 89 Illustrations. Crown 8vo., 10s. 6d.

DRIVING. By the DUKE OF BEAUFORT. With 65 Illustrations. Cr. 8vo., 10s. 6d.

FENCING, BOXING. AND WRESTLING. By WALTER H. POLLOCK, F. C. GROVE. C. PREVOST, E. B. MITCHELL, and WALTER ARMSTRONG. With 42 Illustrations. Crown 8vo., 10s. 6d.

FISHING. By H. CHOLMONDELEY-PENNELL. With Contributions by the MARQUIS OF EXETER, HENRY R. FRANCIS, Major JOHN P. TRAHERNE, G. CHRISTOPHER DAVIES, R. B. MARSTON, &c.

Vol. I. Salmon, Trout, and Grayling. With 158 Illustrations. Crown 8vo., 10s. 6d.

Vol. II. Pike and other Coarse Fish. With 133 Illustrations. Crown 8vo., 10s. 6d.

GOLF. By HORACE G. HUTCHINSON, the Rt. Hon. A. J. BALFOUR, M.P., Sir W. G. SIMPSON, Bart., LORD WELLWOOD, H. S. C. EVERARD, ANDREW LANG, and other Writers. With 89 Illustrations. Crown 8vo., 10s. 6d.

HUNTING. By the DUKE OF BEAUFORT, K.G., and MOWBRAY MORRIS. With Contributions by the EARL OF SUFFOLK AND BERKSHIRE, Rev. E. W. L. DAVIES, DIGBY COLLINS, and ALFRED E. T. WATSON. With 53 Illustrations Crown 8vo., 10s. 6d.

MOUNTAINEERING. By C. T. DENT, Sir F. POLLOCK, Bart., W. M. CONWAY, DOUGLAS FRESHFIELD, C. E. MATHEWS, &c. With 108 Illustrations. Crown 8vo., 10s. 6d.

RACING AND STEEPLE-CHASING. By the EARL OF SUFFOLK AND BERKSHIRE, W. G. CRAVEN, ARTHUR COVENTRY, &c. With 58 Illustrations. Crown 8vo., 10s. 6d.

RIDING AND POLO. By Captain ROBERT WEIR, J. MORAY BROWN, the DUKE OF BEAUFORT, K.G., the EARL of SUFFOLK AND BERKSHIRE, &c. With 59 Illustrations. Cr. 8vo., 10s. 6d.

SHOOTING. By Lord WALSINGHAM and Sir RALPH PAYNE-GALLWEY, Bart. With Contributions by LORD LOVAT, LORD C. L. KERR, the Hon. G. LASCELLES, and A. J. STUART-WORTLEY.
Vol. I. Field and Covert. With 105 Illustrations. Crown 8vo., 10s. 6d.
Vol. II. Moor and Marsh. With 65 Illustrations. Cr. 8vo., 10s. 6d.

SKATING, CURLING, TOBOGANING, AND OTHER ICE SPORTS. By J. M. HEATHCOTE, C. G. TEBBUTT, T. MAXWELL WITHAM, the Rev. JOHN KERR, ORMOND HAKE, and Colonel BUCK With 284 Illustrations. Crown 8vo., 10s. 6d.

SWIMMING. By ARCHIBALD SINCLAIR and WILLIAM HENRY. With 119 Illustrations. Cr. 8vo., 10s. 6d.

TENNIS, LAWN TENNIS, RACQUETS, AND FIVES.. By J. M. and C. G. HEATHCOTE, E. O. PLEYDELL-BOUVERIE and A. C. AINGER. With Contributions by the Hon. A. LYTTELTON, W. C. MARSHALL, Miss L. DOD, &c. With 79 Illustrations. C.8vo., 10s. 6d.

YACHTING.
Vol. I. Cruising, Construction, Racing, Rules, Fitting-Out, &c. By Sir EDWARD SULLIVAN, Bart., LORD BRASSEY, K.C.B., C. E. SETH-SMITH, C.B., &c. With 114 Illust. Cr. 8vo., 10s. 6d.
Vol. II. Yacht Clubs. Yachting in America and the Colonies, Yacht Racing, &c. By R. T. PRITCHETT, the EARL OF ONSLOW, G.C.M.G., &c. With 195 Illus. Crown 8vo., 10s. 6d.

Sport and Pastime—*continued.*
FUR AND FEATHER SERIES.
Edited by A. E. T. WATSON.

THE PARTRIDGE. Natural History, by the Rev. H. A. MACPHERSON; Shooting, by A. J. STUART-WORTLEY; Cookery, by GEORGE SAINTSBURY. With 11 Illustrations by A. THORBURN, A. J. STUART-WORTLEY, and C. WHYMPER, and various Diagrams in the Text. Crown 8vo., 5s.

WILDFOWL. By the Hon. JOHN SCOTT-MONTAGU, M.P., &c. Illustrated by A. J. STUART WORTLEY, A. THORBURN, and others. [*In preparation.*

THE GROUSE. Natural History by the Rev. H. A. MACPHERSON; Shooting, by A. J. STUART-WORTLEY; Cookery, by GEORGE SAINTSBURY. With 13 Illustrations by J. STUART-WORTLEY and A. THORBURN, and various 'Diagrams in the Text. Crown 8vo., 5s.

THE PHEASANT. Natural History by the Rev. H. A. MACPHERSON; Shooting, by A. J. STUART-WORTLEY; Cookery, by ALEXANDER INNES SHAND. With 10 Illustrations by A. THORBURN, and various Diagrams in the Text. Cr. 8vo., 5s.

THE HARE AND THE RABBIT. By the Hon. GERALD LASCELLES, &c. [*In preparation.*

Bickerdyke.—DAYS OF MY LIFE ON WATERS FRESH AND SALT; and other Papers. By JOHN BICKERDYKE. With Photo-Etched Frontispiece and 8 Full-page Illustrations. Crown 8vo., 6s.

Campbell-Walker.—THE CORRECT CARD: or, How to Play at Whist; a Whist Catechism. By Major A. CAMPBELL-WALKER. Fcp. 8vo., 2s. 6d.

DEAD SHOT (THE): or, Sportsman's Complete Guide. Being a Treatise on the Use of the Gun, with Rudimentary and Finishing Lessons on the Art of Shooting Game of all kinds, also Game Driving, Wild-Fowl and Pigeon Shooting, Dog Breaking, etc. By MARKSMAN. Crown 8vo., 10s. 6d.

Falkener.—GAMES, ANCIENT AND ORIENTAL, AND HOW TO PLAY THEM. By EDWARD FALKENER. With numerous Photographs & Diagrams. 8vo., 21s.

Ford.—THE THEORY AND PRACTICE OF ARCHERY. BY HORACE FORD. New Edition, thoroughly Revised and Re-written by W. BUTT, M.A. With a Preface by C. J. LONGMAN, M.A. 8vo., 14s.

Francis.—A BOOK ON ANGLING: or, Treatise on the Art of Fishing in every Branch; including full Illustrated List of Salmon Flies. By FRANCIS FRANCIS. With Portrait and Plates. Cr. 8vo., 15s.

Gibson.—TOBOGGANING ON CROOKED RUNS. By the Hon. HARRY GIBSON. With Contributions by F. DE B. STRICKLAND and 'LADY-TOBOGGANER'. With 40 Illustrations. Crown 8vo., 6s.

Hawker.—THE DIARY OF COLONEL PETER HAWKER, author of "Instructions to Young Sportsmen". With an Introduction by Sir RALPH PAYNE-GALLWEY, Bart. 2 vols. 8vo., 32s.

Lang.—ANGLING SKETCHES. By A. LANG. With 20 Illus. Cr. 8vo., 3s. 6d.

Longman.—CHESS OPENINGS. By FRED. W. LONGMAN. Fcp. 8vo., 2s. 6d.

Maskelyne.—SHARPS AND FLATS: a Complete Revelation of the Secrets of Cheating at Games of Chance and Skill. By JOHN NEVIL MASKELYNE. With 62 Illustrations. Crown 8vo., 6s.

Payne-Gallwey.—Works by Sir RALPH PAYNE-GALLWEY, Bart.
LETTERS TO YOUNG SHOOTERS (First Series). On the Choice and Use of a Gun. With 41 Illustrations. Cr. 8vo., 7s. 6d.

LETTERS TO YOUNG SHOOTERS, (Second Series). On the Production, Preservation, and Killing of Game. With Directions in Shooting Wood-Pigeons and Breaking-in Retrievers. With 104 Illustrations. Crown 8vo., 12s. 6d.

Pole.—Works by W. POLE, F.R.S.
THE THEORY OF THE MODERN SCIENTIFIC GAME OF WHIST. Fcp. 8vo., 2s. 6d.

THE EVOLUTION OF WHIST: a Study of the Progressive Changes which the Game has undergone from its Origin to the Present Time. Cr. 8vo., 6s.

Proctor.—Works by R. A. PROCTOR.
HOW TO PLAY WHIST: WITH THE LAWS AND ETIQUETTE OF WHIST. Crown 8vo., 3s. 6d.

HOME WHIST: an Easy Guide to Correct Play. 16mo., 1s.

Ronalds.—THE FLY-FISHER'S ENTOMOLOGY. By ALFRED RONALDS. With 20 Coloured Plates. 8vo., 14s.

Wilcocks.—THE SEA FISHERMAN: Comprising the Chief Methods of Hook and Line Fishing in the British and other Seas, and Remarks on Nets, Boats, and Boating. By J. C. WILCOCKS. Illustrated. Crown 8vo., 6s.

Veterinary Medicine, &c.

Steel.—Works by JOHN HENRY STEEL.
A TREATISE ON THE DISEASES OF THE DOG. 88 Illustrations. 8vo., 10s. 6d.

A TREATISE ON THE DISEASES OF THE OX. With 119 Illustrations. 8vo., 15s.

A TREATISE ON THE DISEASES OF THE SHEEP. With 100 Illustrations. 8vo., 12s.

OUTLINES OF EQUINE ANATOMY: a Manual for the use of Veterinary Students in the Dissecting Room. Crown 8vo, 7s. 6d.

Fitzwygram.--HORSES AND STABLES. By Major-General Sir F. FITZWYGRAM, Bart. With 56 pages of Illustrations. 8vo., 2s. 6d. net.

"Stonehenge."–THE DOG IN HEALTH AND DISEASE. By "STONEHENGE". With 84 Illustrations 8vo., 7s. 6d.

Youatt.—Works by WILLIAM YOUATT.
THE HORSE. With numerous Illustrations. 8vo., 7s. 6d.
THE DOG. With numerous Illustrations. 8vo., 6s.

Mental, Moral, and Political Philosophy.
LOGIC, RHETORIC, PSYCHOLOGY, ETC.

Abbott.—THE ELEMENTS OF LOGIC. By T. K. ABBOTT, B.D. 12mo., 3s.

Aristotle.—Works by.
THE POLITICS: G. Bekker's Greek Text of Books I., III., IV. (VII.), with an English Translation by W. E. BOLLAND, M.A.; and short Introductory Essays by A. LANG, M.A. Crown 8vo., 7s. 6d.

THE POLITICS: Introductory Essays. By ANDREW LANG (from Bolland and Lang's 'Politics'). Cr. 8vo., 2s. 6d.

THE ETHICS: Greek Text, Illustrated with Essay and Notes. By Sir ALEXANDER GRANT, Bart. 2 vols. 8vo., 32s.

THE NICOMACHEAN ETHICS: Newly Translated into English. By ROBERT WILLIAMS. Crown 8vo., 7s. 6d.

AN INTRODUCTION TO ARISTOTLE'S ETHICS. Books I.-IV. (Book X. c. vi.-ix. in an Appendix.) With a continuous Analysis and Notes. By the Rev. E. MOORE, D.D. Cr. 8vo., 10s. 6d.

Bacon.—Works by FRANCIS BACON.
COMPLETE WORKS. Edited by R. L. ELLIS, J. SPEDDING, and D. D. HEATH. 7 vols. 8vo., £3 13s. 6d.

LETTERS AND LIFE, including all his occasional Works. Edited by JAMES SPEDDING. 7 vols. 8vo., £4 4s.

THE ESSAYS: with Annotations. By RICHARD WHATELY, D.D. 8vo., 10s. 6d.

THE ESSAYS. With Introduction, Notes, and Index. By E. A. ABBOTT. D.D. 2 vols. Fcp. 8vo., 6s. The Text and Index only, without Introduction and Notes, in One Volume. Fcp. 8vo., 1s. 6d.

Bain.—Works by ALEXANDER BAIN, LL.D.
MENTAL SCIENCE. Crown 8vo., 6s. 6d.
MORAL SCIENCE. Crown 8vo., 4s. 6d.
The two works as above can be had in one volume, price 10s. 6d.
SENSES AND THE INTELLECT. 8vo., 15s.
EMOTIONS AND THE WILL. 8vo., 15s.
LOGIC, DEDUCTIVE AND INDUCTIVE. Part I., 4s. Part II., 6s. 6d.
PRACTICAL ESSAYS. Crown 8vo., 3s.

Bray.—Works by CHARLES BRAY.
THE PHILOSOPHY OF NECESSITY: or Law in Mind as in Matter. Cr. 8vo., 5s.
THE EDUCATION OF THE FEELINGS: a Moral System for Schools. Crown 8vo., 2s. 6d.

Bray.—ELEMENTS OF MORALITY, in Easy Lessons for Home and School Teaching. By Mrs. CHARLES BRAY. Cr. 8vo., 1s. 6d.

Davidson.—THE LOGIC OF DEFINITION, Explained and Applied. By WILLIAM L. DAVIDSON, M.A. Crown 8vo., 6s.

Green.—THE WORKS OF THOMAS HILL GREEN. Edited by R. L. NETTLESHIP.
Vols. I. and II. Philosophical Works. 8vo., 16s. each.
Vol. III. Miscellanies. With Index to the three Volumes, and Memoir. 8vo., 21s.
LECTURES ON THE PRINCIPLES OF POLITICAL OBLIGATION. With Preface by BERNARD BOSANQUET. 8vo., 5s.

Mental, Moral and Political Philosophy—*continued.*

Hodgson.—Works by SHADWORTH H. HODGSON.

TIME AND SPACE: a Metaphysical Essay. 8vo., 16s.

THE THEORY OF PRACTICE: an Ethical Inquiry. 2 vols. 8vo., 24s.

THE PHILOSOPHY OF REFLECTION. 2 vols. 8vo., 21s.

Hume.—THE PHILOSOPHICAL WORKS OF DAVID HUME. Edited by T. H. GREEN and T. H. GROSE. 4 vols. 8vo., 56s. Or separately, Essays. 2 vols. 28s. Treatise of Human Nature. 2 vols. 28s.

Justinian.—THE INSTITUTES OF JUSTINIAN: Latin Text, chiefly that of Huschke, with English Introduction, Translation, Notes, and Summary. By THOMAS C. SANDARS, M.A. 8vo. 18s.

Kant.—Works by IMMANUEL KANT.

CRITIQUE OF PRACTICAL REASON, AND OTHER WORKS ON THE THEORY OF ETHICS. Translated by T. K. ABBOTT, B.D. With Memoir. 8vo., 12s. 6d.

INTRODUCTION TO LOGIC, AND HIS ESSAY ON THE MISTAKEN SUBTILTY OF THE FOUR FIGURES. Translated by T. K. ABBOTT, and with Notes by S. T. COLERIDGE. 8vo., 6s.

Killick.—HANDBOOK TO MILL'S SYSTEM OF LOGIC. By Rev. A. H. KILLICK, M.A. Crown 8vo., 3s. 6d.

Ladd.—Works by GEORGE TURMBULL LADD.

ELEMENTS OF PHYSIOLOGICAL PSYCHOLOGY. 8vo., 21s.

OUTLINES OF PHYSIOLOGICAL PSYCHOLOGY. A Text-Book of Mental Science for Academies and Colleges. 8vo., 12s.

PSYCHOLOGY, DESCRIPTIVE AND EXPLANATORY: a Treatise of the Phenomena, Laws, and Development of Human Mental Life. 8vo., 21s.

PRIMER OF PSYCHOLOGY. Crown 8vo., 5s. 6d.

PHILOSOPHY OF MIND: an Essay on the Metaphysics of Physiology. 8vo., 16s.

Lewes.—THE HISTORY OF PHILOSOPHY, from Thales to Comte. By GEORGE HENRY LEWES. 2 vols. 8vo., 32s.

Max Müller.—Works by F. MAX MÜLLER.

THE SCIENCE OF THOUGHT. 8vo., 21s.

THREE INTRODUCTORY LECTURES ON THE SCIENCE OF THOUGHT. 8vo., 2s. 6d.

Mill.—ANALYSIS OF THE PHENOMENA OF THE HUMAN MIND. By JAMES MILL. 2 vols. 8vo., 28s.

Mill.—Works by JOHN STUART MILL.

A SYSTEM OF LOGIC. Cr. 8vo., 3s. 6d.

ON LIBERTY. Cr. 8vo., 1s. 4d.

ON REPRESENTATIVE GOVERNMENT. Crown 8vo., 2s.

UTILITARIANISM. 8vo., 2s. 6d.

EXAMINATION OF SIR WILLIAM HAMILTON'S PHILOSOPHY. 8vo., 16s.

NATURE, THE UTILITY OF RELIGION, AND THEISM. Three Essays. 8vo., 5s.

Stock.—DEDUCTIVE LOGIC. By ST. GEORGE STOCK. Fcp. 8vo., 3s. 6d.

Sully.—Works by JAMES SULLY.

THE HUMAN MIND: a Text-book of Psychology. 2 vols. 8vo., 21s.

OUTLINES OF PSYCHOLOGY. 8vo., 9s.

THE TEACHER'S HANDBOOK OF PSYCHOLOGY. Crown 8vo., 5s.

Swinburne.—PICTURE LOGIC: an Attempt to Popularise the Science of Reasoning. By ALFRED JAMES SWINBURNE, M.A. With 23 Woodcuts. Post 8vo., 5s.

Thomson.—OUTLINES OF THE NECESSARY LAWS OF THOUGHT: a Treatise on Pure and Applied Logic. By WILLIAM THOMSON, D.D., formerly Lord Archbishop of York. Post 8vo., 6s.

Mental, Moral and Political Philosophy—*continued*.

Whately.—Works by R. WHATELY, D.D.

BACON'S ESSAYS. With Annotation. By R. WHATELY. 8vo., 10s. 6d.

ELEMENTS OF LOGIC. Cr. 8vo., 4s. 6d.

ELEMENTS OF RHETORIC. Cr. 8vo., 4s. 6d.

LESSONS ON REASONING. Fcp. 8vo., 1s. 6d.

Zeller.—Works by Dr. EDWARD ZELLER, Professor in the University of Berlin.

THE STOICS, EPICUREANS, AND SCEPTICS. Translated by the Rev. O. J. REICHEL, M.A. Crown 8vo., 15s.

Zeller.—Works by Dr. EDWARD ZELLER. —*continued*.

OUTLINES OF THE HISTORY OF GREEK PHILOSOPHY. Translated by SARAH F. ALLEYNE and EVELYN ABBOTT. Crown 8vo., 10s. 6d.

PLATO AND THE OLDER ACADEMY. Translated by SARAH F. ALLEYNE and ALFRED GOODWIN, B.A. Crown 8vo., 18s.

SOCRATES AND THE SOCRATIC SCHOOLS. Translated by the Rev. O. J. REICHEL, M.A. Crown 8vo., 10s. 6d.

MANUALS OF CATHOLIC PHILOSOPHY.

(Stonyhurst Series.)

A MANUAL OF POLITICAL ECONOMY. By C. S. DEVAS, M.A. Cr. 8vo., 6s. 6d.

FIRST PRINCIPLES OF KNOWLEDGE. By JOHN RICKABY, S.J. Crown 8vo., 5s.

GENERAL METAPHYSICS. By JOHN RICKABY, S.J. Crown 8vo., 5s.

LOGIC. By RICHARD F. CLARKE, S.J. Crown 8vo., 5s.

MORAL PHILOSOPHY (ETHICS AND NATURAL LAW). By JOSEPH RICKABY, S.J. Crown 8vo., 5s.

NATURAL THEOLOGY. By BERNARD BOEDDER, S.J. Crown 8vo., 6s. 6d.

PSYCHOLOGY. By MICHAEL MAHER, S.J. Crown 8vo., 6s. 6d.

History and Science of Language, &c.

Davidson.—LEADING AND IMPORTANT ENGLISH WORDS: Explained and Exemplified. By WILLIAM L. DAVIDSON, M.A. Fcp. 8vo., 3s. 6d.

Farrar.—LANGUAGE AND LANGUAGES. By F. W. FARRAR, D.D., F.R.S., Cr. 8vo., 6s.

Max Müller.—Works by F. MAX MÜLLER.

THE SCIENCE OF LANGUAGE, Founded on Lectures delivered at the Royal Institution in 1861 and 1863. 2 vols. Crown 8vo., 21s.

BIOGRAPHIES OF WORDS, AND THE HOME OF THE ARYAS. Crown 8vo., 7s. 6d.

Max Müller.—Works by F. MAX MÜLLER—*continued*.

THREE LECTURES ON THE SCIENCE OF LANGUAGE, AND ITS PLACE IN GENERAL EDUCATION, delivered at Oxford, 1889. Crown 8vo., 3s.

Roget.—THESAURUS OF ENGLISH WORDS AND PHRASES. Classified and Arranged so as to Facilitate the Expression of Ideas and assist in Literary Composition. By PETER MARK ROGET, M.D., F.R.S. Recomposed throughout, enlarged and improved, partly from the Author's Notes, and with a full Index, by the Author's Son, JOHN LEWIS ROGET. Crown 8vo., 10s. 6d.

Political Economy and Economics.

Ashley.—ENGLISH ECONOMIC HISTORY AND THEORY. By W. J. ASHLEY, M.A. Crown 8vo., Part I., 5*s.* Part II., 10*s.* 6*d.*

Bagehot.—ECONOMIC STUDIES. By WALTER BAGEHOT. Crown 8vo., 3*s.* 6*d.*

Barnett.—PRACTICABLE SOCIALISM : Essays on Social Reform. By the Rev. S. A. and Mrs. BARNETT. Cr. 8vo., 6*s.*

Brassey.—PAPERS AND ADDRESSES ON WORK AND WAGES. By Lord BRASSEY. Edited by J. POTTER, and with Introduction by GEORGE HOWELL, M.P. Crown 8vo., 5*s.*

Devas.—A MANUAL OF POLITICAL ECONOMY. By C. S. DEVAS, M.A. Crown 8vo., 6*s.* 6*d.* (*Manuals of Catholic Philosophy.*)

Dowell.—A HISTORY OF TAXATION AND TAXES IN ENGLAND, from the Earliest Times to the Year 1885. By STEPHEN DOWELL (4 vols. 8vo.) Vols. I. and II. The History of Taxation, 21*s.* Vols. III. and IV. The History of Taxes, 21*s.*

Macleod.—Works by HENRY DUNNING MACLEOD, M.A.
BIMETALISM. 8vo., 5*s.* net.
THE ELEMENTS OF BANKING. Crown 8vo., 3*s.* 6*d.*
THE THEORY AND PRACTICE OF BANKING. Vol. I. 12*s.* Vol. II. 14*s.*
THE THEORY OF CREDIT. 8vo. Vol. I. 10*s.* net. Vol. II., Part I., 10*s.* net. Vol. II. Part II., 10*s.* 6*d.*

Mill.—POLITICAL ECONOMY. By JOHN STUART MILL.
Popular Edition. Crown 8vo., 3*s* 6*d.*
Library Edition. 2 vols. 8vo., 30*s.*

Symes.—POLITICAL ECONOMY: a Short Text-book of Political Economy. With Problems for Solution, and Hints for Supplementary Reading. By Prof. J. E. SYMES, M.A., of University College, Nottingham. Crown 8vo., 2*s.* 6*d.*

Toynbee.—LECTURES ON THE INDUSTRIAL REVOLUTION OF THE 18th CENTURY IN ENGLAND. By ARNOLD TOYNBEE. With a Memoir of the Author by B. JOWETT. 8vo., 10*s.* 6*d.*

Webb.—THE HISTORY OF TRADE UNIONISM. By SIDNEY and BEATRICE WEBB. With Map and full Bibliography of the Subject. 8vo., 18*s.*

Wilson.—Works by A. J. WILSON. Chiefly reprinted from *The Investors' Review.*
PRACTICAL HINTS TO SMALL INVESTORS. Crown 8vo., 1*s.*
PLAIN ADVICE ABOUT LIFE INSURANCE. Crown 8vo., 1*s.*

Evolution, Anthropology, &c.

Babington. — FALLACIES OF RACE THEORIES AS APPLIED TO NATIONAL CHARACTERISTICS. Essays by WILLIAM DALTON BABINGTON, M.A. Crown 8vo., 6*s.*

Clodd.—Works by EDWARD CLODD.
THE STORY OF CREATION : a Plain Account of Evolution. With 77 Illustrations. Crown 8vo., 3*s.* 6*d.*
A PRIMER OF EVOLUTION: being a Popular Abridged Edition of 'The Story of Creation'. With Illustrations. Fcp. 8vo., 1*s.* 6*d.*

Lang.—CUSTOM AND MYTH: Studies of Early Usage and Belief. By ANDREW LANG, M.A. With 15 Illustrations. Crown 8vo., 3*s.* 6*d.*

Lubbock.—THE ORIGIN OF CIVILISATION and the Primitive Condition of Man. By Sir J. LUBBOCK, Bart., M.P. With 5 Plates and 20 Illustrations in th· Text. 8vo. 18*s.*

Romanes.—Works by GEORGE JOH· ROMANES, M.A., LL.D., F.R.S.
DARWIN, AND AFTER DARWIN : an Exposition of the Darwinian Theor, and a Discussion on Post-Darwinia Questions.
Part I. THE DARWINIAN THEOF. With Portrait of Darwin and 15 Illustrations. Crown 8vo., 10*s.* 6*d.*
Part II. POST-DARWINIAN QUSTIONS : Heredity and Utility. [*In the Prs.*
AN EXAMINATION OF WEISMANNM. Crown 8vo., 6*s.*
MIND MOTION AND MONISM. Crvn 8vo., 4*s.* 6*d.*

Classical Literature and Translations, &c.

Abbott.—HELLENICA. A Collection of Essays on Greek Poetry, Philosophy, History, and Religion. Edited by EVELYN ABBOTT, M.A., LL.D. 8vo., 16s.

Æschylus.—EUMENIDES OF ÆSCHYLUS. With Metrical English Translation. By J. F. DAVIES. 8vo., 7s.

Aristophanes.—The ACHARNIANS OF ARISTOPHANES, translated into English Verse. By R. Y. TYRRELL. Cr. 8vo., 1s.

Becker.—Works by Professor BECKER.

GALLUS: or, Roman Scenes in the Time of Augustus. Illustrated. Cr. 8vo., 3s. 6d.

CHARICLES: or, Illustrations of the Private Life of the Ancient Greeks. Illustrated. Cr 8vo., 3s. 6d.

Cicero.—CICERO'S CORRESPONDENCE. By R. Y. TYRRELL. Vols. I., II., III. 8vo., each 12s. Vol. IV., 15s.

Farnell.—GREEK LYRIC POETRY: a Complete Collection of the Surviving Passages from the Greek Song-Writing. By GEORGE S. FARNELL, M.A. With 5 Plates. 8vo., 16s.

Lang.—HOMER AND THE EPIC. By ANDREW LANG. Crown 8vo., 9s. net.

Mackail.—SELECT EPIGRAMS FROM THE GREEK ANTHOLOGY. By J. W. MACKAIL 8vo., 16s.

Rich.—A DICTIONARY OF ROMAN AND GREEK ANTIQUITIES. By A. RICH, B.A. With 2000 Woodcuts. Crown 8vo., 7s. 6d.

Sophocles.—Translated into English Verse. By ROBERT WHITELAW, M.A., Assistant Master in Rugby School: late Fellow of Trinity College, Cambridge. Crown 8vo., 8s. 6d.

Tyrrell.—TRANSLATIONS INTO GREEK AND LATIN VERSE. Edited by R. Y. TYRRELL. 8vo., 6s.

Virgil.—THE ÆNEID OF VIRGIL. Translated into English Verse by JOHN CONINGTON. Crown 8vo., 6s.

THE POEMS OF VIRGIL. Translated into English Prose by JOHN CONINGTON. Crown 8vo., 6s.

THE ÆNEID OF VIRGIL, freely translated into English Blank Verse. By W. J. THORNHILL. Crown 8vo., 7s. 6d.

THE ÆNEID OF VIRGIL. Books I. to VI. Translated into English Verse by JAMES RHOADES. Crown 8vo., 5s.

Wilkins.—THE GROWTH OF THE HOMERIC POEMS. By G. WILKINS. 8vo. 6s.

Poetry and the Drama.

Acworth.—BALLADS OF THE MARATHAS. Rendered into English Verse from the Marathi Originals. By HARRY ARBUTHNOT ACWORTH. 8vo., 5s.

Allingham.—Works by WILLIAM ALLINGHAM.

IRISH SONGS AND POEMS. With Frontispiece of the Waterfall of Asaroe. Fcp. 8vo., 6s.

LAURENCE BLOOMFIELD. With Portrait of the Author. Fcp. 8vo., 3s. 6d.

FLOWER PIECES; DAY AND NIGHT SONGS; BALLADS. With 2 Designs by D. G. ROSSETTI. Fcp. 8vo., 6s.; large paper edition, 12s.

LIFE AND PHANTASY: with Frontispiece by Sir J. E. MILLAIS, Bart., and Design by ARTHUR HUGHES. Fcp. 8vo., 6s.; large paper edition, 12s.

THOUGHT AND WORD, AND ASHBY MANOR: a Play. Fcp. 8vo., 6s.; large paper edition, 12s.

BLACKBERRIES. Imperial 16mo., 6s.

Sets of the above 6 vols. may be had in uniform half-parchment binding, price 30s.

Poetry and the Drama—*continued.*

Armstrong.—Works by G. F. SAVAGE-ARMSTRONG.

POEMS: Lyrical and Dramatic. Fcp. 8vo., 6*s.*

KING SAUL. (The Tragedy of Israel, Part I.) Fcp. 8vo. 5*s.*

KING DAVID. (The Tragedy of Israel, Part II.) Fcp. 8vo., 6*s.*

KING SOLOMON. (The Tragedy of Israel, Part III.) Fcp. 8vo., 6*s.*

UGONE: a Tragedy. Fcp. 8vo., 6*s.*

A GARLAND FROM GREECE: Poems. Fcp. 8vo., 7*s.* 6*d.*

STORIES OF WICKLOW: Poems. Fcp. 8vo., 7*s.* 6*d.*

MEPHISTOPHELES IN BROADCLOTH: a Satire. Fcp. 8vo., 4*s.*

ONE IN THE INFINITE: a Poem. Cr. 8vo., 7*s.* 6*d.*

Armstrong.—THE POETICAL WORKS OF EDMUND J. ARMSTRONG. Fcp. 8vo., 5*s.*

Arnold.—Works by Sir EDWIN ARNOLD, K.C.I.E.

THE LIGHT OF THE WORLD: or, the Great Consummation. Cr. 8vo., 7*s.* 6*d.* net.

THE TENTH MUSE, AND OTHER POEMS. Crown 8vo., 5*s.* net.

POTIPHAR'S WIFE, and other Poems. Crown 8vo., 5*s.* net.

ADZUMA: or, the Japanese Wife. A Play. Crown 8vo., 6*s.* 6*d.* net.

Beesly.—BALLADS, AND OTHER VERSE. By A. H. BEESLY. Fcp. 8vo., 5*s.*

Bell.—CHAMBER COMEDIES: a Collection of Plays and Monologues for the Drawing Room. By Mrs. HUGH BELL. Crown 8vo., 6*s.*

Cochrane.—THE KESTREL'S NEST, and other Verses. By ALFRED COCHRANE. Fcp. 8vo., 3*s.* 6*d.*

Goethe.

FAUST, Part I., the German Text, with Introduction and Notes. By ALBERT M. SELSS, Ph.D., M.A. Cr. 8vo., 5*s.*

FAUST. Translated, with Notes. By T. E. WEBB. 8vo., 12*s.* 6*d.*

Ingelow.—Works by JEAN INGELOW

POETICAL WORKS. 2 vols. Fcp. 8vo., 12*s.*

LYRICAL AND OTHER POEMS. Selected from the Writings of JEAN INGELOW. Fcp. 8vo., 2*s.* 6*d.*; cloth plain, 3*s.*; cloth gilt.

Kendall.—SONGS FROM DREAMLAND. By MAY KENDALL. Fcp. 8vo., 5*s.* net.

Lang.—Works by ANDREW LANG.

BAN AND ARRIÈRE BAN. A Rally of Fugitive Rhymes Fcp. 8vo., 5*s.* net.

GRASS OF PARNASSUS. Fcp. 8vo., 2*s.* 6*d.* net.

BALLADS OF BOOKS. Edited by ANDREW LANG. Fcp. 8vo., 6*s.*

THE BLUE POETRY BOOK. Edited by ANDREW LANG. With 12 Plates and 88 Illustrations in the Text by H. J. FORD and LANCELOT SPEED. Crown 8vo., 6*s.*

Special Edition, printed on Indian paper. With Notes, but without Illustrations. Crown 8vo., 7s. 6d.

Lecky.—POEMS. By W. E. H. LECKY. Fcp. 8vo., 5*s.*

Peek. — Works by HEDLEY PEEK (FRANK LEYTON).

SKELETON LEAVES: Poems. With a Dedicatory Poem to the late Hon. Roden Noel. Fcp. 8vo., 2*s.* 6*d.* net.

THE SHADOWS OF THE LAKE, and other Poems. Fcp. 8vo., 2*s.* 6*d.* net.

Lytton.—Works by THE EARL OF LYTTON (OWEN MEREDITH).

MARAH. Fcp. 8vo., 6*s.* 6*d.*

KING POPPY: a Fantasia. With 1 Plate and Design on Title-Page by Sir ED. BURNE-JONES, A.R.A. Crown 8vo., 10*s.* 6*d.*

THE WANDERER. Cr. 8vo., 10*s.* 6*d.*

LUCILE. Crown 8vo., 10*s.* 6*d.*

SELECTED POEMS. Cr. 8vo., 10*s.* 6*d.*

Poetry and the Drama—*continued.*

Macaulay.—LAYS OF ANCIENT ROME, &c. By Lord MACAULAY.

Illustrated by G. SCHARF. Fcp. 4to., 10s. 6d.

——————— Bijou Edition. 18mo., 2s. 6d., gilt top.

——————— Popular Edition. Fcp. 4to., 6d. sewed, 1s. cloth.

Illustrated by J. R. WEGUELIN. Crown 8vo., 3s. 6d.

Annotated Edition. Fcp. 8vo., 1s. sewed, 1s. 6d. cloth.

Murray.—(ROBERT F.), Author of 'The Scarlet Gown'. His Poems, with a Memoir by ANDREW LANG. Fcp. 8vo., 5s. net.

Nesbit.—LAYS AND LEGENDS. By E. NESBIT (Mrs. HUBERT BLAND). First Series. Crown 8vo., 3s. 6d. Second Series, with Portrait. Crown 8vo., 5s.

Piatt.—Works by SARAH PIATT.

POEMS. With portrait of the Author. 2 vols. Crown 8vo., 10s.

AN ENCHANTED CASTLE, AND OTHER POEMS: Pictures, Portraits and People in Ireland. Crown 8vo., 3s. 6d.

Piatt.—Works by JOHN JAMES PIATT.

IDYLS AND LYRICS OF THE OHIO VALLEY. Crown 8vo., 5s.

LITTLE NEW WORLD IDYLS. Cr. 8vo., 5s.

Rhoades.—TERESA AND OTHER POEMS. By JAMES RHOADES. Crown 8vo., 3s. 6d.

Riley.—Works by JAMES WHITCOMB RILEY.

OLD FASHIONED ROSES: Poems. 12mo., 5s.

POEMS HERE AT HOME. Fcap. 8vo., 6s. net.

Shakespeare.—BOWDLER'S FAMILY SHAKESPEARE. With 36 Woodcuts. 1 vol. 8vo., 14s. Or in 6 vols. Fcp. 8vo., 21s.

THE SHAKESPEARE BIRTHDAY BOOK. By MARY F. DUNBAR. 32mo., 1s. 6d. Drawing-Room Edition, with Photographs. Fcp. 8vo., 10s. 6d.

Sturgis.—A BOOK OF SONG. By JULIAN STURGIS. 16mo., 5s.

Works of Fiction, Humour, &c.

Anstey.—Works by F. ANSTEY, Author of 'Vice Versâ'.

THE BLACK POODLE, and other Stories. Crown 8vo., 2s. boards, 2s. 6d. cloth.

VOCES POPULI. Reprinted from 'Punch'. First Series. With 20 Illustrations by J. BERNARD PARTRIDGE. Cr. 8vo., 3s. 6d.

THE TRAVELLING COMPANIONS. Reprinted from 'Punch'. With 25 Illustrations by J. BERNARD PARTRIDGE. Post 4to., 5s.

THE MAN FROM BLANKLEY'S: a Story in Scenes, and other Sketches. With 24 Illustrations by J. BERNARD PARTRIDGE. Fcp. 4to., 6s.

Astor.—A JOURNEY IN OTHER WORLDS, a Romance of the Future. By JOHN JACOB ASTOR. With 10 Illustrations. Cr. 8vo., 6s.

Baker.—BY THE WESTERN SEA. By JAMES BAKER, Author of 'John Westacott'. Crown 8vo., 3s. 6d.

Beaconsfield.—Works by the Earl of BEACONSFIELD.

NOVELS AND TALES. Cheap Edition. Complete in 11 vols. Cr. 8vo., 1s. 6d. each.

Vivian Grey. | Henrietta Temple.
TheYoungDuke,&c. | Venetia. Tancred.
Alroy, Ixion, &c. | Coningsby. Sybil.
Contarini Fleming, &c. | Lothair. Endymion.

NOVELS AND TALES. The Hughenden Edition. With 2 Portraits and 11 Vignettes. 11 vols. Cr. 8vo., 42s.

Boulton.— JOSEPHINE CREWE. By HELEN M. BOULTON.

Clegg.—DAVID'S LOOM: a Story of Rochdale life in the early years of the Nineteenth Century. By JOHN TRAFFORD CLEGG. Crown 8vo. 2s. 6d.

Works of Fiction, Humour, &c.—*continued.*

Deland.—Works by MARGARET DE-LAND, Author of 'John Ward'.
THE STORY OF A CHILD. Cr. 8vo., 5s.
MR. TOMMY DOVE, and other Stories. Crown 8vo., 6s.
PHILIP AND HIS WIFE. Cr. 8vo., 6s.

Dougall.—Works by L. DOUGALL.
BEGGARS ALL. Crown 8vo., 3s. 6d.
WHAT NECESSITY KNOWS. Crown 8vo., 6s.

Doyle.—Works by A. CONAN DOYLE.
MICAH CLARKE: a Tale of Monmouth's Rebellion. With Frontispiece and Vignette. Cr. 8vo., 3s. 6d.
THE CAPTAIN OF THE POLESTAR, and other Tales. Cr. 8vo., 3s. 6d.
THE REFUGEES: a Tale of Two Continents. With Illustrations. Crown 8vo., 3s. 6d.

Farrar.—DARKNESS AND DAWN: or, Scenes in the Days of Nero. An Historic Tale. By F. W. FARRAR, Dean of Canterbury. Cr. 8vo., 7s. 6d.

Froude.—THE TWO CHIEFS OF DUN-BOY: an Irish Romance of the Last Century. By J. A. FROUDE. Cr. 8vo., 3s. 6d.

Fowler.—THE YOUNG PRETENDERS. A Story of Child Life. By EDITH H. FOWLER. With 12 Illustrations by PHILIP BURNE-JONES. Crown 8vo., 6s.

Gerard.—AN ARRANGED MARRIAGE. By DOROTHEA GERARD. Crown 8vo., 6s.

Gilkes. — THE THING THAT HATH BEEN: or, a Young Man's Mistake. By A. H. GILKES, M.A., Master of Dulwich College. Crown 8vo., 6s.

Haggard.—Works by H. RIDER HAG-GARD.
JOAN HASTE. With Illustrations. Cr. 8vo., 6s.
THE PEOPLE OF THE MIST. With 16 Illustrations. Crown 8vo., 6s.
SHE. With 32 Illustrations. Crown 8vo., 3s. 6d.
ALLAN QUATERMAIN. With 31 Illustrations. Crown 8vo., 3s. 6d.
MAIWA'S REVENGE; or, The War of the Little Hand. Cr. 8vo., 1s. boards, 1s. 6d. cloth.
COLONEL QUARITCH, V.C. Cr. 8vo., 3s. 6d.
CLEOPATRA. With 29 Illustrations Crown 8vo., 3s. 6d.
BEATRICE. Cr. 8vo., 3s. 6d.
ERIC BRIGHTEYES. With 51 Illustrations. Cr. 8vo., 3s. 6d.

Haggard.—Works by H. RIDER HAG-GARD—*continued.*
NADA THE LILY. With 23 Illustrations. Cr. 8vo., 3s. 6d.
MONTEZUMA'S DAUGHTER. With 24 Illustrations. Crown 8vo., 6s.
ALLAN'S WIFE. With 34 Illustrations. Crown 8vo., 3s. 6d.
THE WITCH'S HEAD. With 16 Illustrations. Crown 8vo., 3s. 6d.
MR. MEESON'S WILL. With 16 Illustrations. Crown 8vo., 3s. 6d.
DAWN. With 16 Illustrations. Crown 8vo., 3s. 6d.

Haggard and Lang.—THE WORLD'S DESIRE. By H. RIDER HAGGARD and ANDREW LANG. With 27 Illustrations by M. GREIFFENHAGEN. Cr. 8vo., 3s. 6d.

Harte. — IN THE CARQUINEZ WOODS, and other Stories. By BRET HARTE. Cr. 8vo., 3s. 6d.

Hornung.—THE UNBIDDEN GUEST. By E. W. HORNUNG. Cr. 8vo., 3s. 6d.

Lemon.—MATTHEW FURTH. By IDA LEMON. Crown 8vo., 6s.

Lyall.—Works by EDNA LYALL, Author of 'Donovan,' &c.
THE AUTOBIOGRAPHY OF A SLANDER. Fcp. 8vo., 1s. sewed.
Presentation Edition. With 20 Illustrations by LANCELOT SPEED. 8vo., 2s. 6d. net.
DOREEN: The Story of a Singer. Cr. 8vo., 6s.

Melville.—Works by G. J. WHYTE MELVILLE.

The Gladiators.	Holmby House.
The Interpreter.	Kate Coventry.
Good for Nothing.	Digby Grand.
The Queen's Maries.	General Bounce.

Cr. 8vo., 1s. 6d. each.

Oliphant.—Works by Mrs. OLIPHANT.
MADAM. Cr. 8vo., 1s. 6d.
IN TRUST. Cr. 8vo., 1s. 6d.

Payn.—Works by JAMES PAYN.
THE LUCK OF THE DARRELLS. Cr. 8vo., 1s. 6d.
THICKER THAN WATER. Cr. 8vo., 1s. 6d.

Works of Fiction, Humour, &c.—*continued*.

Phillipps-Wolley.—SNAP: a Legend of the Lone Mountain. By C. PHILLIPPS-WOLLEY. With 13 Illustrations by H. G. WILLINK. Cr. 8vo., 3s. 6d.

Prince.—THE STORY OF CHRISTINE ROCHEFORT. By HELEN CHOATE PRINCE. Crown 8vo., 6s.

Rhoscomyl.—THE JEWEL OF YNYS GALON : being a hitherto unprinted Chapter in the History of the Sea Rovers. By OWEN RHOSCOMYL. Cr. 8vo., 6s.

Robertson.—NUGGETS IN THE DEVIL'S PUNCH BOWL, and other Australian Tales. By ANDREW ROBERTSON. Cr. 8vo., 3s. 6d.

Sewell.—Works by ELIZABETH M. SEWELL.

A Glimpse of the World.	Amy Herbert.
Laneton Parsonage.	Cleve Hall.
Margaret Percival.	Gertrude.
Katharine Ashton.	Home Life.
The Earl's Daughter.	After Life.
The Experience of Life.	Ursula. Ivors.

Cr. 8vo., 1s. 6d. each cloth plain. 2s. 6d. each cloth extra, gilt edges.

Stevenson.—Works by ROBERT LOUIS STEVENSON.
STRANGE CASE OF DR. JEKYLL AND MR. HYDE. Fcp. 8vo., 1s. sewed. 1s. 6d. cloth.
THE DYNAMITER. Cr. 8vo., 3s. 6d.

Stevenson and Osbourne.—THE WRONG BOX. By ROBERT LOUIS STEVENSON and LLOYD OSBOURNE. Cr. 8vo., 3s. 6d.

Suttner.—LAY DOWN YOUR ARMS *Die Waffen Nieder:* The Autobiography of Martha Tilling. By BERTHA VON SUTTNER. Translated by T. HOLMES. Cr. 8vo., 1s. 6d.

Trollope.—Works by ANTHONY TROLLOPE.
THE WARDEN. Cr. 8vo., 1s. 6d.
BARCHESTER TOWERS. Cr. 8vo., 1s. 6d.

TRUE, A, RELATION OF THE TRAVELS AND PERILOUS ADVENTURES OF MATHEW DUDGEON, Gentleman : Wherein is truly set down the Manner of his Taking, the Long Time of his Slavery in Algiers, and Means of his Delivery. Written by Himself, and now for the first time printed Cr. 8vo., 5s.

Walford.—Works by L. B. WALFORD.
MR. SMITH : a Part of his Life. Crown 8vo., 2s. 6d.
THE BABY'S GRANDMOTHER. Crown 8vo., 2s. 6d.
COUSINS. Crown 8vo. 2s. 6d.
TROUBLESOME DAUGHTERS. Crown 8vo., 2s. 6d.
PAULINE. Crown 8vo. 2s. 6d.
DICK NETHERBY. Crown 8vo., 2s. 6d.
THE HISTORY OF A WEEK. Crown 8vo. 2s. 6d.
A STIFF-NECKED GENERATION. Crown 8vo. 2s. 6d.
NAN, and other Stories. Cr. 8vo., 2s. 6d.
THE MISCHIEF OF MONICA. Crown 8vo., 2s. 6d.
THE ONE GOOD GUEST. Cr. 8vo. 2s. 6d.
'PLOUGHED,' and other Stories. Crown 8vo., 6s.
THE MATCHMAKER. Cr. 8vo., 6s.

West.—Works by B. B. WEST.
HALF-HOURS WITH THE MILLIONAIRES : Showing how much harder it is to spend a million than to make it. Cr. 8vo., 6s.
SIR SIMON VANDERPETTER, AND MINDING HIS ANCESTORS. Two Reformations. Crown 8vo., 5s.

Weyman.—Works by S. J. WEYMAN.
THE HOUSE OF THE WOLF. Cr. 8vo., 3s. 6d.
A GENTLEMAN OF FRANCE. Cr. 8vo., 6s.

Popular Science (Natural History, &c.).

Butler.—OUR HOUSEHOLD INSECTS. An Account of the Insect-Pests found in Dwelling-Houses. By EDWARD A. BUTLER, B.A., B.Sc. (Lond.). With 113 Illustrations. Crown 8vo., 6s.

Clodd.—A PRIMER OF EVOLUTION : being a Popular Abridged Edition of 'The Story of Creation'. By EDWARD CLODD. With Illus. Fcp. 8vo., 1s. 6d.

Furneaux.—Works by W. FURNEAUX.
THE OUTDOOR WORLD; or, The Young Collector's Handbook. With 18 Plates, 16 of which are coloured, and 549 Illustrations in the Text. Crown 8vo., 7s. 6d.

Furneaux.—Works by W. FURNEAUX —*continued*.

BUTTERFLIES AND MOTHS (British). With 12 coloured Plates and 241 Illustrations in the Text. Crown 8vo., 10s. 6d. net.

Graham.—COUNTRY PASTIMES FOR BOYS. By P. ANDERSON GRAHAM. With numerous Illustrations from Drawings and Photographs. Crown 8vo., 6s.

Popular Science (Natural History, &c.).

Hartwig.—Works by Dr. GEORGE HARTWIG.

THE SEA AND ITS LIVING WONDERS. With 12 Plates and 303 Woodcuts. 8vo., 7s. net.

THE TROPICAL WORLD. With 8 Plates and 172 Woodcuts. 8vo., 7s. net.

THE POLAR WORLD. With 3 Maps, 8 Plates and 85 Woodcuts. 8vo., 7s. net.

THE SUBTERRANEAN WORLD. With 3 Maps and 80 Woodcuts. 8vo., 7s. net.

THE AERIAL WORLD. With Map, 8 Plates and 60 Woodcuts. 8vo., 7s net.

HEROES OF THE POLAR WORLD. 19 Illustrations. Crown 8vo., 2s.

WONDERS OF THE TROPICAL FORESTS. 40 Illustrations. Crown 8vo., 2s.

WORKERS UNDER THE GROUND. 29 Illustrations. Crown 8vo., 2s.

MARVELS OVER OUR HEADS. 29 Illustrations. Crown 8vo., 2s.

SEA MONSTERS AND SEA BIRDS. 75 Illustrations. Crown 8vo., 2s. 6d.

DENIZENS OF THE DEEP. 117 Illustrations. Crown 8vo., 2s. 6d.

VOLCANOES AND EARTHQUAKES. 30 Illustrations. Crown 8vo., 2s. 6d.

WILD ANIMALS OF THE TROPICS. 66 Illustrations. Crown 8vo., 3s. 6d.

Hayward.—BIRD NOTES. By the late JANE MARY HAYWARD. Edited by EMMA HUBBARD. With Frontispiece and 15 Illustrations by G. E. LODGE. Cr. 8vo., 6s.

Helmholtz.—POPULAR LECTURES ON SCIENTIFIC SUBJECTS. By HERMANN VON HELMHOLTZ. With 68 Woodcuts. 2 vols. Crown 8vo., 3s. 6d. each.

Hudson. — BRITISH BIRDS. By W. H. HUDSON, C.M.Z.S. With a Chapter on Structure and Classification by FRANK E. BEDDARD, F.R.S. With 17 Plates (8 of which are Coloured), and over 100 Illustrations in the Text. Crown 8vo., [*Nearly ready.*

Proctor.—Works by RICHARD A. PROCTOR.

LIGHT SCIENCE FOR LEISURE HOURS. Familiar Essays on Scientific Subjects. 3 vols. Crown 8vo., 5s. each.

CHANCE AND LUCK: a Discussion of the Laws of Luck, Coincidence, Wagers, Lotteries and the Fallacies of Gambling, &c. Cr. 8vo., 2s. boards, 2s. 6d. cloth.

ROUGH WAYS MADE SMOOTH. Familiar Essays on Scientific Subjects. Silver Library Edition. Cr. 8vo., 3s. 6d.

PLEASANT WAYS IN SCIENCE. Cr. 8vo., 5s. Silver Library Edition. Crown 8vo., 3s. 6d.

Proctor. — Works by RICHARD A. PROCTOR—*continued.*

THE GREAT PYRAMID, OBSERVATORY, TOMB AND TEMPLE. With Illustrations. Crown 8vo., 5s.

NATURE STUDIES. By R. A. PROCTOR, GRANT ALLEN, A. WILSON, T. FOSTER and E. CLODD. Crown 8vo., 5s. Sil. Lib. Ed. Cr. 8vo., 3s. 6d.

LEISURE READINGS. By R. A. PROCTOR, E. CLODD, A. WILSON, T. FOSTER, and A. C. RANYARD. Cr. 8vo., 5s.

Stanley.—A FAMILIAR HISTORY OF BIRDS. By E. STANLEY, D.D., formerly Bishop of Norwich. With Illustrations. Cr. 8vo., 3s. 6d.

Wood.—Works by the Rev. J. G. WOOD.

HOMES WITHOUT HANDS : a Description of the Habitation of Animals, classed according to the Principle of Construction. With 140 Illustrations. 8vo., 7s. net.

INSECTS AT HOME : a Popular Account of British Insects, their Structure, Habits and Transformations. With 700 Illustrations. 8vo., 7s. net.

INSECTS ABROAD : a Popular Account of Foreign Insects, their Structure, Habits and Transformations. With 600 Illustrations. 8vo., 7s. net.

BIBLE ANIMALS : a Description of every Living Creature mentioned in the Scriptures. With 112 Illustrations. 8vo., 7s. net.

PETLAND REVISITED. With 33 Illustrations. Cr. 8vo., 3s. 6d.

OUT OF DOORS ; a Selection of Original Articles on Practical Natural History. With 11 Illustrations. Cr. 8vo., 3s. 6d.

STRANGE DWELLINGS : a Description of the Habitations of Animals, abridged from 'Homes without Hands'. With 60 Illustrations. Cr. 8vo., 3s. 6d.

BIRD LIFE OF THE BIBLE. 32 Illustrations. Cr. 8vo., 3s. 6d.

WONDERFUL NESTS. 30 Illustrations. Cr. 8vo., 3s. 6d.

HOMES UNDER THE GROUND. 28 Illustrations. Cr. 8vo., 3s. 6d.

WILD ANIMALS OF THE BIBLE. 29 Illustrations. Cr. 8vo., 3s. 6d.

DOMESTIC ANIMALS OF THE BIBLE. 23 Illustrations. Cr. 8vo., 3s. 6d.

THE BRANCH BUILDERS. 28 Illustrations. Cr. 8vo., 2s. 6d.

SOCIAL HABITATIONS AND PARASITIC NESTS. 18 Illustrations. Cr. 8vo., 2s.

Works of Reference.

Maunder's (Samuel) Treasuries.

BIOGRAPHICAL TREASURY. With Supplement brought down to 1889. By Rev. JAMES WOOD. Fcp. 8vo., 6s.

TREASURY OF NATURAL HISTORY: or, Popular Dictionary of Zoology. With 900 Woodcuts. Fcp. 8vo., 6s.

TREASURY OF GEOGRAPHY, Physical, Historical, Descriptive, and Political. With 7 Maps and 16 Plates. Fcp. 8vo., 6s.

THE TREASURY OF BIBLE KNOWLEDGE. By the Rev. J. AYRE, M.A. With 5 Maps, 15 Plates, and 300 Woodcuts. Fcp. 8vo., 6s.

HISTORICAL TREASURY: Outlines of Universal History, Separate Histories of all Nations. Fcp. 8vo., 6s.

TREASURY OF KNOWLEDGE AND LIBRARY OF REFERENCE. Comprising an English Dictionary and Grammar, Universal Gazeteer, Classical Dictionary, Chronology, Law Dictionary, &c. Fcp. 8vo., 6s.

Maunder's (Samuel) Treasuries —*continued.*

SCIENTIFIC AND LITERARY TREASURY. Fcp. 8vo., 6s.

THE TREASURY OF BOTANY. Edited by J. LINDLEY, F.R.S., and T. MOORE, F.L.S. With 274 Woodcuts and 20 Steel Plates. 2 vols. Fcp. 8vo., 12s.

Roget.--THESAURUS OF ENGLISH WORDS AND PHRASES. Classified and Arranged so as to Facilitate the Expression of Ideas and assist in Literary Composition. By PETER MARK ROGET, M.D., F.R.S. Recomposed throughout, enlarged and improved, partly from the Author's Notes, and with a full Index, by the Author's Son, JOHN LEWIS ROGET. Crown 8vo., 10s. 6d.

Willich.—POPULAR TABLES for giving information for ascertaining the value of Lifehold, Leasehold, and Church Property, the Public Funds, &c. By CHARLES M. WILLICH. Edited by H. BENCE JONES. Crown 8vo., 10s. 6d.

Children's Books.

Crake.—Works by Rev. A. D. CRAKE.

EDWY THE FAIR; or, the First Chronicle of Æscendune. Crown 8vo., 2s. 6d.

ALFGAR THE DANE: or, the Second Chronicle of Æscendune. Cr. 8vo., 2s. 6d.

THE RIVAL HEIRS: being the Third and Last Chronicle of the Æscendune. Cr. 8vo., 2s. 6d.

THE HOUSE OF WALDERNE. A Tale of the Cloister and the Forest in the Days of the Barons' Wars. Crown 8vo., 2s. 6d.

BRIAN FITZ-COUNT. A Story of Wallingford Castle and Dorchester Abbey. Cr. 8vo., 2s. 6d.

Lang.—Works edited by ANDREW LANG.

THE BLUE FAIRY BOOK. With 138 Illustrations by H. J. FORD and G. P. JACOMB HOOD. Crown 8vo., 6s.

THE RED FAIRY BOOK. With 100 Illustrations by H. J. FORD and LANCELOT SPEED. Cr. 8vo., 6s.

THE GREEN FAIRY BOOK. With 101 Illustrations by H. J. FORD and L. BOGLE. Crown 8vo., 6s.

THE YELLOW FAIRY BOOK. With 104 Illustrations by H. J. FORD. Cr. 8vo., 6s.

THE BLUE POETRY BOOK. With 100 Illustrations by H. J. FORD and LANCELOT SPEED. Crown 8vo., 6s.

Lang.—Works edited by ANDREW LANG —*continued.*

THE BLUE POETRY BOOK. School Edition, without Illustrations. Fcp. 8vo., 2s. 6d.

THE TRUE STORY BOOK. With 66 Illustrations by H. J. FORD, LUCIEN DAVIS, C. H. M. KERR, LANCELOT SPEED, and LOCKHART BOGLE. Crown 8vo., 6s.

Meade.—Works by L. T. MEADE.

DADDY'S BOY. Illustrated. Crown 8vo., 3s. 6d.

DEB AND THE DUCHESS. Illustrated. Crown 8vo., 3s. 6d.

THE BERESFORD PRIZE. Crown 8vo., 3s. 6d.

Molesworth.—Works by Mrs. MOLESWORTH.

SILVERTHORNS. Illustrated. Cr. 8vo., 5s.

THE PALACE IN THE GARDEN. Illustrated. Crown 8vo., 2s. 6d.

NEIGHBOURS. Illus. Crown 8vo., 2s. 6d.

Soulsby.—STRAY THOUGHTS FOR GIRLS. By LUCY H. M. SOULSBY, Head Mistress of Oxford High School. 16mo. 1s. 6d. net.

Stevenson.—A CHILD'S GARDEN OF VERSES. By ROBERT LOUIS STEVENSON. Small fcp. 8vo., 5s.

Longmans' Series of Books for Girls.

Crown 8vo., price 2s. 6d. each

ATELIER (THE) DU LYS: or an Art Student in the Reign of Terror.
BY THE SAME AUTHOR.
MADEMOISELLE MORI: a Tale of Modern Rome.
THAT CHILD.
UNDER A CLOUD.
THE FIDDLER OF LUGAU.
A CHILD OF THE REVOLUTION.
HESTER'S VENTURE.
IN THE OLDEN TIME: a Tale of the Peasant War in Germany.
THE YOUNGER SISTER.
THE THIRD MISS ST. QUENTIN. By Mrs. MOLESWORTH.

ATHERSTONE PRIORY. By L. N. COMYN.
THE STORY OF A SPRING MORNING, &c. By Mrs. MOLESWORTH. Illustrated.
NEIGHBOURS. By Mrs. MOLESWORTH.
VERY YOUNG; and QUITE ANOTHER STORY. By JEAN INGELOW.
CAN THIS BE LOVE? By Louis A. Parr.
KEITH DERAMORE. By the Author of ' Miss Molly '.
SIDNEY. By MARGARET DELAND.
LAST WORDS TO GIRLS ON LIFE AT SCHOOL AND AFTER SCHOOL. By Mrs. W. GREY.

The Silver Library.

CROWN 8vo. 3s. 6d. EACH VOLUME.

Arnold's (Sir Edwin) Seas and Lands. With 71 Illustrations. 3s. 6d.
Bagehot's (W.) Biographical Studies. 3s. 6d.
Bagehot's (W.) Economic Studies. 3s. 6d.
Bagehot's (W.) Literary Studies. 3 vols. 10s. 6d.
Baker's (Sir S. W.) Eight Years in Ceylon. With 6 Illustrations. 3s. 6d.
Baker's (Sir S. W.) Rifle and Hound in Ceylon. With 6 Illustrations. 3s. 6d.
Baring-Gould's (Rev. S.) Curious Myths of the Middle Ages. 3s. 6d.
Baring-Gould's (Rev. S.) Origin and Development of Religious Belief. 2 vols. 3s. 6d. each.
Becker's (Prof.) Gallus: or, Roman Scenes in the Time of Augustus. Illus. 3s. 6d.
Becker's (Prof.) Charicles: or, Illustrations of the Private Life of the Ancient Greeks. Illustrated. 3s. 6d.
Bent's (J. T.) The Ruined Cities of Mashoanland: being a Record of Excavation and Exploration in 1891. With 117 Illustrations. 3s. 6d.
Brassey's (Lady) A Voyage in the ' Sunbeam '. With 66 Illustrations. 3s. 6d.
Clodd's (E.) Story of Creation: a Plain Account of Evolution. With 77 Illustrations. 3s. 6d.
Conybeare (Rev. W. J.) and Howson's (Very Rev. J. S.) Life and Epistles of St. Paul. 46 Illustrations. 3s. 6d.
Dougall's (L.) Beggars All; a Novel. 3s. 6d.
Doyle's (A. Conan) Micah Clarke: a Tale of Monmouth's Rebellion. 3s. 6d.
Doyle's (A. Conan) The Captain of the Polestar, and other Tales. 3s. 6d.
Doyle's (A. Conan) The Refugees: A Tale of Two Continents. With Illustrations. 3s. 6d.
Froude's (J. A.) Short Studies on Great Subjects. 4 vols. 3s. 6d. each.

Froude's (J. A.) Cæsar: a Sketch. 3s. 6d.
Froude's (J. A.) Thomas Carlyle: a History of his Life.
1795-1835. 2 vols. 7s.
1834-1881. 2 vols. 7s.
Froude's (J. A.) The Two Chiefs of Dunboy: an Irish Romance of the Last Century. 3s. 6d.
Froude's (J. A.) The History of England, from the Fall of Wolsey to the Defeat of the Spanish Armada. 12 vols. 3s. 6d. each.
Froude's (J. A.) The English in Ireland. 3 vols. 10s. 6d.
Froude's (J. A.) The Spanish Story of the Armada, and other Essays. 3s. 6d.
Gleig's (Rev. G. R.) Life of the Duke of Wellington. With Portrait. 3s. 6d.
Haggard's (H. R.) She: A History of Adventure. 32 Illustrations. 3s. 6d.
Haggard's (H. R.) Allan Quatermain. With 20 Illustrations. 3s. 6d.
Haggard's (H. R.) Colonel Quaritch, V.C.: a Tale of Country Life. 3s. 6d.
Haggard's (H. R.) Cleopatra. With 29 Full-page Illustrations. 3s. 6d.
Haggard's (H. R.) Eric Brighteyes. With 51 Illustrations. 3s. 6d.
Haggard's (H. R.) Beatrice. 3s. 6d.
Haggard's (H. R.) Allan's Wife. With 34 Illustrations. 3s. 6d.
Haggard's (H. R.) The Witch's Head. With Illustrations. 3s. 6d.
Haggard's (H. R.) Mr. Meeson's Will. With Illustrations. 3s. 6d.
Haggard's (H. R.) Dawn. With 16 Illustrations. 3s. 6d.
Haggard's (H. R.) and Lang's (A.) The World's Desire. With 27 Illus. 3s. 6d.
Haggard's (H. R.) Nada the Lily. With Illustrations by C. M. KERR. 3s. 6d.
Harte's (Bret) In the Carquinez Woods, and other Stories. 3s. 6d.

The Silver Library—*continued.*

Helmholtz's (Hermann von) Popular Lectures on Scientific Subjects. With 68 Woodcuts. 2 vols. 3*s.* 6*d.* each.

Hornung (E. W.) The Unbidden Guest. 3*s.* 6*d.*

Howitt's (W.) Visits to Remarkable Places. 80 Illustrations. 3*s.* 6*d.*

Jefferies' (R.) The Story of My Heart: My Autobiography. With Portrait. 3*s.* 6*d.*

Jefferies' (R.) Field and Hedgerow. Last Essays of. With Portrait. 3*s.* 6*d.*

Jefferies' (R.) Red Deer. With 17 Illust. by J. CHARLTON and H. TUNALY. 3*s.* 6*d.*

Jefferies' (R.) Wood Magic: a Fable. With Frontispiece and Vignette by E. V. B. 3*s.* 6*d.*

Jefferies' (R.) The Toilers of the Field. With Portrait from the Bust in Salisbury Cathedral. 3*s.* 6*d.*

Knight's (E. F.) The Cruise of the 'Alerte': the Narrative of a Search for Treasure on the Desert Island of Trinidad. With 2 Maps and 23 Illustrations. 3*s.* 6*d.*

Knight (E. F.) Where Three Empires Meet: a Narrative of Recent Travel in Kashmir, Western Tibet, Baltistan, Gilgit, and the adjoining Countries. With a Map and 54 Illust. 3*s.* 6*d.*

Lang's (A.) Angling Sketches. 3*s.* 6*d.*

Lang's (A.) Custom and Myth: Studies of Early Usage and Belief. 3*s.* 6*d.*

Lees (J. A.) and Clutterbuck's (W. J.) B.C. 1887, A Ramble in British Columbia. With Maps and 75 Illustrations. 3*s.* 6*d.*

Macaulay's (Lord) Essays and Lays of Ancient Rome. With Portrait and Illustrations. 3*s.* 6*d.*

Macleod (H. D.) The Elements of Banking. 3*s.* 6*d.*

Marshman's (J .C.) Memoirs of Sir Henry Havelock. 3*s.* 6*d.*

Max Müller's (F.) India, what can it teach us? 3*s.* 6*d.*

Max Müller's (F.) Introduction to the Science of Religion. 3*s.* 6*d.*

Merivale's (Dean) History of the Romans under the Empire. 8 vols. 3*s.* 6*d.* ea.

Mill's (J. S.) Political Economy. 3*s.* 6*d.*

Mill's (J. S.) System of Logic. 3*s.* 6*d.*

Milner's (Geo.) Country Pleasures. 3*s.* 6*d.*

Nansen's (F.) The First Crossing of Greenland. With Illustrations and a Map. 3*s.* 6*d.*

Phillipps-Wolley's (C.) Snap: a Legend of the Lone Mountain. With 13 Illustrations. 3*s.* 6*d.*

Proctor's (R. A.) The Orbs Around Us. Essays on the Moon and Planets, Metors and Comets, the Sun and Coloured Pairs of Suns. 3*s.* 6*d.*

Proctor's (R. A.) The Expanse of Heaven. Essays on the Wonders of the Firmament. 3*s.* 6*d.*

Proctor's (R. A.) Other Worlds than Ours. 3*s.* 6*d.*

Proctor's (R. A.) Rough Ways made Smooth. 3*s.* 6*d.*

Proctor's (R. A.) Pleasant Ways in Science. 3*s.* 6*d.*

Proctor's (R. A.) Myths and Marvels of Astronomy. 3*s.* 6*d.*

Proctor's (R. A.) Nature Studies. 3*s.* 6*d.*

Rossetti's (Maria F.) A Shadow of Dante: being an Essay towards studying Himself, his World and his Pilgrimage. 3*s.* 6*d.*

Smith's (R. Bosworth) Carthage and the Carthaginians. 3*s.* 6*d.*

Stanley's (Bishop) Familiar History of Birds. 160 Illustrations. 3*s.* 6*d.*

Stevenson (Robert Louis) and Osbourne's (Lloyd) The Wrong Box. 3*s.* 6*d.*

Stevenson (Robert Louis) and Stevenson (Fanny van de Grift) More New Arabian Nights. — The Dynamiter. 3*s.* 6*d.*

Weyman's (Stanley J.) The House of the Wolf: a Romance. 3*s.* 6*d.*

Wood's (Rev. J. G.) Petland Revisited. With 33 Illustrations. 3*s.* 6*d.*

Wood's (Rev. J. G.) Strange Dwellings. With 60 Illustrations. 3*s.* 6*d.*

Wood's (Rev. J. G.) Out of Doors. 11 Illustrations. 3*s.* 6*d.*

Cookery, Domestic Management, &c.

Acton.—MODERN COOKERY. By ELIZA ACTON. With 150 Woodcuts. Fcp. 8vo., 4*s.* 6*d.*

Bull.—Works by THOMAS BULL, M.D.
HINTS TO MOTHERS ON THE MANAGEMENT OF THEIR HEALTH DURING THE PERIOD OF PREGNANCY. Fcp. 8vo., 1*s.* 6*d.*

THE MATERNAL MANAGEMENT OF CHILDREN IN HEALTH AND DISEASE. Fcp. 8vo., 1*s.* 6*d.*

De Salis.—Works by Mrs. DE SALIS.
CAKES AND CONFECTIONS À LA MODE. Fcp. 8vo., 1*s.* 6*d.*

DOGS: a Manual for Amateurs. Fcp. 8vo., 1*s.* 6*d.*

DRESSED GAME AND POULTRY À LA MODE. Fcp. 8vo., 1*s.* 6*d.*

DRESSED VEGETABLES À LA MODE. Fcp. 8vo., 1*s.* 6*d.*

DRINKS À LA MODE. Fcp. 8vo., 1*s.* 6*d.*

ENTRÉES À LA MODE. Fcp. 8vo., 1*s.* 6*d.*

Cookery, Domestic Management, &c.—*continued.*

De Salis.—Works by Mrs. DE SALIS *continued.*

FLORAL DECORATIONS. Fcp. 8vo., 1s. 6d.

GARDENING À LA MODE. Part I. Vegetables, 1s. 6d.; Part II. Fruits, 1s. 6d.

NATIONAL VIANDS À LA MODE. Fcp. 8vo., 1s. 6d.

NEW-LAID EGGS: Hints for Amateur Poultry Rearers. Fcp. 8vo., 1s. 6d.

OYSTERS À LA MODE. Fcp. 8vo., 1s. 6d.

PUDDINGS AND PASTRY À LA MODE. Fcp. 8vo., 1s. 6d.

SAVOURIES À LA MODE. Fcp. 8vo., 1s. 6d.

SOUPS AND DRESSED FISH À LA MODE. Fcp. 8vo., 1s. 6d.

SWEETS AND SUPPER DISHES À LA MODE. Fcp. 8vo., 1s. 6d.

TEMPTING DISHES FOR SMALL INCOMES. Fcp. 8vo., 1s. 6d.

WRINKLES AND NOTIONS FOR EVERY HOUSEHOLD. Cr. 8vo., 1s. 6d.

Lear.—MAIGRE COOKERY. By H. L SIDNEY LEAR. 16mo., 2s.

Poole.—COOKERY FOR THE DIABETIC By W. H. and Mrs. POOLE. With Preface by Dr. PAVY. Fcp. 8vo., 2s. 6d.

Walker.—A HANDBOOK FOR MOTHERS: being Simple Hints to Women on the Management of their Health during Pregnancy and Confinement, together with Plain Directions as to the Care of Infants. By JANE H. WALKER, L.R.C.P. and L.M., L.R.C.S. and M.D. (Brux.). Cr. 8vo., 2s. 6d.

West.—THE MOTHER'S MANUAL OF CHILDREN'S DISEASES. By CHARLES WEST, M.D. Fcp. 8vo., 2s. 6d.

Miscellaneous and Critical Works.

Allingham.—VARIETIES IN PROSE. By WILLIAM ALLINGHAM. 3 vols. Cr. 8vo, 18s. (Vols. 1 and 2, Rambles, by PATRICIUS WALKER. Vol. 3, Irish Sketches, etc.)

Armstrong.—ESSAYS AND SKETCHES. By EDMUND J. ARMSTRONG. Fcp. 8vo., 5s.

Bagehot.—LITERARY STUDIES. By WALTER BAGEHOT. 3 vols. Crown 8vo., 10s. 6d.

Baring-Gould.—CURIOUS MYTHS OF THE MIDDLE AGES. By Rev. S. BARING-GOULD. Crown 8vo., 3s. 6d.

Battye. — PICTURES IN PROSE OF NATURE, WILD SPORT, AND HUMBLE LIFE. By AUBYN TREVOR BATTYE, B.A. Crown 8vo., 6s.

Baynes.—SHAKESPEARE STUDIES, AND OTHER ESSAYS. By the late THOMAS SPENCER BAYNES, LL.B., LL.D. With a biographical Preface by Prof. LEWIS CAMPBELL. Crown 8vo., 7s. 6d.

Boyd ('A. K. H. B.').—Works by A. K. H. BOYD, D.D., LL.D.

And see MISCELLANEOUS THEOLOGICAL WORKS, p. 24.

AUTUMN HOLIDAYS OF A COUNTRY PARSON. Crown 8vo., 3s. 6d.

COMMONPLACE PHILOSOPHER. Crown 8vo., 3s. 6d.

CRITICAL ESSAYS OF A COUNTRY PARSON. Crown 8vo., 3s. 6d.

EAST COAST DAYS AND MEMORIES. Crown 8vo., 3s. 6d.

Boyd ('A. K. H. B.').—Works by A. K. H. BOYD, D.D., LL.D.—*continued.*

LANDSCAPES, CHURCHES AND MORALITIES. Crown 8vo., 3s. 6d.

LEISURE HOURS IN TOWN. Crown 8vo., 3s. 6d.

LESSONS OF MIDDLE AGE. Cr. 8vo., 3s. 6d

OUR LITTLE LIFE. Two Series. Cr. 8vo., 3s. 6d. each.

OUR HOMELY COMEDY: AND TRAGEDY. Crown 8vo., 3s. 6d.

RECREATIONS OF A COUNTRY PARSON. Three Series. Cr. 8vo., 3s. 6d. each. Also First Series. Popular Ed. 8vo., 6d.

Butler.—Works by SAMUEL BUTLER.

EREWHON. Cr. 8vo., 5s.

THE FAIR HAVEN. A Work in Defence of the Miraculous Element in our Lord's Ministry. Cr. 8vo., 7s. 6d.

LIFE AND HABIT. An Essay after a Completer View of Evolution. Cr. 8vo., 7s. 6d

EVOLUTION, OLD AND NEW. Cr. 8vo., 10s. 6d.

ALPS AND SANCTUARIES OF PIEDMONT AND CANTON TICINO. Illustrated. Pott 4to., 10s. 6d.

LUCK, OR CUNNING, AS THE MAIN MEANS OF ORGANIC MODIFICATION? Cr. 8vo., 7s. 6d.

EX VOTO. An Account of the Sacro Monte or New Jerusalem at Varallo-Sesia. Crown 8vo., 10s. 6d.

Miscellaneous and Critical Works—*continued.*

Gwilt.—AN ENCYCLOPÆDIA OF ARCHITECTURE. By JOSEPH GWILT, F.S.A. Illustrated with more than 1100 Engravings on Wood. Revised (1888), with Alterations and Considerable Additions by WYATT PAPWORTH. 8vo., £2 12s. 6d.

Hart.—STUDIES IN AMERICAN EDUCATION. By ALBERT BUSHNELL HART, Ph.D. Crown 8vo., 5s.

James.—MINING ROYALTIES: their Practical Operation and Effect. By CHAS. ASHWORTH JAMES, of Lincoln's Inn, Barrister-at-Law. Fcp. 4to., 5s.

Jefferies.—Works by R. JEFFERIES.
FIELD AND HEDGEROW: last Essays. With Portrait. Crown 8vo., 3s. 6d.
THE STORY OF MY HEART: With Portrait and New Preface by C. J. LONGMAN. Crown 8vo., 3s. 6d.
RED DEER. 17 Illusts. Cr. 8vo., 3s. 6d.
THE TOILERS OF THE FIELD. With Portrait. Crown 8vo., 3s. 6d.
WOOD MAGIC. With Frontispiece and Vignette by E. V. B. Cr. 8vo., 3s. 6d.
THOUGHTS FROM THE WRITINGS OF RICHARD JEFFERIES. Selected by H. S. HOOLE WAYLEN. 16mo., 3s. 6d.

Johnson.—THE PATENTEE'S MANUAL: a Treatise on the Law and Practice of Letters Patent. By J. & J. H. JOHNSON, Patent Agents, &c. 8vo., 10s. 6d.

Lang.—Works by ANDREW LANG.
LETTERS TO DEAD AUTHORS. Fcp. 8vo., 2s. 6d. net.
LETTERS ON LITERATURE. Fcp. 8vo., 2s. 6d. net.
BOOKS AND BOOKMEN. With 19 Illustrations. Fcp. 8vo., 2s. 6d. net.
OLD FRIENDS. Fcp. 8vo., 2s. 6d. net.
COCK LANE AND COMMON SENSE. Fcp. 8vo., 6s. 6d. net.

Laurie.—HISTORICAL SURVEY OF PRE-CHRISTIAN EDUCATION. By S. S. LAURIE, A.M., LL.D. Crown 8vo., 12s.

Leonard.—THE CAMEL: Its Uses and Management. By Major ARTHUR GLYN LEONARD. Royal 8vo., 21s. net.

Macfarren.—LECTURES ON HARMONY. By GEO. A. MACFARREN. 8vo., 12s.

Max Müller.—Works by F. MAX MÜLLER. [8vo., 3s. 6d.
INDIA: WHAT CAN IT TEACH US? Cr.
CHIPS FROM A GERMAN WORKSHOP.
Vol. I., Recent Essays and Addresses. Cr. 8vo., 6s. 6d. net.
Vol. II., Biographical Essays. Cr. 8vo., 6s. 6d. net.
Vol. III., Essays on Language and Literature. Cr. 8vo., 6s. 6d. net.
Vol. IV., Essays on the Sciences of Language, of Thought, and of Mythology. [*In Preparation.*

Mendelssohn.—THE LETTERS OF FELIX MENDELSSOHN. Translated by Lady WALLACE. 2 vols. Cr. 8vo., 10s.

Milner.—Works by GEORGE MILNER.
COUNTRY PLEASURES: the Chronicle of a Year chiefly in a Garden. Cr. 8vo., 3s. 6d.

STUDIES OF NATURE ON THE COAST OF ARRAN. With Illustrations by W. NOEL JOHNSON. Cr. 8vo., 6s. 6d. net.

Poore.—ESSAYS ON RURAL HYGIENE. By GEORGE VIVIAN POORE, M.D., F.R.C.P. With 13 Illustrations. Cr. 8vo., 6s. 6d.

Proctor.—Works by R. A. PROCTOR.
STRENGTH AND HAPPINESS. With 9 Illustrations. Crown 8vo., 5s.

STRENGTH: How to get Strong and keep Strong, with Chapters on Rowing and Swimming, Fat, Age, and the Waist. With 9 Illus. Cr. 8vo., 2s.

Richardson.—NATIONAL HEALTH. A Review of the Works of Sir Edwin Chadwick, K.C.B. By Sir B. W. RICHARDSON, M.D. Cr. 8vo., 4s. 6d.

Rossetti.—A SHADOW OF DANTE: being an Essay towards studying Himself, his World, and his Pilgrimage. By MARIA FRANCESCA ROSSETTI. Cr. 8vo., 10s. 6d. Cheap Edition, 3s. 6d.

Solovyoff.—A MODERN PRIESTESS OF ISIS (MADAME BLAVATSKY). Abridged and Translated on Behalf of the Society for Psychical Research from the Russian of VSEVOLOD SERGYEEVICH SOLOVYFF. By WALTER LEAF, Litt. D. With Appendices. Crown 8vo., 6s.

Stevens.—ON THE STOWAGE OF SHIPS AND THEIR CARGOES. With Information regarding Freights, Charter-Parties, &c. By ROBERT WHITE STEVENS, Associate Member of the Institute of Naval Architects. 8vo. 21s.

Van Dyke.—A TEXT-BOOK OF THE HISTORY OF PAINTING. By JOHN C. VAN DYKE, of Rutgers College, U.S. With Frontispiece and 109 Illustrations in the Text. Crown 8vo., 6s.

West.—WILLS, AND HOW NOT TO MAKE THEM. With a Selection of Leading Cases. By B. B. WEST. Fcp. 8vo., 2s. 6d.

Miscellaneous Theological Works.

• For Church of England and Roman Catholic Works see MESSRS. LONGMANS & CO.'s
Special Catalogues.

Balfour.—THE FOUNDATIONS OF BE-
LIEF: being Notes Intooductory to the
Study of Theology. By the Right Hon.
ARTHUR J. BALFOUR, M.P. 8vo., 12s. 6d.

Boyd.—Works by A. K. H. BOYD, D.D.
COUNSEL AND COMFORT FROM A CITY
PULPIT. Crown 8vo., 3s. 6d.
SUNDAY AFTERNOONS IN THE PARISH
CHURCH OF A SCOTTISH UNIVERSITY
CITY. Crown 8vo., 3s. 6d.
CHANGED ASPECTS OF UNCHANGED
TRUTHS. Crown 8vo., 3s. 6d.
GRAVER THOUGHTS OF A COUNTRY
PARSON. Three Series. Crown 8vo.,
3s. 6d. each.
PRESENT DAY THOUGHTS. Crown 8vo.,
3s. 6d.
SEASIDE MUSINGS. Cr. 8vo., 3s. 6d.
'TO MEET THE DAY' through the
Christian Year; being a Text of Scrip-
ture, with an Original Meditation and
a Short Selection in Verse for Every
Day. Crown 8vo., 4s. 6d.

Darmesteter.—SELECTED ESSAYS OF
JAMES DARMESTETER. Edited, with
an Introductory Memoir, BY MORRIS
JASTROW, Jun. With Portrait, crown
8vo., 6s. 6d.

De La Saussaye.—A MANUAL OF
THE SCIENCE OF RELIGION. By Prof.
CHANTEPIE DE LA SAUSSAYE. Crown
8vo., 12s. 6d.

Kalisch.—Works by M. M. KALISCH,
BIBLE STUDIES. Part I. The Pro-
phecies of Balaam. 8vo., 10s. 6d. Part
II. The Book of Jonah. 8vo., 10s. 6d.
COMMENTARY ON THE OLD TESTAMENT:
with a new Translation. Vol. I.
Genesis. 8vo., 18s. Or adapted for the
General Reader. 12s. Vol. II. Exodus.
15s. Or adapted for the General
Reader. 12s. Vol. III. Leviticus, Part
I. 15s. Or adapted for the General
Reader. 8s. Vol. IV. Leviticus, Part
II. 15s. Or adapted for the General
Reader. 8s.

Martineau.—Works by JAMES MAR-
TINEAU, D.D., LL.D.
HOURS OF THOUGHT ON SACRED
THINGS: Sermons. 2 Vols. Crown
8vo., 7s. 6d. each.
ENDEAVOURS AFTER THE CHRISTIAN
LIFE. Discourses. Cr. 8vo., 7s. 6d.
THE SEAT OF AUTHORITY IN RELIGION.
8vo., 14s.
ESSAYS, REVIEWS, AND ADDRESSES. 4
Vols. Crown 8vo., 7s. 6d. each. I.
Personal; Political. II. Ecclesiastical;
Historical. III. Theological; Philo-
sophical. IV. Academical; Religious.
HOME PRAYERS, with Two Services for
Public Worship. Crown 8vo. 3s. 6d.

Macdonald.—Works by GEORGE MAC-
DONALD, LL.D.
UNSPOKEN SERMONS. Three Series.
Crown 8vo., 3s. 6d. each.
THE MIRACLES OF OUR LORD. Crown
8vo., 3s. 6d.
A BOOK OF STRIFE, IN THE FORM OF
THE DIARY OF AN OLD SOUL: Poems
18mo., 6s.

Max Müller.—Works by F. MAX
MÜLLER.
HIBBERT LECTURES ON THE ORIGIN
AND GROWTH OF RELIGION, as illus-
trated by the Religions of India.
Crown 8vo., 7s. 6d.
INTRODUCTION TO THE SCIENCE OF
RELIGION: Four Lectures delivered at
the Royal Institution. Cr. 8vo., 3s. 6d.
NATURAL RELIGION. The Gifford
Lectures, delivered before the Uni-
versity of Glasgow in 1888. Cr. 8vo.,
10s. 6d.
PHYSICAL RELIGION. The Gifford
Lectures, delivered before the Uni-
versity of Glasgow in 1890. Cr. 8vo.,
10s. 6d.
ANTHROPOLOGICAL RELIGION. The Gif-
ford Lectures, delivered before the
University of Glasgow in 1891. Cr.
8vo., 10s. 6d.
THEOSOPHY OR PSYCHOLOGICAL RELI-
GION. The Gifford Lectures, delivered
before the University of Glasgow in 1892.
Cr. 8vo., 10s. 6d.
THREE LECTURES ON THE VEDANTA
PHILOSOPHY, delivered at the Royal
Institution in March, 1894. 8vo., 5s.

Phillips.—THE TEACHING OF THE VE-
DAS. What Light does it Throw on the
Origin and Development of Religion?
By MAURICE PHILLIPS, London Mission,
Madras. Crown 8vo., 6s.

Scholler.—A CHAPTER OF CHURCH
HISTORY FROM SOUTH GERMANY: being
Passages from the Life of Johann Evan-
gelist Georg Lutz, formerly Parish Priest
and Dean in Oberroth, Bavaria. By L.
W. SCHOLLER. Translated from the
German by W. WALLIS. Crown 8vo.,
3s. 6d.

SUPERNATURAL RELIGION: an
Inquiry into the Reality of Divine Revelation. 3 vols. 8vo., 36s.
REPLY (A) TO DR. LIGHTFOOT'S ESSAYS.
By the Author of 'Supernatural Religion'. 8vo., 6s.
THE GOSPEL ACCORDING TO ST. PETER:
a Study. By the Author of 'Supernatural Religion'. 8vo., 6s.